Dynamic
Women
of the Bible

Dynamic
Women
of the Bible

WHAT WE CAN LEARN FROM THEIR SURPRISING STORIES

RUTH A. TUCKER

BakerBooks

a division of Baker Publishing Group
Grand Rapids, Michigan

Published by Baker Books
a division of Baker Publishing Group
P.O. Box 6287, Grand Rapids, MI 49516-6287
www.bakerbooks.com

Printed in the United States of America

Library of Congress Cataloging-in-Publication Data is on file at the Library of Congress, Washington, DC.

ISBN 978-0-8010-1610-3 (pbk.)

14   15   16   17   18   19   20   7   6   5   4   3   2

In Loving Memory
of Myra Jean Kraker Worst
my very dear friend
and beloved late wife
of my husband John Worst

Sit tibi terra levis

Contents

Contents

Acknowledgments

"Appreciation is a wonderful thing," wrote Voltaire. "It makes what is excellent in others belong to us as well."

How true these words are as I acknowledge my heartfelt appreciation for the professional excellence that I continue to experience at Baker Publishing Group. This excellence is not simply their own, but it belongs to me as well. Ours is a collaborative effort on every level and on every project. I'm sure this collaboration begins at the top of the organization, but for me the one who pulls everything together is Executive Editor Robert Hosack. His insights and efforts in bringing an idea to life and nurturing it from manuscript to bookshelf are commendable indeed.

I also offer sincere appreciation to James Korsmo, my project editor, who has patiently worked with me from manuscript submission to indexing and many steps in between. It is the good fortune of an author when she knows the editor, has met with him face-to-face, and can stir up some dust without creating a storm. James is adept at diffusing tension, interjecting humor, and interacting in a way that invariably improves the text.

For the work of Heather Dean Brewer, who designed the cover, I am most grateful. You can go to New York or London for cover design, but she's the best in the business. The marketing and publicity team is also top-notch. To Ruth Anderson, Brianna DeWitt, and Lauren Carlson, I extend my deepest thanks. Our collaboration has not only involved countless emails and phone calls but also a very profitable project luncheon that included Bob and James as well. Here animated conversation spilled into concrete strategies.

As I have acknowledged many times before, my writing would seriously suffer were it not for my beloved husband, John Worst. We disagree and bicker and sometimes howl with laughter as we trudge through the muck of the manuscript, always clearing the way for improved content, clarity— and charisma. He repeatedly reads and refines and bends and molds my straggling sentences and paragraphs. For his efforts I am most grateful.

Regardless of this remarkable collaboration, my name alone, for better and for worse, appears on the cover, and thus I take full responsibility for its contents, including errors.

Introduction

What if there had been no story?
No Abraham and Sarah, no Isaac and Rebekah,
and no Esau and Jacob, and no Rachel and Leah.
What if no one had remembered?
What if no one had cared enough to write it down?
What if there had been no God of Adam and Eve, Cain and
    Abel,
and the ten generations from Noah to Abraham had never
    existed?
What if there had been no creation and there was only chaos
    and the void?
What if God himself was only a hole in the darkness?

                        Anne Roiphe, *Water from the Well*

What if, indeed, there had been no story—no Bible that has brought balance and richness and spiritual direction to countless faithful through the ages? And where else in history or literature could we find such an assortment of colorful women as in the Bible? And where could we find women whose issues and aspirations are as contemporary as our own? From Eve to Phoebe and Priscilla, these women seek to understand and serve God and to deal with sin and personal struggles in their lives. It's all in the Bible, whether anger, infertility, rape, incest, adultery, mental illness, marital problems, racism, sister rivalry—even idolatry and murder. Almost any problem we can imagine is found among these women in the pages of Scripture. But we also find joyful celebrations and ingenuity and quick wit and cooperation and courage and sacrificial ministry.

Some of these fascinating women in both the Old and the New Testaments are not even named. We know them only by a description or a feminine pronoun. She is buried in the book of Judges, this unnamed daughter of a man whose name is either mispronounced or misspelled or entirely forgotten. Her story is shocking. She is her daddy's little girl—absolutely adored. Then in an insane set of circumstances her world is upended. Is she slain as a ritual sacrifice by her doting father, or is she forced into a lifetime of secluded celibacy? The text is unclear. Jephthah's daughter, forever nameless, is just one of the captivating women in the Bible.

How we might wish the Bible came with footnotes expanding the stories and points of view of these female characters. But even the women who have become household names are barely known to us. That the Bible offers few biographical details, however, is not necessarily an obstacle to the one who wishes to draw inspiration and understanding from its pages. In fact, one might argue that the power of the text is often bolstered by its very brevity. The purpose of the writers, rather than to simply present biography, is to relate events or perhaps put forward beliefs and laws of behavior and worship. So we're frustrated when we discover their profiles are so puny.

When I was growing up, we took the Bible seriously, and so it ought to be. But there is also a place for fun and even hilarity. If we don't laugh with the writers of the Bible, we will surely cry because almost every book is soaked in blood and sadness. In fact, we join with generations of old who see right through the desolation into the very heart of humor. We imagine the patriarchs and their descendants sitting around campfires telling and retelling these same stories, sometimes slapping their knees and howling with laughter. So also women baking bread and drawing water reminding each other of Rebekah and Rachel and Rahab. What merriment these recollections would bring.

Women comprise a distinct minority—often a marginalized minority—in the biblical text. Of the some three thousand named Bible characters, fewer than 10 percent are women. But positioned as *other*, they play a key role. They are the ones who bring new blood into the family of God. Israelite men marry them. Such stalwarts as Esau, Judah, Moses, Boaz, and King David marry *outsiders*. The prophet Hosea marries a prostitute. Jesus interacted with a Samaritan as well as a Syrophoenician woman. And of course Jesus himself had *outsider* blood running through his veins. This only serves to make the women of the Bible approachable and authentic.

In addition to the down-to-earth reality of these women, their symbolic wallop is enormous. Eve is a case in point, as is Mary. Perhaps more than any other biblical characters, they are suffused with symbolism, particularly through the course of church history. But they are surely not alone. Sarah and Hagar and Lot's wife are cited metaphorically by none other than Paul—and Jesus himself.

The individual in Scripture whose persona takes on the most striking symbolism is arguably Jezebel, rivaled only by Judas. In John's Revelation, she is a prophet in Thyatira luring people into false religious beliefs, even as Jezebel, the wife of Ahab, rallied the prophets of Baal and lured the Israelites into false worship. Today referring to a woman as a *Jezebel* carries obvious negative connotations. Other symbolic women have very positive connotations, as Job's daughters do. In fact, there is an international youth organization named Job's Daughters. Their website (www.jobsdaughters international.org) explains the symbolic nature of the name: "Job's Daughters is based on . . . Job 42:15, 'And in all the land were no women found so fair as the Daughters of Job.'"

Job's wife, on the other hand, symbolizes the lament summed up in one's *disappointment with God*. "Curse God and die" are her most memorable words. The Proverbs 31 woman is a grand composite of the faithful and competent wife. The Song of Songs is packed full of symbolism depicting most notably a sexually alluring woman. Gomer is a prostitute who becomes a prophet's wife, a striking metaphor of Israel's unfaithfulness.

The New Testament is also rich in symbolism. Mary is the ultimate icon of purity. The woman of Sychar stands in for the seeking sinner set free. Richard Blanchard's song lyrics of "Fill My Cup, Lord" speak for themselves. The first line is familiar: "Like the woman at the well I was seeking . . ."[1] She, like Mary Magdalene, represents the *fallen woman*.

Men, of course, are depicted similarly. Adam's symbolic significance is immense as is Father Abraham's. Joseph is a *type* of Christ. *The patience of Job* is a common figure of speech, and Judas represents the ultimate betrayal. In Sunday school when we sang "Dare to be a Daniel," no one had to ask what *being a Daniel* meant. The prodigal son and the good Samaritan also stand as powerful symbols. Yet, for their numbers, women rank high in symbolism, and failure to recognize this richness diminishes any study of them.

Nevertheless, the symbolic dimension of these women must not be their defining measurement. In Eve we must see far more than a temptress who offered her husband forbidden fruit. Mary is more than a pregnant virgin. And both are far more than mothers, as some books on biblical women categorize them. They are complex women who deserve another look, despite the brevity of their stories.

As we peer into these fascinating lives, it helps when we exercise our imaginations and ask more questions than we answer. In fact, I often think it is helpful to steal a sentence from Spinoza (the eminent seventeenth-century philosopher). He writes that the purpose of the Bible "is not to convince the reason, but to attract and lay hold of the imagination."[2]

> **The Historical Imagination**
>
> The historian's picture of the past is . . . in every detail an imaginary picture. . . . As works of imagination, the historian's work and the novelist's do not differ. Where they do differ is that the historian's picture is meant to be true.
>
> R. G. Collingwood,
> "The Historical Imagination"

We will become ensnared in a dense thicket if we demand that everything we find in these pages pass the test of reason. Some things, pure and simple, just don't make sense to a rational questioning mind. That's okay. Such is not the purpose of Scripture.

Likewise, we ought to be wary of the kind of sermonizing that too easily simplifies and sterilizes these characters—sermonizing, for example, that pegs women like Mary and Martha as opposites who are easily categorized as personality types. Their lives, however, are full of joy and sorrow and perhaps boredom, consumed with daily activities involving family, friends, and neighbors. That they lived in a very different time and culture utterly foreign to what most of us experience is easily ignored.

Cultural differences are truly vast. Today in the West, for example, women often choose not to marry or to delay pregnancy or forgo motherhood altogether. Those with infertility issues have medical and adoption options. Rarely are they defined by their barrenness, as was often true in biblical times. Imagine defining Oprah by her lack of children. But in the Palestine of three thousand years ago, she would have been perceived in a very different light.

Unlike their male counterparts, women of the Bible, with the exception of the Virgin Mary, are rarely associated with incredible miracles or fantastic feats. No woman builds an ark and then packs it full of animals. No woman calls down plagues on whole populations, nor does she command the waters of the Red Sea or the Jordan River to separate for easy passage. No woman kills a giant with a slingshot and a stone. For her, the sun does not stand still. No woman is ever swallowed by a big fish, nor does she even snatch a coin from the mouth of an ordinary-sized fish to pay taxes.

Nevertheless, while the circumstances surrounding these women typically relate to domestic life, their stories are no less interesting than those of their male counterparts. True, their wombs are opened by God, including the jaw-dropping instance when Sarah becomes pregnant in her old age. But for the most part, because of their very ordinariness, the women are often easier to relate to than the men in the Bible.

That is not to say that the Bible, even when it focuses on women, is easy to understand. There are countless questions that arise as we read through the text. How do Adam and Eve fit into the scheme of prehistoric humanity? Was there no evil in this world before Eve reached for and then ate the forbidden fruit? How could Adam have lived nearly a thousand years? Did Sarah actually give birth in her nineties? For the inquisitive reader, the issues are almost endless. The simplest response is that the Bible is a sacred book loaded with miracles and mysteries. But many readers want more-specific and concrete answers. This volume does not address these matters, thoughtful and valid though they may be. We leave these issues to experts, while here we embrace the mystery.

This book is ideally read in small groups, where there is greater opportunity for interaction and understanding. But some may say: *we need an expert. We need a scholarly Bible teacher.* Perhaps. But biblical experts

Embracing Biblical Mystery

Kierkegaard's simple man makes a simple mistake: he wants to translate the mystery of the biblical story into terms that he can comprehend. His failure has something to teach us. Sometimes it is when we stop trying to understand or interrogate apparently "absurd" phenomena . . . [that] we become more open to them.

Zadie Smith, "Some Notes on Attunement"

often disagree among themselves. A group setting offers an opportunity to ask questions and stimulate thinking. "Questions to Think About" conclude each chapter, some serious, some more frivolous and fun.

If I were in a book group studying this volume, I would welcome points of view that differ from my own. And I would be eager for someone to challenge my own perspective. As a college and seminary professor for some three decades, I have learned to love the lively discussions in class and the wide-ranging points of view. I can only hope such would be the atmosphere among groups digging into this presentation of biblical women.

I seek to avoid making these women over into my own image, but I do recognize my own subjectivity. We all must take care not to fall into this temptation. Deep down we unconsciously remake them, if not in our own image, then into our ideal portrait of what a woman should be. I want to shout: *Leave them alone!* Rahab is a prostitute. *Get over it!* We must take her as she is. No matter how hard we try, we simply cannot remake her into a virtuous massage therapist.

So also with many other biblical women. Poor Mary. She has suffered the most. From the early centuries to the present, she has been idealized as the perpetual virgin fossilized into a saintly statue or, if not that, the definitive model of a perfect submissive woman. We will see that she was a sturdy, strong-willed, small-town girl who seamlessly developed into a respected Jewish matriarch. We seek to imagine her not as a *saint* but rather as a neighbor who might be sharing a recipe for stew or giving us some tips on keeping the tomato hornworm at bay.

We imagine best what we know. My imagination, like all imaginations, arises out of my own worldview, one formed in the northern Wisconsin farming community in which I was raised, never far away from the country church on the corner of County H and Lewis Road. My worldview has been stretched by such diverse cultures as those found in East Texas; Newark,

New Jersey; Crown Point, Indiana; Kijabe, Kenya; Moscow; and Singapore, places where I set up temporary residence. For twenty-eight years, I made my home in an integrated neighborhood in Grand Rapids, Michigan, and after that in a nearby river-rat neighborhood on a floodplain in Comstock Park, where I am writing today. Add to that a slew of Asian, African, and Latino students, and you might think I am a model of diversity. Far from it. Open these pages, and a white middle-class woman is writing every line.

I long to be truly multicultural. Indeed, how many times have I popped in next door to weep my pain in Claretha's arms and sit at her kitchen table eating ribs and fried chicken? I have loved her as I've loved no other neighbor in my entire life. But there is no way I can enter into her worldview or that of any other black women transplanted from Mississippi, and surely not Kenyan or Korean women. So it is left up to other writers to situate these women in settings that are even closer to biblical cultures than mine is. May this book then be one that spawns many such volumes, each with its own cultural flair.

When my editor initially proposed this project to me, my first reaction was: *Is there a need for another book on women in the Bible? Enough already!* But then I began perusing what is available, and I found mainly fictional volumes or profile overviews (mostly A–Z) that left me wondering and wanting. The truth is, I'm still wondering and wanting, but I have come to appreciate these women as I never have before. What incredibly fascinating individuals they are. Why hadn't I long ago dug deeper into their lives?

So as we unleash our imaginations and begin this journey by considering the reality as well as the symbolic nature of biblical women, let us get

> ## Annie Dillard and the Art of Biblical Imagination
>
> A blur of romance clings to our notions of "publicans," "sinners," "the poor," "the people in the marketplace," "our neighbors," as though of course God should reveal himself, if at all, to these simple people, these Sunday school watercolor figures, who are so purely themselves in their tattered robes, who are single in themselves, while we now are various, complex, and full at heart. Yet, some have imagined well, with honesty and art, the detail of such a life, and have described it with such grace, that we mistake vision for history, dream for description, and fancy that life has devolved.
>
> Annie Dillard, *Holy the Firm*, quoted in *Pilgrim Souls*

ready for the ride of our lives. We must never be fooled, however, by assuming we truly understand them. We hardly know our own selves. How can we possibly know these elusive women of millennia past? All we can do is to invite them to live again and be ever grateful for the enrichment they bring to our lives.

> The LORD God said, "It is not good for the man to be alone." . . . She is clothed with strength and dignity; she can laugh at the days to come. . . . Honor her for all that her hands have done, and let her works bring her praise at the city gate.[3]

1

Eve and Noah's Wife

Mothers of Us All

If I were an accomplished portrait artist, my primary subject would be Eve. I would set my pastels aside and paint her in living color. My painting would never be mistaken for one by the great sixteenth-century artist Lucas Cranach, whose Eve is a thin, flat-chested, demure Caucasian lady offering Adam an apple. My Eve, rather, is a robust and voluptuous black woman with toned arms. She has unblemished ebony skin with a sheen that glistens in the sun filtering through the tropical rainforest. She is lying on a bed of moss, attired only in flowering hibiscus and ferns, her long legs and breasts partially exposed. Her hair is lush, her lips full and slightly parted, her eyes sparkling, her head tilted. The expression on her face is one of bemusement as much as utter contentment.

Eve is typically depicted in art and defined in commentaries by her sin—her one-time fall from grace. I look back on my own life and can easily enumerate temptations to which I have succumbed. How would I feel if the most egregious of these sins were what defined who I am? I understand such defining of individuals like Susan Smith, who is remembered—if remembered at all—for her crime of drowning her two young sons. But

Eve, the Most Misunderstood Woman of the Bible

With the possible exception of Mary, Eve is the most misunderstood woman of the Bible. She has been wrenched from the actual words of the text, then shoved and pounded into various shapes to fit whatever void a culture feels in the collective psyche. So many alterations has she undergone, so many cultural re-constructions has she suffered, so many private purposes has she served, that it is next to impossible to get past this most symbolic of all females to examine the "real" woman. . . . From the apostle Paul to C. S. Lewis, writers have used her to make theological points about human nature. This was inevitable, of course. . . . And, according to which theologian one reads, Eve's story is proof of women's inferior reason, their innate feminine guile, or their superior daring and courage.

Virginia Stem Owens, *Daughters of Eve*

Eve? Really? She was deceived by the serpent's cunning, the Bible says, and she ate the fruit and urged Adam to sample it as well. Sure, she disobeyed God's clear commandment. But haven't I also, even more blatantly than did Eve?

Eve's persona is ever so scantily revealed in Scripture. Although there are more books featuring her than any other biblical woman aside from Mary the mother of Jesus, her story commands very little space in the canon. She is featured in less than two full chapters of Genesis (2:22–4:2, 4:25). Yet Eve grabs our imaginations. She's inquisitive and feisty as the woman who stands forever as the mother of us all.

Noah's wife has an entirely different role to play, but in a very significant sense, she too is the mother of us all. In fact, she is the only woman in the Bible besides Eve who could be considered as such.

Eve: Mother of All Living

Like Adam, weeks or months earlier, Eve had awakened to an environment that must have seemed both strange and natural. She is seeing and breathing and smelling for the first time. A baby breathes and begins to smell and see things as weeks pass. Sitting, walking, talking, and understanding come much later. Was Eve created with a capacity for all adult aptitudes? Did she naturally stand up and walk about? Did she greet Adam as though he were an acquaintance or friend? Or was she fearful or shy? Any attempt to re-create Eve's first moments of life is, of course, purely speculative.

But if she is to have meaning for our own lives, we are well served by a questioning imagination.

Eve has no way of knowing that she had been formed out of this man-creature's rib. Nor would she have had any means of fully understanding, even if she did indeed hear him say, "This is now bone of my bones and flesh of my flesh; she shall be called 'woman,' for she was taken out of man."[1] All the text reveals about her is that she was naked and she saw him naked and she did not even blush.

Time passes—a day, a week, a month, a year or more—and Eve finds herself in the company of a snake. It apparently doesn't occur to her to shriek. She has no fear nor, for that matter, surprise when the snake asks her a question. Only curiosity. How was she to know that snakes don't talk? And, of course, this was no ordinary snake. This "serpent was more crafty than any of the wild animals the LORD God had made." His question is straightforward, while at the same time shading the truth: "Did God really say, 'You must not eat from any tree in the garden'?"[2]

For anyone who is tracking only the verses about Eve, the question makes no sense. There are only two verses between her creation and this question. *Say what?* might have been her response. God had interacted and communed with Adam, but there is no indication that Eve had enjoyed this same privilege. She is on the ground floor of humanity at a time when God is walking through the Garden. But does she know God personally as Adam does?

It is clear, however, that she had learned from Adam about the forbidden fruit on the Tree of Knowledge of Good and Evil. We now hear Eve speaking for the first time. In fact, this is the first time any individual in Scripture has actually engaged in a conversation. Adam had identified each creature as God paraded it before him, and he had identified Eve as *bone of my bones* and more. But Eve answers a question, and her response is unequivocal:

> We may eat fruit from the trees in the garden, but God did say, "You must not eat fruit from the tree that is in the middle of the garden, and you must not touch it, or you will die."[3]

Here she adds an interesting twist. God had previously said nothing specific to Adam about *touching* the fruit. It seems entirely possible that Adam, in his concern to keep his wife from eating the fruit, added this restriction. As parents, we have all magnified restrictions to young children: *The stove is hot. Don't touch it. Don't even get close to it.* Adam's concern for Eve and his awareness of her natural sense of curiosity might have prompted him to exaggerate the danger.

Now the snake speaks again. He doesn't simply offer an opinion. He comes across as an authority—sounding to her as though he knows his way around better than Adam does. His words are presented as outright fact: "You will not certainly die . . . for God knows that when you eat from it your eyes will be opened, and you will be like God, knowing good and evil."[4]

Had Eve thought about the matter, she might have already wondered why God would restrict them from eating from one particular tree, and she might have been tantalized by this tree of *Knowledge*. Today if there were a fruit that, for example, freed up brain cells so that we could store and remember more knowledge, we might be tempted to give it a try even if we were warned of the risk factors. This may have been similar to the temptation Eve was confronting. Indeed, she now sees that this fruit offers her an opportunity "for gaining wisdom."[5]

She touches. Nothing happens. She eats. Nothing. She gives some to Adam, who, by the way, was with her all along. He touches. Nothing. The moment he eats it, however, the scales fall off. Time stands still. Their eyes are opened. They suddenly have a *knowledge of good and evil* that they had not possessed before. They realize for the first time that they are naked, and in that instant they feel shame. Eve blushes. Had she looked like Lucas Cranach's fair maiden, she would have been as red as a beet.

What, one may ask, was Adam thinking as he stood by listening to the serpent? This is not the place to try to sort out his thoughts, but needless to say, he didn't jump into the conversation and talk down the snake. He neither defended God nor protected Eve. He simply stood by and watched his wife disobey God's explicit orders. At this point, however, there is no thought of fussing and fighting over that shortcoming. They are so overcome with embarrassment by their nudity that they grab fig leaves, sew them together, and cover their private parts. Aren't they husband and wife? Why the shame? After all, they are not in Times Square in broad daylight. Nevertheless, their naked bodies are now properly covered.

God's warning had been unambiguous. All they can do is wait for the other shoe to fall. And fall it does. Indeed, *the Fall* is the subject of long-standing doctrinal disputations. The doctrine of *original sin* finds its origin in Adam and Eve. In the Reformed faith this sin takes on a magnitude of massive proportions when it is sandwiched on a theological grid between two other major concepts: Creation, *Fall*, Redemption. So now in both a personal and a cosmic sense sin has entered God's perfect creation, and there is hell to pay.

Both Eve and her husband hear the sound of the Lord walking in the Garden of Eden in the late afternoon as the sun is setting. They know the jig is up, and they hide. God calls to Adam and asks where he is. He responds that he was afraid and hid because he was naked. But God is on to him and asks where he got the idea that he was naked. Who told him? Before he can answer, God quickly moves to the heart of the matter, asking him if he has eaten from the Tree of Knowledge of Good and Evil. Adam's answer is classic. He places the blame squarely on Eve: "The woman you put here with me—she gave me some fruit from the tree, and I ate it."[6]

If Eve thinks Adam alone will be questioned, she's mistaken. God speaks to her directly, asking her what she has done. Taking a cue from Adam, she blames the snake. Without missing a beat, God turns to the snake, not to question but to curse—make the snake the most cursed of animals. That the serpent will crawl on its belly and eat dirt is easily understood, but the second half of the curse is more confusing:

> And I will put enmity
>   between you and the woman,
>   and between your offspring and hers;

Eve, Sarah, and Radical Grace

No longer can I isolate chapter three, reading it as the story of the Fall appended to two creation accounts. . . . [Walter] Brueggemann, the biblical exegete, disallows my tendency as a theologian to turn story into dogma. . . . Of course, this is not to deny the proud disobedience and consequent alienation portrayed in the story. But, contends Brueggemann, there is not one "fall" story but rather, in Genesis 1–11, four "falls," four stories of invitation and refusal, all of which form the prelude to the story of God's radical grace in the creation of a people out of the barrenness of Sarah's womb.

Richard A. Rhem, "The Continuing Adventure of Faith"

---

he will crush your head,
    and you will strike his heel.[7]

Whether or not Eve had any notion of what this meant, theologians have since generally agreed that this is God's warning that Satan, as represented by the snake, will be defeated by Christ, who will redeem the sins of the world. After cursing the serpent, God turns to Eve. Her life will never be the same. She will have pain in childbearing. Until this point, she apparently has no concept of pain. Things will also change in her relationship with her husband. She will have a desire for him, sexually and otherwise, and he will rule over her. Exactly how this rule would play out is not specified, but historically and even today in certain cultures women suffer severely under male domination and rule.

Eve also hears God's words to Adam that the ground will now be cursed with thorns and thistles, and he will work by the sweat of his brow just to stay alive. Though God is speaking to Adam, this curse on the ground has also had profound implications for Eve and all women who have toiled in fields throughout biblical times and since.

Although Eve's sin is not mentioned again in the Old Testament or in the Gospels, Paul refers to it in his letters. In 2 Corinthians 11:3, he warns fellow believers, men and women alike: "But I am afraid that just as Eve was deceived by the serpent's cunning, your minds may somehow be led astray from your sincere and pure devotion to Christ." In 1 Timothy 2:14–15, the statement is less clear.

> And Adam was not the one deceived; it was the woman who was deceived and became a sinner. But women will be saved through childbearing—if they continue in faith, love and holiness with propriety.

One might wonder why it was that Adam ate the fruit if he had not been deceived. Did he act with full awareness of his rebellion against God? And how is a woman *saved* through childbearing? Paul states elsewhere that all are saved by God's grace, through faith. So his words could hardly have reference to salvation and eternal life. Some have interpreted his words to refer to being physically saved. But that is also problematic. Have faithful women in any era been physically saved from the perils of childbirth?

6

Hardly. Overseas missionary women in past generations, for example, died frequently in childbirth, and not because of any lack of holiness and propriety. These verses have rightly been labeled one of the "desperately difficult" passages of the Bible.

Although Paul, speaking of Adam, states in Romans 5:12 that "sin entered the world through one man," Eve as temptress has received the brunt of the blame. Writing in the early third century, Tertullian (c. 160–225) laid the guilt squarely on her:

> God's judgment on this sex lives on in our age; the guilt necessarily lives on as well. You are the Devil's gateway; you are the unsealer of that tree; you are the first foresaker of the divine law; you are the one who persuaded him whom the Devil was not brave enough to approach; you so lightly crushed the image of God, the man Adam; because of your punishment, that is, death, even the Son of God had to die.[8]

Also reflecting on the first chapters of Genesis, the celebrated fourth-century "golden-mouthed" preacher, John Chrysostom, made the case that the man only was created in the image of God: "Therefore the man is in the 'image of God' since he had no one above him, just as God has no superior but rules over everything. The woman, however, is 'the glory of man,' since she is subjected to him."[9]

Augustine, considered the greatest theologian of the first millennium of the church, took the argument a step further, tying Adam's superiority not only to Eve's subjection but also to her "small intelligence."

> That a man endowed with a spiritual mind could have believed this [the lie of the serpent] is astonishing. And just because it is impossible to believe it, woman was given to man, woman who was of small intelligence and who perhaps still lives more in accordance with the promptings of the inferior flesh than by the superior reason.[10]

There is surely nothing in the text that would indicate that Eve is of small intelligence, nor is there any evidence in the continuing biblical narrative that men have an edge over women intellectually. As for Eve herself, she is banished from the Garden with her husband. God is taking no chances for fear they will try to return in order to "live forever." So he drives them out to make a life in the deserted land east of Eden; there can be no return to the Garden for the gate is obstructed by "cherubim and a flaming sword flashing back and forth to guard the way to the tree of life."[11]

At this point, we can only wonder about Eve's personal relationship with God. What was it founded upon? It is true that, unlike many of us today, she actually had a one-on-one conversation with God, albeit short. But that was in the context of a dressing-down. She tries to defend herself only to learn of the pain she will endure the rest of her life. Her next encounter with God—though not verbal—is the equivalent of sirens, flashing lights, and armed guards preventing her from going back to the only home she has ever known.

But that is behind them. We now learn that Adam has "made love to his wife Eve." She conceives, and when Cain is born, she credits God: "With the help of the LORD I have brought forth a man."[12] She conceives again and gives birth to Abel. Apart from their sexual intimacies, nothing more is said or implied about the relationship between Eve and Adam. They are hardscrabble subsistence farmers barely eking a living out of the weed-prone rocky soil. After that the story line fades away.

No woman can read this biblical account without wondering how it was for Eve as she raised her boys, from teething and potty training to becoming responsible young men. There are many blanks to be filled in. Imagine telling your own story of raising children and moving from infancy to adulthood without any reference to the two decades in between. Was she a doting mother who was ever watchful of dangers, or did she let them spend hours unsupervised while discovering the world for themselves? If they are typical kids, she endures their terrible twos and years of mischief making and perhaps adolescent rebellion and butting heads with each other long before they arrive at their final showdown.

Then there is that devastating day. How much Eve might have known of her sons' two different offerings to God is not disclosed. Were the boys spiritually inclined? Had she spoken to them about God and the perils of disobedience? All we know is that in an instant she becomes the first member of the most awful exclusive club a parent can ever join. She receives news that her own child is dead, her boy whom it seemed like just yesterday she had cradled in her arms and nursed. And worse than that, her other son, her beloved firstborn, has killed him.

Unless a mother has buried a child, she is unable to enter this surreal realm of utter anguish. Those of us who have not can only try to imagine the stabbing pain that Eve endures. There are no words that encompass such grief, and the author of Genesis does not try. We are not privy to even a glimpse of her tears. How does she pull her life together after such a crushing blow? Does she go through the standard stages of grief? Does she ever speak of her dear sons again? Life goes on—the day-to-day grind of eking out an existence. Amid the gloom, she conceives once again, and Seth is born. She is a woman who knows deep sadness, but we can also imagine her as a woman who knows how to celebrate moments of joy and laughter.

The joy and pain no doubt continue as Eve eases into her role as a grandmother. Cain has been banished from east of Eden to become a wanderer—wandering in the land of Nod, where his son Enoch is born and his grandson Irad. Fast forward three generations to Lamech, who like great-grandpa Cain (four times removed) has a fight and kills a man. Was Eve still living, and did she hear about this murder? In the meantime, she has had another grandson, Enosh, the son of Seth.

The Bible does not say when Eve died or how old she was. Adam, as far as the text reveals, had no other wife than Eve and, besides Seth, "had other sons and daughters."[13] He died at age 930.

Noah's Wife

Though her three sons are named, she is not, nor are her three daughters-in-law. But we are curious to know more about this nameless woman. Noah is a very old man, five hundred years old to be precise, when he begins building the ark. What was she doing in those centuries before, or might she have been a few hundred years younger than he? How would she have felt about his building such a vessel? Did he explain to her that his marching orders came directly from God? At this point in time, there is no evidence that God was verbally interacting with people on a regular basis. Did she think her husband had gone stark raving mad?

Once the ark is constructed, there are other concerns that affect her far more than had the procurement of gopher wood. (That indeed may have been the main topic of dinner conversation for decades on end.) Now the old man is out lassoing antelope. The neighbors' eye-rolling has progressed to head-shaking and just plain pity—at least for her. For them it's a show. Their gathering to watch the daily activity is a social diversion. The usual routine of manual labor, broken only by drunken, rowdy vice, is itself marked by boredom. Now there's something to talk about.

During the last days before the deluge, Noah's wife and daughters-in-law must have been busy themselves. While the men herded wild and domesticated animals into the ark, they would have been busy packing and preparing for a long voyage. They may have recoiled at the whole idea of it, but Noah's authority apparently holds sway.

Then the day arrives. They are safe and secure inside, as their neighbors look on with as much amusement as bewilderment. Rain begins with an unusual suddenness. Noah paces back and forth on the inside decks, checking the peepholes. His wife peeks out as well. She's never seen so much water. Their once-freestanding house is coming apart and floating away. Worse, she hears the voices of children and women she's known all her life. They're screaming for help. There's nothing—absolutely nothing—she can do.

Those first terrible hours are forever etched in her psyche. Never is she far from the sounds of those cries for help. The weeks and months drag on. Eventually, however, there is hope of dry land once again. But the land is never really dry again, at least not in her lifetime. There is decay, that awful smell of rotting dead bodies, both animal and human. The thorns and thistles that Eve had encountered were but irritations in comparison to the land that Noah's wife steps into. The smelly ark was no paradise, and if she had imagined it, there was surely no pot of gold at the end of the rainbow. Only a reminder of how bad it once was.

Concluding Observations

Eve as the mother of us all is hidden in the dense tropical ferns in paradise, barely visible to the naked eye. When she is banished from her lush surroundings, she is almost lost entirely, fading into the distant rugged landscape. Wisdom warns us to say very little about her that could ever be confused with fact.

It is unfortunate that Eve has for so long been used as a political—or social—football. She has been kicked around more than any other biblical woman, beginning particularly with certain of the church fathers. During the Reformation, Catholic clerics labeled the outspoken Protestant Argula von Stauffer an "insolent daughter of Eve." Anne Hutchinson was accused by Puritan divines of being "an Eve" who was influencing other women and trying to "catch their husbands also."

In recent years, Eve has been branded the first feminist and hailed as the founder of the New Age movement for her desire for higher wisdom. She has been used to bolster both sides of the headship debate that has raged for years among certain Evangelicals. But if we are honest she eludes us—except in our imaginations.

Noah's wife is rarely featured in commentaries or other writings. She became the butt of jokes, however, in medieval street plays that portrayed her as a nagging wife, refusing to leave her "gossips" and come into the ark until Noah grabbed a stick and hit her on the backside. It was an old joke even then, but it always drew a hearty laugh.

When we actually take the time to contemplate her, she is a pitiful character. While Noah would forever go down as a great man of faith, she would be no more than a footnote, perhaps her mournful cry echoed in the distant thunder. The rainbow of hope would be for future generations. Her soggy, putrefied world would be a constant reminder of deep sadness.

Questions to Think About

Have artistic renditions of Eve wrongly represented her? How would you describe her or paint her portrait? Would her nationality and features be similar to your own?

What issues and problems relevant to women today may have also confronted Eve? Is there anything in the biblical text that gives us insight into her relationships and emotions? Is there anything you can draw on that helps you understand the loss of a child? Have you or anyone you've known endured such a terrible loss?

In what specific ways has Eve been most egregiously misinterpreted since New Testament times? Are we also sometimes unfairly sized up by others? Does Eve remind us that we ought to ask ourselves how we will be regarded after we die?

Why do women have a reputation for shrieking in horror at the sight of a snake? Is that part of our DNA, or is it a learned reaction?

Do you suppose that Eve ever reminisced and longed for the perfection of Eden? Do you look back with nostalgia for the *good old days*?

Imagine yourself as Eve. How might you describe your relationship with God? Was God's presence in some way closer and more readily available then than it is for us today? If you were to encounter Eve in heaven and had the opportunity to ask her one question, what would you want to know?

Does a paradise of perfection appeal to you? Would life be less exciting in such perfection?

Are you able to contemplate Noah's wife and daughters-in-law and their terrible loss of extended family members and friends in the great deluge? Do you think that the horror of the flood is often diminished in Noah's ark picture books and various ark-related kitsch?

2

Sarah and Hagar

Bad Blood Down to the Present Day

Before my mother enrolled in teacher's training in the late 1920s to prepare for a series of jobs in one-room country schools, she worked as a maid in Saint Paul, Minnesota. She despised the work, not because the hours were long and the work was arduous but because she was treated badly by the mistress and her young son. The woman was a wealthy socialite who lounged in her silk pajamas and looked condescendingly on my mother as wholly beneath her.

Despite her hard work, my mother was unable to do anything that actually pleased the mistress. Their different cultural backgrounds may have contributed to the ongoing tension: the maid from a poor, hardscrabble farm family of Scandinavian descent, the mistress from a nouveau riche Jewish family that had endured generations of anti-Semitism.

For most of a year, the older and the younger endured each other, but not without resentment and seething anger on the part of the younger. The mistress wielded power and sometimes seemed to purposely create incidents whereby she could vent her rage. But the maid was clever enough to occasionally escape the abuse.

The story that sticks with me most is a tale of spoiled milk and a spoiled son. My mother had prepared the boy's breakfast in the kitchen, as she always did, while the mother remained in bed. After he was picked up for school, my mother would bring the mistress breakfast in her chamber. On this particular morning, the boy was silent as usual, the table set before him. Without warning he jumped up and cried out as he ran to his mother's room: *The milk is spoiled.*

Thinking quickly, my mother poured the spoiled milk down the drain and grabbed a bottle that had only minutes earlier been delivered at the door. When the mistress marched out of her boudoir to test the milk and rage at the maid, she was stopped short. The milk was fresh, and the spoiled brat was told to finish his breakfast.

Scroll backward some four thousand years, and we find a mistress and a maid, Sarah and Hagar. Sarah is the rich wife of the grand old patriarch Abraham, and as such she wields the power. But Hagar, her Egyptian servant, has her own defenses, and we see them in a prolonged struggle. In the end, Sarah wins, though the struggle is hardly over. In fact, today the Jewish descendants of Sarah are often at war with Muslims, who consider Hagar and her son, Ishmael, their biblical forebearers.

Sarah

Sarah is anything but an enviable character. She comes from Ur of the Chaldees and is married to her half brother Abraham—same father, different mothers. An arranged marriage, we presume. But why? She's classy, competent, and, without a doubt, a looker. Was there no one else in the clan who regarded her highly enough to fork over a hefty bride-price? And why would Terah want to marry his own daughter to his son? And how did Sarah feel about it? How well did they know each other? Was he the big brother she looked up to, and did he play the role of protector? Or, considering their age difference, did they basically ignore each other?

Sarah is surely an enigma, and not just because the text holds her secrets tight. Her daughter-in-law Rebekah (whom she would never know) and her granddaughter Rachel are both aware of betrothal negotiations and appear to consent to their marriages. Whether Sarah was in any way involved is not revealed. Was she a child when she was married, or was she an old maid in her fifties?

Today we recoil at such incestuous relationships, and we naturally wonder if she cringed at the idea as we would. There are other times as well when we wonder if she might have been tempted to balk. She's obviously a strong woman, but she does not stand up for herself when her husband puts her in jeopardy in order to protect himself. Yet on other occasions she behaves very badly when we wish she would show more restraint.

We first meet Sarah when she is sixty-five, what we think of today as retirement age. She is a homemaker with no children or grandchildren running underfoot. It would have been nice to have daughters helping with the housework and carrying on the family traditions of meal preparation and holiday celebrations. Only sons, however, would give her true fulfillment as a wife and as an honored matriarch. But now she is too old. Her biological clock had run out decades ago. Life is miserable.

In fact, her barrenness is what defines her. When she is introduced in the Genesis account, the reference is unambiguous: "Now Sarai was childless because she was not able to conceive."[1]

The first in a line of biblical women who lament their barrenness, Sarah treads a painful path that others will follow—that of watching concubines or lesser wives making babies for her own husband. She is a woman caught in the patriarchal web that envelops the ancient world. The pain associated with childbearing does not begin to match the curse of bearing no children at all.

There have been so many monthly periods she cannot begin to count them. Cramps and PMS sometimes lasting for days. And what a mess! No corner drugstore where she could stock up on tampons and sanitary napkins or buy a bottle of Midol. If she were like most women, she would have begun "the change" in her late forties or fifties, bleeding at times like a stuck pig. Then would come the near fainting spells and what could only be described as grand-mal hot flashes—never-ending menopause. How long has it been since she made love with Abraham? Years? She doesn't keep track.

And now Abraham is talking about relocating again, this time to Canaan. What a massive undertaking such a move will be. True, she has servants,

15

but packing up such a large household still requires a lot of exertion on her part. Has he told her that his decision is based on a *call* from God? If he has, how might she have reacted? *What a crock! Is he hearing voices—hallucinating?* She certainly isn't hearing anything. And there is no reason to believe that they were like a modern missionary couple, discussing together God's will for their lives.

In fact, it is hard to imagine that Abraham would reveal to her the most astounding aspect of this call. It's one thing to claim God is giving instructions to move—quite another to claim that God is going to make you the head of a *great nation*.

If she had been told about a promised land, she might have wondered once they arrived how promising it really was. For one thing, it is inhabited, and there is certainly no Welcome Wagon committee to mark their arrival. Twice they stop long enough for Abraham to build an altar and make a sacrifice. Does he tell her that the voice is speaking again? At Shechem, he hears God saying: "To your offspring I will give this land."[2] What offspring? No doubt Abraham kept that promise to himself. Again they are on the move, only to pitch their tents in Bethel, where he builds another altar and makes a sacrifice.

But famine keeps them from settling in Canaan. So they head off into the Negev, a rocky, parched desert, making their way slowly to Egypt. To avoid the severe famine in Canaan, they settle down for a time in Egypt, where there is grazing land and plenty of food. While it is true that nomads with their tents and herds roam the region, one could wonder why Abraham has assumed he will be safe in Egypt, where God has surely not called him. But from this point on, Abraham is flying by the seat of his pants.

What is she thinking when he presents her with his latest plan? It might be a clever idea, and not entirely untrue, if it did not risk her well-being.

> I know what a beautiful woman you are. When the Egyptians see you, they will say, "This is his wife." Then they will kill me but will let you live. Say you are my sister, so that I will be treated well for your sake and my life will be spared because of you.[3]

To treat even a sister in such a way is unconscionable, but a wife—*bone of my bone and flesh of my flesh?* How could he do it? Far better to have remained in a land of famine than to betray one's wife. Her response, if she gave any, is not recorded. As anticipated, the royal officials tell the Pharaoh that an incredibly beautiful woman has entered their domain. She is summoned to live in the palace.

We can only wonder what might have happened to her next. The Pharaoh is not simply looking for a potted plant. He wants action. We do know that Abraham, her brother, receives from the Pharaoh as payment for her "sheep and cattle, male and female donkeys, male and female servants, and camels."[4]

How long she remains with the Pharaoh

> **Sarah and the Pharaoh**
>
> Abram's wife becomes another man's wife. Becoming a wife, in these narratives, always implies sexual relations. The curse for sexual relations, in fact, comes true: "And the Lord afflicted Pharaoh and his household with terrible plagues because of Sarai, the wife of Abram." Instead of bringing blessing to all nations, Abram has brought curse.
>
> Paul Borgman, *Genesis*

and how she feels about her sudden move from tent to palace is not disclosed. We can only imagine the conflicting sensations. How long has it been since she's had a bath? Has she ever had a bath? Or has she used a wet towel, ever conscious of the scarcity of water? Scented soap and perfume are probably new to her. Nor has she ever slept in such a luxuriant bed. The tapestries and tiled floors and statuary make tent living seem so commonplace, even shabby. She eats fruits and sweets and delectables that are tastier than anything she's previously known. Makeup and colorful gowns and priceless jewelry enhance her beauty.

She's no longer defined by that odious word *barren*. Now she sizzles. She is so dazzling she commands the eye of the king.

From the beginning of recorded history to the present time, the splendor of Egypt has captured the collective imagination of specialists and ordinary people alike. Here was Sarah experiencing the most glorious wealth the world had to offer. But it would not last. Word comes that some mysterious disease is spreading through the royal household—and she is blamed. Or rather Abraham, who pawned her off as his sister, is blamed. The Pharaoh is furious. He knows he's been duped. He has four bitter words for Abraham: "Take her and go!"[5]

So Sarah finds herself back in tents headed out into the Negev once again. She shouldn't be too harshly censured if she looked back with fleeting regret. Once again she is mistress of a large, unwieldy household and worse, a barren wife to a husband (and brother) she hardly knows. Besides the forbidding terrain and the unforgiving sun, there are serious family tensions. Something has got to give.

By the time they arrive back in Canaan, the whole encampment is ready to explode. Early on she may have been pleased to have her nephew Lot traveling with them. But ever since Egypt, he has taken on an air of equality if not superiority. With all his cattle and servants, he is every bit the equal of Abraham. Now his herdsmen are fighting with her husband's. Will it never end?

Too soon she learns that Abraham has given Lot the choice grazing land. *That lowdown scoundrel. Sure, Abraham offered it to him, but if he'd had any manners at all he would have declined.*

They settle down in what she considers a wasteland, and life becomes routine—that is until a messenger arrives to inform them that Lot has been taken captive by enemy armies. Abraham doesn't hesitate a minute. He calls together all 318 of his herdsmen, forms them into a makeshift militia, and marches them off to rescue his dear nephew. Sarah has no say in the matter, and she is left essentially alone with the children and womenfolk to manage the camp.

Abraham returns home, having waged a successful campaign, with recognition and respect previously unknown. He has been honored by kings. He has been blessed by a priest of God Most High, and he has sworn an oath by that same God not to take the spoils of war. Even more significant is further word from God, promising him a son. He sacrifices "a heifer, a goat and a ram, each three years old, along with a dove and a young pigeon," after which he is told how to cut and arrange them on an altar.[6] At nightfall he falls asleep, and God sends him prophetic dreams.

We easily read over such material thinking that all of this makes perfect sense to Abraham, and perhaps it does. But it is only natural to wonder if Sarah at this point has any real conception of God. How much does she know—if anything—about the creation of the world, of Adam and Eve and their sin and banishment from the Garden, of Noah and his ark full of creatures? Perhaps she knows stories, but does she know the God to whom Abraham builds altars and sacrifices? The text is silent as to whether God has ever spoken to her or if Abraham has ever spoken to her about God speaking to him.

We know nothing at all about her spiritual life—that is until we hear her very first recorded words. And they are anything but words of praise. Rather she accuses the Lord of closing her womb. How is it that she would point her finger at God? Life has again been chugging along in a daily grind. Lot, his wife, and his daughters are safe. The herdsmen are back tending the flocks. Then one day, seemingly out of the blue, she says to Abraham: "The LORD has kept me from having children. Go, sleep with my slave; perhaps I can build a family through her."[7]

One wonders how long this resentment has been festering. Her choice of words is most interesting. She orders him to have sex with *her* slave so that *she* can build a family. Both the husband and the slave are to breed for her benefit. Is she still chafing over Abraham's betrayal of her in Egypt?

Abraham, the man who can maneuver his paltry militia to crush the enemy, throws up a white flag when it comes to Sarah. He does what she tells him to do, and when the slave becomes pregnant, Sarah again accuses him: "You are responsible for the wrong I am suffering. I put my slave in your arms, and now that she knows she is pregnant, she despises me. May the LORD judge between you and me."[8]

Why doesn't he man up and remind her that he was simply following orders—her orders? Instead, he gives his calculating wife carte blanche in dealing with the helpless slave. So badly does Sarah oppress the slave girl that she fears for her life and runs away, only to return before her son is born.

Soon after this, Sarah realizes that her husband is again getting instructions from God. First there are to be name changes. His name, for most of a century Abram, is now to be Abraham to signal that he will be the father of many nations, through Ishmael, she must presume. Her given name,

> ### Sarah an Echo of Eve
>
> Sarah takes her maid and gives her to Abraham in an echo of the way Eve takes the fruit and gives it to Adam. . . . Sarah is trying to wrest control of creation, which Abraham and God are already struggling over. Abraham may be wavering in his faith, but Sarah seems to have abandoned hers. Her act may be selfless, but it's also faithless. . . . Sarah's gesture sets up a tension that will occupy history forever.
>
> Bruce Feiler, *Abraham*

19

Sarai, is now to be Sarah. Abraham perhaps thinks better of telling her that the reason for her name change is because he will have a son by *her*.

She can handle the name changes, but what comes next is shocking. Abraham is telling her that God has ordered him and all the men and his young son, Ishmael, to be circumcised. She has never heard of such a thing. Has Abraham lost his mind? We can only imagine her shuddering and shaking her head in utter bewilderment.

The surgery heals, and the men are again going about their work when one day while Abraham is sitting at the door of his tent, three visitors arrive. It's not every day they have company, and Abraham offers a hearty Palestinian welcome and bows before them. After inviting them to have their feet washed and enjoy a feast with him, he rushes back into the tent and instructs Sarah to quickly bake bread and orders a servant to kill a calf and prepare a succulent veal roast.

After the meal is over, one of the men tells Abraham that he will return in a year, at which time his wife will have given birth to a son. All the while Sarah has been eavesdropping, wondering what is going on. She hears the bizarre prediction, and she laughs aloud. The very idea is preposterous. She's long past menopause; she couldn't possibly give birth.

One of the men, who is actually the Lord in disguise, asks Abraham why she has laughed. Overhearing these words, Sarah stiffens up. Who is this talking? A dreadful fear comes over her, so she lies. She says, apparently to anyone in earshot: "I did not laugh."⁹

Sarah's is one of the few times of laughter recorded in the Bible. Because of her denial, we can assume it was a laugh of derision rather than delight. Her true laughter of delight is yet to come.

Shortly after this visit by the three men, Sodom and Gomorrah are destroyed, and Lot's wife is turned into a pillar of salt. Does Sarah grieve when she hears the news of the catastrophe, or does she think that Lot's wife and all the residents got what they deserved? Abraham looks across the plain to the smoldering cities, but there is no mention of her doing the same.

Abraham has failed in his bargaining with God to save the cities, and he is anxious to get out of the area, so he moves to the region of the Negev and settles in Gerar. One could wish that the Bible were silent about this sojourn, but it is not. Once again Abraham convinces his beautiful wife to go along with his scheme and let it be known that she is only his sister. Predictably, the king of Gerar, Abimelek, ushers her into his harem. But before he brings her to his bed, God informs him in a dream that he is *dead meat* if he does not return her to her rightful husband.

Now the king demands that Abraham explain why he has carried out this awful deception. The reader might answer the question by accusing the devious old patriarch of trying to make a buck. In fact, Abraham does come away from the encounter with a boatload of gifts: sheep, cattle, slaves, and a thousand shekels of silver. But Abraham reveals to Abimelek an even worse indictment against himself, admitting that his deceptive ways began when he left his father's household and was on his own:

> I said to myself, "There is surely no fear of God in this place, and they will kill me because of my wife." Besides, she really is my sister, the daughter of my father though not of my mother; and she became my wife. And when God had me wander from my father's household, I said to her, "This is how you can show your love to me: Everywhere we go, say of me, 'He is my brother.'"[10]

Imagine having your husband insist that you show your love by protecting him by offering yourself to other men. Is it any wonder that Sarah is at times harsh with him? But this circus in Gerar will give way to celebration. At ninety years of age, Sarah gives birth to Isaac. After the baby is circumcised on the eighth day and when she has had time to recover, she gives a toast, and what a toast it is: "God has brought me laughter, and everyone who hears about this will laugh with me." Then she tags on a little addendum: "Who would have said to Abraham that Sarah would nurse children? Yet I have borne him a son in his old age."[11]

The next we learn, however, Sarah is back to her cranky self. During a feast that Abraham has thrown to celebrate Isaac's weaning, she catches the adolescent Ishmael poking fun at him. So what's the big deal? He's all boy after all. Punish him if it will make you feel better. Send him to bed without any dessert. But not Sarah. She goes ballistic. She shouts at Abraham: "Get rid of that slave woman and her son, for that woman's son will never share in the inheritance with my son Isaac."[12]

21

Here again one might seriously wonder about this marriage. It is easy to imagine there is little love lost between the two of them. Abraham admits that he uses her for self-defense, and she obviously allows herself to be used and abused. She almost appears to be biding her time until she can get back at him, as she is doing now. The boy she is banishing is none other than Abraham's firstborn son. Abraham is distressed, but now when he should be putting a clamp on Sarah's malice, he is mute. God intervenes, however, and tells him not to "be so distressed about the boy and [his] slave woman."[13] God goes a step further and tells him to heed Sarah's words.

From what the text implies, Sarah keeps a close watch on her beloved young son. She appears to be entirely out of the loop, however, when Abraham, having yet again heard the voice of God, takes him away for several days to sacrifice him on Mount Moriah. In the end, God stops him before he kills his son.

As for Sarah, we hear from her no more. Does Isaac return and tell her of the nightmare he has just endured? Or does she go to her grave having been spared the story? She lives on until Isaac is thirty-seven years old, still unmarried. When Isaac does marry three years later, he takes his bride into his mother's tent and is only then comforted in his grief.

If the bond between Sarah and her husband, Abraham, appears weak, the same could not be said for the attachment to her son—perhaps so strong as to be unhealthy.

Hagar

She is one of the few named individuals in Scripture who is referred to as a slave. And more than that. Hagar is an Egyptian, quite possibly part of the booty that Abraham left with after having been sent away for deceiving the Pharaoh. Where else would he have acquired a slave from Egypt? Egyptian slaves had more options for freedom than did most slaves in other cultures and eras. In fact, they sometimes voluntarily served as slaves, trading their manual labor or skills for room and board.

As for Hagar, she might have been a royal servant, thus one who could have been given away or sold without being consulted in any such transaction. If that were the case, we can assume that her status does not improve when she enters Sarah's household. Her presence is first mentioned after she had been living for a decade with Sarah, shortly after the sudden fiery destruction of the cities of Sodom and Gomorrah.

Unbeknownst to her, Sarah proposes that Abraham breed with her. Perhaps such a term is harsh. This proposal was far more than a transaction between, for example, dog breeders, whereby the owner of the bitch receives the pick of the litter. But the fact is, Sarah owns the slave, will get the pick of the litter, and the slave has no say in the matter. "Go, sleep with my slave," she orders Abraham, with more than a hint of bitterness; "perhaps I can build a family through her."[14] A more favorable term for this slave might be that of *surrogate mother*, but surrogates, at least in contemporary situations, are not only consulted but freely offer their services.

The "breeder" whom neither Sarah nor Abraham call by name becomes pregnant, and she is changed, at least in her own mind, into a full-fledged mother. She is transformed. It's more than hormones and morning sickness and an expanding waistline. She feels that first kick, and her maternal instincts take over. This baby is hers, and any thought of it being taken from her is dreadful—nothing short of kidnapping. Her mind is racing. Will she herself be sold off, never to see her baby again?

The text is less than clear about her attitude toward Sarah. That she *despises* her fits the context—despising a woman who plans to snatch your baby. Other translations suggest rather that Sarah becomes *slight* in her eyes—that her respect for Sarah diminishes with her fertile one-upmanship. It may have been all the above. From Hagar's perspective, Sarah holds the power; she herself is powerless; she is *other*; she is marginalized.

More than that, Sarah is now mistreating her. Does she slap Hagar, perhaps still in her teens? Does she call her a slut? Does she assign impossible tasks and berate her for not completing them? All we know is that Hagar feels so desperate that she runs away into the desert. What is she thinking? She surely cannot survive alone in the wilderness. Danger lurks on every side, not the least of which are rowdy traders, who, for all she knows, might gang-rape her.

She travels a caravan route and gets as far as a wayside spring. Imagine the loneliness and despair that are suddenly interrupted by a voice: "Hagar, slave of Sarai, where have you come from, and where are you going?"[15]

<table>
<tr><td>

Hagar's Affliction

Sarah "afflicts" Hagar, the text says, using the same words later invoked to describe how the Israelites are treated by the pharaohs in Egypt, and Hagar responds the same way, by fleeing into the desert. The place Hagar goes—the wilderness of Shur—is the *exact same place* the Israelites go immediately after crossing the Red Sea. Again the Bible is sending a subtle message. All of God's children are afflicted in some way. And when they are, God looks after them.

Bruce Feiler, *Abraham*

</td></tr>
</table>

An angel has found her and is apparently visible. He knows who she is and calls her by name. We might expect her at least to express an exclamation of surprise. No. She simply answers the question and tells the angel that she is running away from Sarah. The angel orders her to go back and submit to her mistress, and then gives her some incredible news—the very words given years earlier to Abraham: "I will increase your descendants so much that they will be too numerous to count."[16]

But this talkative angel doesn't stop there. Hagar can't believe what she is hearing. He confirms her pregnancy and goes far beyond the readings of a sonogram. Not only will she give birth to a son, but she will name him Ishmael because the Lord knows her desolation. More than that, the angel offers a personality analysis of the fetus in her womb:

> He will be a wild donkey of a man;
>   his hand will be against everyone
>   and everyone's hand against him,
> and he will live in hostility
>   toward all his brothers."[17]

Is she actually assimilating these words? At minimum they seem to be a mixed bag. Yet, as a slave, she must feel empowered by this *wild donkey* in her womb. And, in fact, she now recognizes that it is the Lord himself who has brought this message. She's ecstatic. God has called her by name, as neither Sarah nor Abraham ever did. Even as she recognizes God, she recognizes herself. She is not merely a pregnant slave, the mother-to-be of Ishmael. She is *Hagar*, God's child. This father God, she exclaims, is "the God who sees me." And equally astounding is her daring acknowledgment: "I have now seen the One who sees me."[18]

24

Hagar returns home and gives birth, and the text records that Abraham named his son Ishmael. What Hagar discloses about her encounter with God to the eighty-six-year-old father is not revealed. She is submissive and subdued, biding her time, knowing that she is the mother of a great nation.

The years fly by, and the energetic, and perhaps unruly, colt of a boy is growing up an only child. Hagar no doubt pushes him outside with the herdsmen away from the critical eye of her mistress. Her days are consumed with hard labor. Then one day she hears the shocking news that her mistress is pregnant. At age ninety? The very idea is preposterous. But it's true. She should be happy, but she's confused. Ishmael is the promised son of Abraham. How does this affect him (and her) if Sarah has a boy?

> **Proud Father, Nursing Mother**
>
> Abram was eighty-six when Hagar bore his child. Later that day, he went to her tent and sat on a rug beside her pallet. Hagar had just nursed her newborn, and the boy was asleep on her breast. A gentle breeze drifted in through the open tent flap, and the warm glow of the afternoon sun reflected in on the young mother and her child. Earlier, the midwife had scrubbed the infant with salt, cleansed him with olive oil, and swaddled him with linen bindings.
>
> J. SerVaas Williams, *Abraham and Sarah*

She could hardly have trusted Abraham to stand up for her and their son. He is easily pushed around by Sarah. She knows all too well what a flawed individual he is. From now on, Sarah will surely have the upper hand. Then when the baby boy is born, she cannot help notice how happy Abraham is. He's behaving as though this is his firstborn son. And her mistress—the old biddy—is giddy with laughter. What an unfortunate turn of events!

Fast-forward three years. Hagar has been working day and night to get everything ready for the big celebration. Sarah's boy, Isaac, is now weaned. Big deal. There was no grand party for Ishmael's weaning. She must often wonder if her encounter with God had been a figment of her imagination as she peered into a desert mirage.

The guests have all arrived and there is much merrymaking—eating and drinking and celebrating. Feasts like this last for hours, and then there is cleanup. What a relief it will be when she can finally get to bed. But suddenly she hears a commotion. Her mistress is raging at Abraham. Not again. *Just leave him alone for once,* Hagar is no doubt thinking. But then she hears a reference to her and to Ishmael. Oh dear, what antics has Ishmael been up to now? But this is sounding far more dramatic than one of Sarah's typical flare-ups. She moves quickly to discipline Ishmael only to meet a barrage of angry words.

Indeed, Sarah's vicious tirade is like none Hagar has ever heard. Ishmael has been poking fun of Isaac—maybe more than ordinary teasing. Was Hagar's adolescent son hurling insults at the little boy, calling him stupid or dumb? Had Hagar herself noticed that little Isaac was developmentally slower than most children? Whatever the case may have been, Sarah is irate. Ishmael has said or done something that simply cannot be tolerated, and Sarah has no doubt been waiting for this moment.

Her words are defiant: "Get rid of that slave woman and her son, for that woman's son will never share in the inheritance with my son Isaac."[19] Is it possible that at the very moment Ishmael ridiculed Isaac, Sarah's eyes had been fully opened to the deficiencies of her own son? Ishmael is clever, smart as a whip. Her own son, the sweetest little boy she has ever laid eyes on, is a slow learner.

Abraham, true to his nature, does not tell Sarah to *put a clamp on it.* He is upset to be sure, but he will not challenge his wife. If Hagar had taken notice of him, she might have been terrified by how quickly he seemed to calm down. She would not have known that God had spoken.

It is doubtful that Hagar got any sleep that night. There was cleanup after the party and then presumably packing. After dawn, Abraham comes to her with some food and a canteen of water—more than what we would find in an ordinary bag lunch, for he hefts them and sets the baggage on her shoulders. He then sends the two of them away into the desert. There they wander in the vast Desert of Beersheba for who knows how long.

Now the food and water are gone, and Hagar simply gives up. She has Ishmael lie down under a bush, and she walks away so that she does not have to watch him die. As she begins to weep, we wonder how she could do this. If the poor child is going to die, he shouldn't have to die alone. But hardly has the boy begun to cry when the angel of the Lord calls down from heaven. He knows Hagar's name, and we can assume he is the same one who had met her at the spring some years earlier. He reassures her of the same promise he had given before, and he tells her to take the boy to a nearby well and let him drink.

It is most interesting that the text tells us that "God was with the boy as he grew up."[20] There is no parallel statement for Isaac. Hagar is also with him as he grows up. They make their home in the desert, and he becomes an archer. She travels to Egypt, where she finds a wife for him. We can imagine Hagar, unlike her mistress, Sarah, being surrounded by grandchildren and even great-grandchildren.

Concluding Observations

When we reflect on the Genesis accounts, we typically discover them to be complex while woefully incomplete. We seek to make sense of them as closed biblical stories. But in many cases they are not. Eve was deceived; Adam was not. Huh? So says Paul in his first letter to Timothy. Lot was righteous? Peter claims he was. And Sarah and Hagar? Paul writes in Galatians of the one as a free woman, the other as a slave, an obvious conclusion from the Genesis text. But then he makes a shocking analogy, though he clearly prefaces his words with the phrase: "These things are being taken figuratively."[21]

Sarah, in Paul's figure of speech, represents the freedom of the new faith, while Hagar represents the Jewish law. It is important to keep in mind that Paul's major theme in Galatians is freedom from the law. Paul might have used two men from the Hebrew Bible to represent freedom and the law, but none are paired as neatly as are Sarah and Hagar. Paul's underlying theme is that the new faith has its heritage deep in Scripture and comes to fulfillment not among the Judaism of his day but rather in the person of Jesus and in his own preaching. "Now you, brothers and sisters," writes Paul, "like Isaac, are children of promise."[22]

So we understand where Paul is going with this. Nevertheless, we easily cringe when he goes on to repudiate Hagar and Ishmael: "But what does Scripture say? 'Get rid of the slave woman and her son, for the slave woman's son will never share in the inheritance with the free woman's son.'"[23] We must remember that Paul is using Sarah's vicious words as a figure of speech.

If we read the Genesis account only, Sarah is the one we might avoid, while Hagar is the one we would seek out as a friend.

Questions to Think About

If you, as an amateur therapist, were to psychoanalyze Sarah, what terms might you use to describe her? Codependent? Bipolar? Suffering from preconception and/or postpartum depression? Needing anger management?

How does Sarah align with what is often regarded as *wifely submission*? Is it ever right to be complicit in wrongdoing as was Sarah in Egypt?

How should we assess Sarah in her sending her slave to bed with Abraham? Do we also unconsciously use *the end justifies the means* as a defense? How have we made wrong choices in our own lives by that way of thinking?

Does the Egyptian Hagar uniquely have something to say today to African American women, whose heritage is slavery? To oppressed women of any culture and era?

What do Sarah and Hagar have in common? Has the patriarchal culture negatively affected both of them?

What do you make of Hagar's encounter with God? Does her spiritual experience far surpass that which Sarah could claim, and is it unique for a biblical woman?

Who would you rather have join your book club, Sarah or Hagar?

3

Lot's Wife and Daughters

Pillar of Salt and Premeditated Incest

I once lived on 532 Pleasant Street in a small Midwestern town surrounded by rich farmland and large dairy herds. It was an idyllic setting, or so it seemed on the surface. But sin and scandal were all too
real. I was a young minister's wife and a new mother. Life was good. Then
there was that unforgettable knock on the door. My world fell apart. We
were forced to leave town unexpectedly and under a cloud as a result of
the exposure of my husband's hidden misdeeds. God might have rained
down fire on that town or on us, but he did not. When we left, I looked
back with anguish and guilt and utter sadness. Yes, I looked back. For me
the shame was searing, and I can still feel that hot metaphorical sulfur
singeing my skin now nearly forty years later.

I'm reminded of Lot's wife. Was she an innocent victim residing amid
the corruption and debauchery of her neighbors, or did she have issues as
well? Though referred to in the Bible as a *city*, Sodom was a small town
on the Jordan River plain, a well-watered garden where cattle grazed and
shepherds tended their flocks. Perhaps she too lived on Pleasant Street and
took pride in her newly wallpapered kitchen and her freshly washed clothes

29

blowing in the breeze. Like me, she fled with her small family, perhaps also burdened with shame and sadness. And she also looked back.

For this parting glance, she was struck down and sculpted into a pillar of salt—forever remembered for her disobedience, if not for her supposed wickedness. Is it even possible for us today to reflect on this woman with objectivity and a sympathetic heart? Can we come alongside her and learn things that perhaps no other woman can teach us?

The English text referring to her is a bare dozen words: "But Lot's wife looked back, and she became a pillar of salt."[1] How can that one sentence possibly frame an entire life? Surely it cannot. Unlike many biblical figures who rate only a sentence, however, her days are lived out in the shadow of her husband and daughters. It is an implied life and legacy, ever so indistinct.

And what can we say about her daughters? Nothing in polite company. We blush to even contemplate it. What if they were our daughters, and we were still alive? We would be sickened to the core. Social workers would be at the door. The scandal would be unbearable.

Lot's Wife

In an effort to better imagine this woman, I have given her dates that correspond in some ways to my own life. From the oldest biblical manuscripts known as the Masoretic text, biblical chronology has been established beginning with the creation of Adam and Eve at the year 0. Adam dies in the year 930, and Noah is born in 1056 and lives to be 950. Abraham is born in 1948 and Sarah in 1958. If I transpose these years to AD, I can relate to them more easily.

Were I to make an educated guess (based on this biblical chronology), I would mark the birth of Lot's wife at 2006. That was the year Noah died, and she might have heard stories about that ancient old man who walked the earth so recently. Her death is more easily established at 2047, the year that

> **We all *Look Back***
>
> And Lot's wife, of course, was told not to look back where all those people and their homes had been. But she did look back, and I love her for that, because it was so human. So she was turned into a pillar of salt. So it goes.
>
> Kurt Vonnegut, *Slaughterhouse-Five*

Sodom was destroyed, which was also the year before Isaac was born. In that case, she would have given birth to her daughters well before barren Aunt Sarah gave birth to Isaac in 2048, and also prior to Ishmael's birth in 2034.

She must have known Sarah and Abraham well. It seems likely that she traveled with them from Haran to the Promised Land, perhaps having married Lot when she was still in her teens. That journey began in 2023, when Abraham was seventy-five. For the next twenty-four years, she would have traveled with the caravan not only to Canaan but also on to Egypt and then back to Canaan, where she settled down with her family on the plain.

The journey would have been arduous and dangerous. There is always a sense of security in numbers, but the caravan passes through enemy territory. Grazing land and water are precious commodities ever in short supply. It's only natural that she often wonders: *Are we there yet? Is there really a promised land?* They do indeed reach the land of Canaan, but it certainly is not an inviting place. Besides enemy tribes, there is parched soil. In fact, there is a famine so severe that Uncle Abraham pulls up stakes and heads south. Now they are wending their weary way on what surely seems like a harebrained scheme, a never-ending trek into a stark wasteland. It is a wilderness that might swallow them up in forty years of wandering—if she were to time-travel more than four hundred years into the future.

Where on earth is her uncle heading? Does he have a plan? Does he have a map? Why would he be taking them to Egypt? In the distant future, God's people would be fleeing Egypt in search of a land flowing with *milk and honey*. But now Abraham is going in reverse. As the caravan passes through the worst of the vast desert, it actually seems to be inching its way into a promised land. They approach a rich river delta. The closer they get, the more awestruck she is, until they reach the very gates of the grand palace. It's like nothing she has ever seen before.

She feels giddy and fearful at the same time. Uncle Abraham is fidgety, nervous as a cat. He's scared silly that Sarah's beauty endangers his very life. So he hatches a plan—actually a lie. He will tell the officials that she is his sister so that they won't have to make her a widow in order for her to join the king's harem.

It's easy to imagine Lot's wife, much younger than Sarah, rolling her eyes. Sure, Aunt Sarah is well preserved, but she's hardly *that* beautiful.

She realizes, however, that she has seriously underestimated the loveliness of her aunt when Sarah is actually escorted to the palace. Does she feel sorry for her, or does she secretly envy her?

We can only imagine her wide-eyed wonder amid all the wealth of this land of plenty. The palace architecture and landscaping are more than she can take in. She is simply astonished by the ostentatious display of riches—royal ladies with their bejeweled headpieces and gold plated strands woven into their hair. Cosmetics of every hue giving color and depth to their facial features and heavy jewelry and gowns that weigh them down so they can hardly walk. She cannot distinguish the queen from the ladies who comprise the king's harem. Does she even recognize Sarah bedecked in such finery?

Even the food is tastier in this abundant land. (It is not for nothing that one day the children of Israel, tired of manna, will hark back to the fleshpots of Egypt.) Uncle Abraham's ruse is working. Life is good. But not for long. When the Pharaoh gets word of the foreigner's deception, he is livid. At this point he might have slain the patriarch and the whole bunch of them. Instead, he banishes the entire household, though allowing them to depart with all the great wealth they have acquired.

Once again they are on the road. She is enjoying the luxuries of affluence as well as her little family. Aunt Sarah is still barren, while she has little ones running underfoot. Is there enmity and rivalry between them? The text is silent, but it is not difficult to imagine Sarah's resentment toward the younger woman with young daughters to lighten otherwise dreary days.

When they eventually return to Canaan and prepare to settle down, life is anything but serene. Bitter conflict soon arises between Uncle Abraham's and her husband's herdsmen. The workers are loyal to their masters, and each side fights with the other for grazing land and water. Though not on the front lines of the bitter conflict, she and no doubt Sarah feel their own blood pressure rising as well.

The only solution is to split up and each household go its separate way. The old patriarch is in charge, and he magnanimously offers her husband first choice of the land. Lot, with no apparent hesitation, chooses the well-watered plain. His wife makes no effort to disguise her smugness. There the two of them, with their daughters and herdsmen, set up camp not far from Sodom.

Lot looked around and saw that the whole plain of the Jordan toward Zoar was well watered, like the garden of the LORD, like the land of Egypt. (This was before the LORD destroyed Sodom and Gomorrah.) So Lot chose for himself the whole plain of the Jordan and set out toward the east.[2]

Now Lot's wife, though perhaps barely thirty years old, is herself the matriarch of a wealthy household. Still living in tents, she shoulders the heavy responsibilities of their large encampment. She has oversight of the servants, some probably married to herdsmen with children of their own. They mend tents, make clothing, cook and clean, and prepare communal meals. There is little time, if she were so inclined, for fun and frivolity.

Daily life on the well-watered plain is routine until it unexpectedly makes a U-turn. They've been attacked by marauding militias and carried away to be—God knows what—raped and murdered? Could she and Lot really have imagined that local tribes would not resent them and their wealth and their massive spread of cattle? Who do they think they are, taking over a large swath of the region that is already claimed by others? But such questions arise too late to even contemplate.

Conflict over Lot's intrusion onto the grassy plain, however, does not actually set off the war that suddenly erupts. External hostilities are at play. Several tribal chieftains (or kings) and their fighting men are at war with another set of allied chieftains. One set (including the kings of Sodom and Gomorrah) has rebelled against King Kedorlaomer and his allies, and for good reason. For twelve years they have been forced to submit to his tyrannical rule.

The rebellion is unsuccessful, and in the end the kings of Sodom and Gomorrah and their allies head for the hills in a hasty retreat, during which some of their men fall into the tar pits that dot the region. The towns of Sodom and Gomorrah are then raided of all their goods (and presumably residents). What a disgrace it is for this uprising to be so soundly squashed in a war that would have been relegated to the dustbin of history had not Lot and his family been taken hostage along with all their goods.

Surely it is a horrifying time for Lot's wife and daughters. Was she raped, as women hostages sometimes were? Did she fear for the very lives of her young daughters? Both she and her husband are no doubt deeply regretting the decision to take the choice land, leaving the less appealing grazing pastures for Uncle Abraham. But the uncle does not hold grudges, and he quickly comes to the rescue with more than three hundred trained men.

King Kedorlaomer and his allies are defeated. Lot and family are freed; their possessions are recovered; and the kings who initiated the rebellion are most grateful to Abraham. In fact, the king of Sodom wants Abraham to take all the goods recovered from his city, but the patriarch adamantly refuses. Nevertheless, the king is most pleased, and Lot and his wife and family are invited to move into town. In fact, the apparent good feeling toward Abraham extends to Lot, who enjoys the honor of sitting at the town gate.

Lot's wife also participates in the benefits of town life. She is wealthy by local standards, and we can imagine her furnishing her new home with tapestries and rugs and other treasures that she might have brought from Egypt. Sodom is no more than a country hamlet compared to Egypt's royal city. But the local residents do not let that deter them from hosting all-night parties and carousing around in unspeakable debauchery.

In fact, the biblical text sums up in a terse sentence the town's notoriety before Lot's family relocated there: "Now the people of Sodom were wicked and were sinning greatly against the LORD."[3] Lot should have known better. But, not surprisingly, in an effort to further advance his own cause, he risks the well-being of his family.

So grievous is Sodom's wickedness that God has determined to simply wipe the town (and neighboring Gomorrah) off the face of the map. Neither Lot nor his wife is aware that God and two angels in the form of men visit Abraham, at which time the old patriarch learns of the planned devastation. He bargains with God to spare the city—even if there are fifty righteous people, forty, thirty, and down to twenty. Furthermore, God agrees to save Sodom if there be a mere ten righteous people in the entire town.

The angels are dispatched to Sodom to take a head count of those who are righteous. They arrive in the evening and find Lot sitting at the city gate. He respectfully greets them, not recognizing them as angels, and warmly invites them to his home. They decline, preferring to sleep in the town square. But he persists until they agree. He prepares the meal; there is no mention of his wife. No sooner are they done eating than they hear clamoring outside and a knock.

Lot opens the door to a large contingent of men, both old and young, demanding that the visitors be sent out so that they can rape them. Lot is horrified. What a terrible thing to do to anyone, much less visitors from out of town. He steps outside and insists that they not bring any harm to the men, while seeking to mollify them by offering his two virgin daughters.

How could a father possibly do such a thing? Is Lot's wife screaming in the background? She surely must be used to her role as wife of a large landowner in a patriarchal society. If she had observed Sarah being handed over to the Pharaoh, she would have been well aware of what was expected of women. But her own daughters? Did she hear her husband say, "Let me bring them out to you, and you can do what you like with them"?[4] How could she have possibly kept her silence? Perhaps she and her daughters were hiding and did not hear this evil offer.

The men of the town will have none of it. They do not want the daughters, and they are furious with Lot, a foreigner who is now acting like a judge over them. They are on the verge of tearing down the door when the angels who are inside reach out and pull Lot in with them and at the same time strike the mob with blindness.

Now for the first time Lot hears from the angels that God intends to destroy the town. Lot rushes out to warn the two young men engaged to his daughters, only to be rebuffed. By now light is creeping into the eastern sky, and the angels are insistent that he and his wife and daughters get out of town immediately. When he hesitates, the angel-men grab him by the hand, his wife and daughters also, and literally pull them out through the gates of the town.

Lot is ordered to hide out in the mountains: "Flee for your lives! Don't look back, and don't stop anywhere in the plain!"[5] The orders are clear, but Lot is not used to being ordered around. He insists rather that they be allowed to find safe haven in the hamlet of Zoar. The angels back down and grant his request. By the time they arrive in the town, the sun is up and another day has begun.

Lot's wife. Imagine what must be going through her mind. She has been in the background, perhaps not even knowing what the commotion was all about the previous night. Sure, a bunch of town rowdies made some trouble. But she had become used to the nighttime shenanigans, and usually by morning it would have been all over and she'd be ready to start another day. But today without warning she is rushed out of the house by two strangers.

No sleep. It's been the craziest night of her life. They are in Zoar now, and she doesn't even have a toothbrush or a pound of meal for breakfast cakes. She looks across the plain to her hometown at the very moment it is hit with what is comparable to an atomic bomb—Sodom and Gomorrah, Hiroshima and Nagasaki. But there is not even a nanosecond to think about it. She is frozen solid, her body becoming a pillar of salt. That is where the biblical account ends—except for Jesus's reference to her some two thousand years later.

Jesus warns his disciples not to go chasing after every televangelist, thinking he might be the Son of Man. "Do not go running after them," Jesus says. No, the true Son of Man "must suffer many things and be rejected by this generation." People will not expect Christ's coming, as was true for those just before the great flood.

> People were eating, drinking, marrying and being given in marriage up to the day Noah entered the ark. Then the flood came and destroyed them all. It was the same in the days of Lot. People were eating and drinking, buying and selling, planting and building. But the day Lot left Sodom, fire and sulfur rained down from heaven and destroyed them all. . . . Remember Lot's wife! . . . Two women will be grinding grain together; one will be taken and the other left.[6]

It is interesting that Jesus does not point to the wickedness in either setting. Rather that people were involved in the routine of daily activities. Lot's wife, like the women grinding grain, is not necessarily wicked. Rather she is not ready. In Jesus's illustration, she is not looking for the coming of the Lord. Rather she is looking back to her old life in Sodom.

Reading Genesis, one might wonder if her punishment for looking back—after she had arrived safely in Zoar—was overkill. After all, her husband did not hasten out of town himself, and he argued against the order to flee to the mountains. But the Bible does not always make sense to its readers.

Who really was Lot's wife? At the end of the day, we are left scratching our heads looking at a pillar of salt.

Lot's Daughters

Born into a culture where boys are prized, and growing up where they never quite fit in, these nameless rich girls are an enigma. They are the only children of Lot and his wife. Most likely born during the first sojourn in Canaan, their earliest memories would have been the spectacular sights of Egypt and perhaps playing dress-up with jewelry and colorful wraps. They must have been in awe of the beautiful and perhaps unapproachable matriarch known to them only as Aunt Sarah. Perhaps they find Hagar, that special servant girl (who is only a few years older than they are), the most lovable—and mysterious—of the entire clan.

When they are still young, their household splits from Uncle Abraham's, and they may have never gotten to know their younger cousin Ishmael, Hagar's little boy. Nor is there any reason to believe that they would have become acquainted later on with their cousin Isaac or their distant kin Bethuel and his children Laban and Rebecca.

After living in tents on the plain for a time, their lives are suddenly up-ended by raiding armies who take them captive. The fighting men on neither side of the conflict are in any way honorable, and we can only imagine how terrified the girls must have felt. But then as quickly as they have been taken captive, they are rescued by none other than dear Uncle Abraham.

Now they encounter a new twist in their lives as scary as it is exciting. The isolated farm girls find themselves coming of age in the raucous town of Sodom, and Daddy is a big shot sitting at the city gate. Did they ever sneak out late and join in the revelry of all-night parties? Probably not. They surely hear the shouts and laughter of neighbors carousing in the streets, but they are most likely secluded behind locked doors.

But during the day they no doubt go outside and walk about town, stopping at the gate to visit with their father. We might imagine that they become friends of the neighborhood youths, but even if they keep themselves apart, they surely must know by sight the young men to whom they will become engaged to marry. As is the custom, their father would have made the arrangements. They surely would not have been out on the dating circuit.

Once they have settled into town, life becomes routine. Nothing too exciting happens, until one day when visitors arrive at the city gates and accept an invitation from their father to come for dinner and stay the night. The men give vivid meaning to the word *strangers*. There certainly is something very different about them, as would be observed even from a peek around the curtain.

At night the noise starts up again, and suddenly the usual rowdies are swelling into a mob, and they are surrounding their house. That's weird, the girls must think. No one ever pays too much attention to their house. There's loud yelling, and now their father is out on the steps trying to calm them down. There is pushing and shoving and the shouts grow louder and the whole house seems to be shaking. They are terrified and hide in the back room, fearing that at any moment the mob will break past their father and yank them into the street and do unspeakable things to them.

What a shock it would have been had they known their own father was actually outside negotiating, begging the loudmouths to let him send the two of them out into the street to be raped. How could their beloved father do such a horrific thing? Why would he not have offered himself to be raped and fought to his death to protect them? They probably never learned what kind of a man their father actually was.

The next thing they know they are being rushed out of town by the strangers, Mom and Dad in tow. Their hearts are pounding; their heads are spinning. They are absolutely exhausted by the time they reach the village of Zoar. The strangers are gone. The sun is now up. Mother is fretting and doesn't know what to do next. Everything she needs to maintain a household is back in Sodom. She looks back, and in an instant the girls are motherless. All they see is a statue of calcified sulfur and salt. Did they cry out in utter anguish? Did they throw themselves on the ground, inconsolable? Only yesterday they were giggling about their wedding gowns. Now the past is obliterated, and their futures are uncertain.

> ### A Pillar of Salt
>
> When one journeys to the Dead Sea region, peculiar salt formations, some almost four feet tall, dot the landscape. Due to its high salt content, the Dead Sea recedes every year. It is not hard to imagine how tall some of the current salt formations would have been at the time the story of Lot's wife was written.
>
> Katherine B. Low, "The Sexual Abuse of Lot's Daughters"

How does anyone deal with such sudden disaster? We would like to think that after a season of grief we would pull ourselves together and carry on in a noble fashion. This, however, is not how the story ends. Indeed, if the account of Lot's wife appears to be confusing or unfair, the story of his daughters is downright deplorable. These two young women conspire to arrange for a night of drunkenness and incest, not just once but twice, and there are no pillars of salt marking their demise.

Some students of Scripture excuse Lot and his daughters for their behavior, as though they had no other options. But the text gives no indication that their situation is necessarily so dire. It is true that after a day or a week or a month or more, they realize they have overstayed their welcome in Zoar. So they head for the hills, which is where the angels had ordered Lot to go in the first place.

Why they would make their home with spiders and rodents in a cave, eating roots and berries, is not explained. After all Uncle Abraham is close by. On the very morning after the family had fled for their lives, "he looked down toward Sodom and Gomorrah, toward all the land of the plain, and he saw dense smoke rising from the land, like smoke from a furnace."[7] There is no indication that he is beside himself searching the landscape for Lot and his family, nor is there any reason to believe that he knows of the terrible demise of Lot's wife.

As for Lot, one would imagine that after finding safety in the mountains for his daughters, he would have, under cover of night and by circling around Zoar, if need be, sought out Abraham and asked for help. His uncle is a wealthy man. Even if Lot had offered to serve him as a herdsman, he would have been far better off than living in a cave. Through his uncle's help, he could have arranged a new wife for himself from his own kinfolk and husbands for his daughters, even as Abraham would later arrange for Isaac.

But no, Lot apparently does nothing, absolutely nothing. One might speculate that he and his daughters were all suffering from post-traumatic stress. And a therapist might conclude that the codependency that resulted is not surprising. Whatever the case may be, the nameless daughters concoct a plan—a plan so scandalous that today some four thousand years later it still shocks our sensibilities.

The daughters are desperate. They have two issues: that their father's line be preserved and that each of them have a child of her own. We might wonder if they had discussed the possibility of their father finding a new wife. That would certainly have been a step in the right direction to preserve their father's line. As far as the two of them having children, from the older daughter's reasoning, the situation is hopeless: "Our father is old, and there is no man around here to give us children."[8]

So the older daughter decides to take matters into her own hands and kill two birds with one stone: have a baby and at the same time preserve their father's line—that is, if her plan results in a son. So that night, with the help of her younger sister, she offers her father so much wine that he is essentially knocked out cold—so cold that he doesn't realize that he's being seduced, or at least that his daughter is the seducer.

The scheme set forth by the older sister seems to have assumed that both daughters would seduce their father. But the next day, the older daughter tells the younger that she has indeed slept with their father, almost implying that the younger did not know that she had actually gone through with it. She suggests that her sister repeat the same scenario that very night. So once again Lot is seduced while so drunk he does not know what is happening. How an old man in such an intoxicated condition is able to perform the sex act is not explained.

Both daughters become pregnant, and both have sons. The older daughter names her son Moab, and her sister's son is named Ben-Ammi. Both boys will one day become leaders of tribes (Moabites and Ammonites) that will often be at war with the descendants of Abraham, Isaac, and Jacob. As for the daughters, they disappear from the text as suddenly as did their mother.

Concluding Observations

Lot's wife is known for one thing, for one spontaneous act that led to her instantaneous death and a reputation forever marked by disobedience. She had safely escaped Sodom without a moment to lose when God rained down burning sulfur as punishment for the wickedness of Sodom and its sister city, Gomorrah. Did she look back in a thoughtless gesture of curiosity, or did she look back in greedy, grasping nostalgia for the life she had left behind? She is only one of two biblical women to be struck down dead in an instant. (Eve's sin, as well as Adam's, brought sin and death into the world, but they would live on for centuries to regret it.) Only Sapphira's death mirrors that of Lot's wife. In her case the sin was premeditated dishonesty, and her death served as a deterrent to others.

Who then is Lot's wife? Why is such a woman without a name or face or personality even mentioned in Scripture, not once but twice? True, she is a warning for all who are so consumed with earthly things that they are not prepared for Christ's return. But she is also a symbol of a lost life—life snuffed out in one of those distant earthquakes or tsunamis where only numbers sum up the tragedy. How else could we speak of the obliteration of Sodom? Here there are people, naughty people, little children saying words they should never utter, but God's creatures nonetheless. One of these individuals whose life was snuffed out on that terrible day of destruction we now know. She is a wife and mother—especially a mother—and that says it all.

Is there any symbolic significance we can give to the daughters? They did manage to carry on their father's line, though the future of the Moabites and Ammonites would generally not serve to further the aims of the Israelites.

Perhaps the most surprising aspect of the story is that Lot's wife and daughters (as well as Lot himself, of course) are in the ancestral line of the Messiah. In fact, it is truly astonishing that an awful act of incest would result in pregnancy and the birth of the Moabites, the people from which Ruth, the great-grandmother of David, descended. The line that eventually comes down to Jesus is messy, and these daughters in some backhanded way symbolize the ultimate meaning of redemption.

Questions to Think About

Of all the men in the Bible, where on the chart might Lot rate as a husband and father? Do you know any men—husbands or fathers—who seem to be as utterly callous as he?

Imagine yourself living in Palestine at the time of Sarah and Lot's wife. What would stand out as the greatest contrast with today? Where would the similarities lie?

What is the most significant (not specifically spiritual) event of your life that might be noted in a sentence or short paragraph a thousand years hence—or even a generation or two in the future?

Has Lot's wife gotten a bad rap? In what ways can you identify with her?

You're a defense attorney standing before the New England town fathers of *The Scarlet Letter* fame. Or a defense attorney today. Your clients are Lot's daughters, the details of whose planned pregnancies have been brought to light. What arguments would you use to defend them?

When we consider separately the transgression of Lot's wife as opposed to that of his daughters, are we often less understanding and forgiving—or more so—than God appears to be in biblical times? How do we account for different standards of behavior in different eras?

4

Rebekah

Maiden, Wife, and Mother

Years ago I worked with a woman whose sense of humor and edgy personality immediately drew me to her. We became good friends and went out to lunch and browsed area art fairs. When I was warned by an acquaintance to be careful about confiding in her, I was defensive. There must have been a misunderstanding. She would not do the things she was being accused of. Again, someone warned me to be careful. I ignored him. After that she betrayed me. I fell victim to her manipulation of the truth. How did this aspect of her personality escape me for more than three years? Was I simply in denial? And why would she want to hurt me? Even today I wonder.

How does an individual acquire qualities that make her or him prone to dishonesty and deception? Is this a matter of nature or nurture—a genetic defect or learned behavior? I ask these questions when I contemplate my former friend. Indeed, when I think of her, her betrayal and dishonesty come to mind first. But she is much more than that. Like Rebekah, she's a daughter and sister and wife and mother. And like this matriarch, she's

43

hardworking, intelligent, and beautiful. Yet, it's easy and often tempting to define her like I am tempted to define Rebekah: as dishonest and manipulative.

In fact, more than two decades ago when I wrote *Multiple Choices*, I titled a chapter "Manipulative Choices," and my opening paragraphs featured Rebekah. Here are some excerpts from that chapter.

> Rebekah lived in a patriarchal, polygamous society. . . . One writer, in discussing her arranged marriage at age twenty, commends her "childlike simplicity." Yet the biblical account gives no indication of this. Indeed, a straightforward reading of the text gives the impression that Rebekah was a very mature and hospitable young woman. . . . But the Rebekah we know best is the middle-aged, manipulative mother of two sons—a strong, forceful woman who had learned how to circumvent the obstacles of sex discrimination.[1]

It is this middle-aged period in the life of Rebekah that is featured most prominently in Genesis, and we cannot escape that fact. But in the back of our minds, we surely know there was far more to her character than deception and dishonesty.

Rebekah

We first meet Rebekah as a young, unmarried woman. Unlike Sarah (the deceased mother of her soon-to-be husband, Isaac), whose sixty-five years of "youth" are a blank slate, Rebekah steps out of the pages of the Bible young and vigorous.

Imagine growing up in the town of Nahor (nearly five hundred miles northeast of Canaan) in Mesopotamia, present-day Iraq. There are vast deserts in this region that can turn bitterly cold in the winter. In summer the blazing sun cracks the desert floor. The sandstorms are fierce. The region is sparsely populated. Nothing much happens in this outpost, same routine day in, day out. As an unmarried young woman, she's still living at home, no pad of her own and no nightlife in town. Her father is rich in land and herds, but that certainly doesn't mean she has a maid at her beck and call.

It is late afternoon, and as usual she heads through the village of tents with an empty jar on her shoulder to fetch water from the well at the nearby spring. As she exits the town gate and winds her way to the spring, she suddenly does a double take. Off in the distance, she sees a man with ten loaded camels kneeling as though they need to be watered. The other women heading for the well are as confused as she. This is not an everyday experience.

The man appears to be an ordinary camel driver, except that he is not looking around or doing anything. It sounds crazy, but he seems to be talking to someone. Is he perhaps praying?

Here is Rebekah's first glimpse of Eliezer, servant of Abraham. She knows nothing of his mission—that he has been sent by her great uncle Abraham from far away in Canaan to find a wife for his son Isaac.

Rebekah is known around town for her take-charge, outgoing personality, so it is no surprise to the other women that she does not hesitate to approach the well. When the stranger kindly requests a cup of water, her response is what the others would expect. Of course, she is most honored to give him a drink, and she'll water all his camels as well. How could she do anything less for a man who is obviously tired after a long journey?

Watering ten thirsty camels is no small task. But Rebekah is used to hard work, and part of her striking beauty is her sturdy and muscular frame, obvious even under her modest dress. She is anything but a frail, skinny size 6. If she had noticed the camel driver looking her over, she might have taken it as an affront, but her concentration is on the camels only.

Finished at last, all she expects is a thank-you. But the man approaches with a large gold ring (which he puts in her nose) and two heavy gold bracelets, which he places on her arms. Then he asks whose daughter she is. And if that is not forward enough, he asks if there is room at her father's house for him to spend the night. Hospitality is second nature to her. This man surely does not have to offer costly jewelry for simple kindness. But she answers without hesitation. Her father is Bethuel, the son of Milkah and her husband, Nahor. *Of course, he can stay the night.* They have feed for the camels and a guest room, perhaps even with a bed already made up.

What happens next is most astonishing. The stranger bows to the ground and thanks God in an audible voice: "Praise be to the LORD, the God of my master Abraham, who has not abandoned his kindness and faithfulness to my master. As for me, the LORD has led me on the journey to the house of my master's relatives."[2]

Without even waiting for an *amen*, Rebekah races home and brings the news to "her mother's household." How her mother may have reacted is not revealed, but how her brother reacts is vintage Laban (as will be noted later on). When he sees the expensive jewelry his sister is now wearing and hears that the man has been sent by a faraway relative, he's on his way to the spring at the speed of a desert goat. His hospitality, no doubt prompted by the glitter of gold, is ever so cordial: "Come, you who are blessed by the LORD. . . . Why are you standing out here? I have prepared the house and a place for the camels."[3]

Laban has done no such thing. If Eliezer sees right through him, he doesn't let on. After all, his own master, Abraham, can be conniving himself. Eliezer and the men who have accompanied him bring their camels to the house. They unload and feed them and then are invited to clean up and wash their feet before they sit down for a meal. But Eliezer insists that he will not have a meal with them until he explains his mission. Laban, no doubt trying to act calm, nevertheless blurts out, "Then tell us," as though he cannot wait to hear what else might be in the heavy baggage removed from the camels.

So Eliezer, having memorized the script, begins by telling how rich his master is. Bethuel and Laban are wide-eyed as he continues. God has given his master, Abraham, "sheep and cattle, silver and gold, male and female servants, and camels and donkeys,"[4] everything he could ever want. But now he's old, and his only heir is his unmarried son, who was born to his elderly wife, Sarah, before she died. Moreover, he's given this son his entire estate. Laban's heart is skipping a beat, waiting for the next words out of the man's lips.

Eliezer goes on to tell how he has prayed to God that the perfect wife for his master's son would give him a drink of water and also water his camels. God has indeed answered his prayer, and Rebekah is the very woman who has met that high standard.

Eyeing the hefty packs of loot, Laban (joined by his father in a breathy duet) sings out:

This is from the LORD. . . .
  Here is Rebekah; take her and go,
and let her become the wife of your master's son,
    as the LORD has directed.[5]

Eliezer is ecstatic. What a stroke of genius! He will be bringing this beautiful specimen of womanhood—and kinfolk—back to his master, Abraham. He wastes no time in unpacking the stuffed bags that contain more costly jewelry for Rebekah as well as exquisite gowns and shawls. Here is this desert family rich in livestock and land, but they have never seen this kind of extravagant wealth before. They have heard about the vast splendor and riches of Egypt, but never in their wildest imaginations did they think they would actually possess some of it.

But there's more, and that's what they are waiting for. Eliezer now begins distributing lavish gifts to Laban and his mother. There is no mention of Rebekah's father getting anything. In the presence of his shrewd son, Bethuel has sunk into the background. Laban is the suave negotiator who must be satisfied, and generosity with the mother of the bride is simply good manners.

Rebekah, for her part, has no doubt donned a priceless robe and is now testing how many bracelets and nose rings she can sport without falling face-forward on the carpet.

After a hearty meal and an evening of drinking, they all hit the sack. The next morning, Eliezer surprises them by saying he desires a speedy send-off for him and his passenger. He is most eager to head back to Canaan. Laban and his mother hesitate. Laban may be wondering if there are a few more gifts to be distributed, and the mother is not prepared to lose her daughter so suddenly. *Let her stay another week or two* is their response.

But Eliezer is chomping at the bit. He can't wait to get back. This is the biggest coup of his life. Abraham will be overjoyed. Before their differences can mar the perfect proceedings, they call Rebekah in. How does she feel about getting on the road without a prolonged good-bye? Without hesitation she agrees to the hasty departure.

We can only imagine her frame of mind. Sure she loves her family, but this is a dream come true. Who else is there for her to marry? She knows the young men around town, all related in one way or another. Not one of them has captured her eye. Perhaps most of them are already married or betrothed. Some feel threatened by her beauty and assertive personality. They can't quite imagine her as a submissive wife.

The send-off includes a family blessing by none other than Laban, not surprisingly with a materialist slant:

> Our sister, may you increase
>   to thousands upon thousands;
> may your offspring possess
>   the cities of their enemies.[6]

With that, she's off on the adventure of a lifetime. Accompanied by her attendant and the kindly Eliezer and his men, they travel southeast on a caravan route to the Promised Land.

We can be certain that Eliezer had made preparations for a comfortable camel trip home, perhaps even a version of a litter or canopy chair mounted on the beast's hump. When they arrive in Canaan, Rebekah is no doubt dead tired from the long journey. If they had made a distance of twenty miles a day, it would have taken them some three weeks on the hot, dusty roads.

As they ride into the encampment, she sees a man in the distance. He is out in the field, though he doesn't appear to be working, instead perhaps praying or meditating or just standing around. Inquiring of Eliezer, she asks who he is and is informed that the man is Isaac himself. She immediately pulls her veil over her face.

Eliezer then walks over to Isaac and tells him the long story from the beginning. Isaac learns for the first time that the veiled stranger is to be his wife. Isaac does what he is told to do. He walks over to Rebekah and brings her into his late mother's tent. Does Rebekah know she's in Sarah's tent? Surely from Eliezer she must have heard about this beautiful matriarch who has preceded her.

With all his wealth, one would imagine that Abraham would have thrown a grand feast to welcome his gorgeous daughter-in-law. But there is no celebration. Why, then, didn't Eliezer at least have a fatted calf prepared, or why didn't Isaac throw his own feast and then dance the night away with his bride? Is there some reason—some kind of an impairment afflicting Isaac—that would preclude such a celebration?

The veiled Rebekah gets her first real look at her husband in the interior dimness of the tent. How we would like to have been a fly on the wall—surely not as a voyeur, but to hear their first greetings and halting sentences. Does she know that by taking Isaac in her arms and doing what couples do on their wedding night, she is finally consoling his grief over his mother's death? He *loves* her. Indeed, so deeply that the writer feels obligated to tell us, almost as though no other man ever was as devoted to his wife.

Whether Isaac would also grieve for his father, who would die many years later, we do not know. The text does say that he met his brother, Ishmael, in Mamre, where they buried Abraham. Did Isaac travel the seventy miles with servants only, or did Rebekah and their teenage twin sons accompany him?

> **Isaac Was Different**
>
> Isaac wasn't a failure; he was just *different*. After all, the people in each generation have to find themselves and be themselves and not spend their lives slavishly trying to imitate their ancestors.
>
> Warren W. Wiersbe, *The Wiersbe Bible Commentary on the Old Testament*

It would be interesting to know how Isaac might have described the old man to Rebekah and to know whether he ever told her about how he was taken to Mount Moriah by his father, who nearly sacrificed him there. It is hard to imagine Rebekah not being curious about the patriarch and his wife, also about Isaac's brother, Ishmael.

What Rebekah does for the next two decades is not recorded. Suffice to say that going through her jewelry box eyeing her costly nose rings and bracelets gets old after a while. It is unlikely there were parties to attend with all her beautiful gowns and glittering jewelry, or that she even did much entertaining amid her colorful tapestries and carpets. But life goes on.

Then after they have been married for twenty years, the barren Rebekah becomes pregnant with twins. The story is familiar. Two babies in her womb are punching each other and her so hard that for a fleeting moment she wishes her life were over. How different from Sarah, whose pregnancy is associated with laughter. Rebekah pleads with God to know the cause of this bitter malice within her only to learn that two nations are warring against each other. The nations, represented by her kicking sons, will carry their prenatal hostility to distant battlefields where the younger will prevail over the older.

This is Rebekah's secret, her very own prophecy from God. And she is bound and determined to help God carry it out in her own deceptive way. It's a patriarchal tradition. Didn't Sarah and Abraham contrive to help God carry out his promise through a plot to impregnate Hagar?

The time of her delivery arrives. Here is an instance of intense pain in childbirth that fulfills the curse that first fell on Eve's ears. The firstborn son moves normally through the birth canal, but the second is coming out arm first, hanging onto the heel of his brother. Arms are supposed to be tucked into the abdomen, but not for this wily twin, who is struggling for his birthright before he is even born.

Like a breech birth (or breech presentation), when the buttocks comes first rather than the head as in the case of a normal birth, an arm presentation is as rare today as it would have been in the ancient world. Interestingly, one of the primary reasons for this anomaly is a multiple birth.

Right from the beginning, Rebekah shows favoritism—favoritism that may have been sparked by God's prophecy and her desire to be on the right side of history. Or it may have been sparked by the sight of her babies, the first one born appearing like a little primate. He is reddish in color with a furry body. She's seen babies before, perhaps even been called in with other women to help in birthing. But never before has she seen a baby like this. She would have hated to admit it, but she's repulsed.

Rebekah's rejection of her firstborn opens the way for her flaccid husband to naturally gravitate toward Esau, the older son. Pushed out of the house by his mother, Esau learns to love the outdoors. He's an expert marksman, stealthily stalking his prey, half-naked, no need for camouflage. He no doubt longs for the approval of his strong and beautiful mother, but knows instinctively that her maternal devotion toward him has never ignited. His father is

> **If the Twins Could Talk**
>
> If Esau and Jacob could talk to us, they might well draw attention to the problems in their family that gradually developed. . . . We hear Jacob and Esau pleading with parents to change the family legacy, to stop the spread of whatever toxic water flows in the family. If the poison is deception, then dam up that flow that has seeped into the family across the generations and deal openly and honestly with each other as parents and . . . children.
>
> Karen and Ron Flowers, "If the Twins Could Talk to Us"

weak and almost pathetic, but Esau knows how to spark his approval. It's not rocket science; it's simply through his stomach. And what fun it is to make the old man's mouth water with antelope steaks on the grill. It gives purpose to the excitement of tracking down game.

Meanwhile, Rebekah is in charge of the household—and perhaps much more. Does she fully trust her husband to keep track of their massive business undertakings? Does she stand in for him as CEO on the organizational chart of herd management? Whatever the case, not much slips under the radar of her watchful eyes. And Jacob is ever close by. She has never loved so fiercely as she does her second-born son. He's handsome, clever, and quick—takes after her in every way.

Rebekah does not encourage Jacob to be an outdoorsman. He spends his time around the encampment, perhaps a homeschooling schedule of reading, music lessons, and stretching exercises. He likewise learns the art of meal preparation, which was not necessarily considered an effeminate activity among the patriarchs. Distant cousin Lot had prepared a meal, with no shame, for his visitors to Sodom, and his own burly brother knows how to cook as well.

Rebekah and Jacob are close, and we would not be surprised if he tells her about the day that Esau came in from the field famished, acting like a great big baby begging for some of the pottage he had just stirred up. Why should he share with Esau? What has he ever done for him? So he toys with the hairy dimwit: *All you can eat for the birthright*. Esau eyes the pottage, no doubt thinking, *What a stupid offer is this!* Besides who cares about a birthright at a time like this? He grabs the bowl of pottage, with a shrug and a *so-be-it*. But Jacob makes him swear an oath. So he does.

If Jacob had told his mother while sporting a sly look of accomplishment, she had probably turned away shaking her head without giving obvious approval. He's a clever boy, and he'll do well in life.

Things, however, are not going well for the herdsmen. A drought has burned up the grazing land, and it's not the right time to sell. So the family moves south. Isaac remembers Gerar from his younger years. His father had moved the encampment there, and it had worked out well. Why not do the same? So now after more than three decades of marriage, Rebekah is in charge of packing up for the relocation. Imagine all she might have accumulated in those years, and she comes across those beautiful betrothal gifts she's almost forgotten. Do they bring back memories of her youth and family? Does she have any regrets? Might there have been a nice hometown lad more suited to her than Isaac? But how could she wish for anything different? Jacob is the light of her life.

They set up camp among the Philistines, though Rebekah knows not for how long. Isaac seems to have livened up since deciding to move. In fact, she probably knows nothing of his visitation from God, a clear warning not to go all the way to Egypt. Is she aware of how his mother was offered to Pharaoh and later to Abimelek so as to protect father Abraham? If she is, she might be getting an uneasy feeling now that they are settling into Abimelek's kingdom.

Like his father, Isaac assumes that the king will want to kill him so that he can have his wife. But had he known the story relating to his mother, he would have realized that his fears were unfounded. Nevertheless, he tells the officials she is his sister. His sister? What is he thinking? This is an outright lie. She is kin, and a relatively distant kin at that, surely no sister as was the case with his mother. Nor is there any evidence that he has ever discussed this with Rebekah, as his father had with his mother before they set out on their journey.

But Rebekah might have gotten wind of what Isaac had done. How else can we explain why she would appear in the courtyard of the palace below the king's window and, dare we assume, encourage her husband to caress her? Rebekah is the smart, domineering side of the duo. Why else would she consent to be *making out* in public? This is no Woodstock of the late 1960s.

Of course, Abimelek questions Isaac about his relationship with Rebekah, and Isaac admits he had feared for his life. Abimelek apparently shrugs it off and allows Isaac and his herdsmen to graze their sheep and livestock. More than that, they plant crops with remarkably high yields—so much so that the local farmers resent him and refuse him water rights.

Despite the bad blood between Isaac's herdsmen and the Philistines, the king recognizes that God is with Isaac, and he approaches him desiring a truce. With that they all settle down in the land, and no surprise, Esau marries a local woman, Judith, a Hittite. But he doesn't stop there;

he takes a second Hittite wife, named Basemath. Though forty years old, he surely must have realized this would upset his parents, particularly his mother, perhaps his way after all these years of getting back at her. Nor does he move out of the household with his wives; they are all living in the same encampment.

Amid her daily grind and troubles with daughters-in-law, one day Rebekah overhears Isaac speaking with Esau. She doesn't trust Esau one bit and knows that he has his father wrapped around his little finger—especially through his tasty meals of wild game. Edging closer to the opening of the tent, she is startled to hear her husband tell Esau that he desires to bless him. Why hasn't he spoken to her first about the matter? A blessing is not something to bestow willy-nilly. Hasn't she repeatedly told Isaac that Esau is not suited to carry on the family line—even before he had brought home those trashy Hittite girls? That was like a kick in the face.

And now the old man is telling Esau to bring home game and cook it up for a celebratory blessing. She's frantic. She's simply got to stop this. She'll tell her husband that he must put a halt to this charade before it happens. But he can be so stubborn despite his utter feebleness. Then an idea strikes her. She has a little time to play with. Esau is off hunting.

Now in her combat mode, she quickly explains to Jacob what has transpired and orders him to bring her the best young goat he can find in the flock so that she can prepare it and he can stand in for his brother and get the blessing. Jacob is no fool. He argues that it simply won't work; no one could ever mistake him for his brother. *Get real!* But his mother has given the command, and he follows her orders.

While the goat stew is cooking, she rummages through Esau's closet, finds some smelly clothes, gathers some hairy skins to fasten on Jacob's bare arms, and voilà! her boy is ready, albeit reluctant, to receive his brother's blessing. The ruse works. The confused, blind old Isaac gives Esau's blessing to Jacob. And what a blessing it is:

> May God give you heaven's dew
>   and earth's richness—
>   an abundance of grain and new wine.
> May nations serve you
>   and peoples bow down to you.

Be lord over your brothers,
>   and may the sons of your mother bow down to you.
May those who curse you be cursed
>   and those who bless you be blessed.[7]

Rebekah is smug.

In her haste to trick her husband, however, she almost forgets a little response she made to Jacob's protest. Amazing as it may seem, this crafty son of hers actually questions the ethics—the rightness—of what she is doing. He is concerned that this blessing might be turned into a curse. She shuts him up with a short sentence that will haunt her for the rest of her life: "Let the curse fall on me."[8]

Now the curse is just beginning. She cannot help but hear Esau's ranting and raving when he learns that Jacob has tricked him. He cries out to his father for a blessing also. Isaac relents and offers some words for his oldest son as well. To Rebekah's ears, they sound ominous:

You will live by the sword
>   and you will serve your brother.
But when you grow restless,
>   you will throw his yoke
>   from off your neck.[9]

Esau is seething when he departs from his father. *I'll kill that low-down scoundrel*, he says under his breath. In fact, he's not just saying it under his breath. Rebekah gets wind of his threat.

Let the curse fall on me. What if he actually goes through with it? What an awful, unspeakable curse that would be. Murder. She's got to act fast. Maybe she can give herself a little time. She will tell the servants and those terrible Hittite daughters-in-law that her beloved husband's condition has worsened and he could die any moment. He's been talking about his imminent death for days, so it will hardly come as a shock to anyone. And surely Esau would not kill his brother while his dear father is on his deathbed. It would not be polite.

With the household preparing for a funeral, Rebekah surreptitiously prepares Jacob to get out of the encampment and flee to Harran, where her brother Laban is now living. Esau will eventually cool off, and then he can come back home. She confides to Isaac that she is sending him off to find a wife, cursing those Hittite hussies even as she speaks.

Jacob flees. Rebekah will never see him again. She no doubt goes to her grave with those fateful words still ringing in her ears: *Let the curse fall on me.*

Concluding Observations

Where did Rebekah go wrong? When we first meet her, she comes across as a most appealing young woman. She is a daughter who would make any parent proud, the very sort of girlfriend we would want our sons to bring home to meet the family. But her charm and allure seem to dissipate as the story of her life unfolds.

> ### Rebekah alongside Herodias and Jezebel
>
> She was willing to be hated by her husband and cursed by God—all so her son might be blessed? Whatever are we to think of Rebekah? She seems as manipulative as "Off-with-his-head!" Herodias, as devious as "I'll-get-you-the-vineyard" Jezebel. Yet, unlike those Glad-to-Be-Bad women, Rebekah served the one true God, making her behavior here all the more inexcusable.
>
> Rebekah's willingness to sacrifice herself for her son wasn't virtuous, it was blasphemous. God alone decides whom he will bless and whom he will curse.
>
> Liz Curtis Higgs, *Slightly Bad Girls of the Bible*

It is important to remember that the author of the Genesis text is primarily focused on the patriarchs themselves. Thus, we learn about her character sandwiched in between Isaac, on the one hand, and her sons, Esau and Jacob, on the other. We might wish that we could peer into her life in other circumstances or as she interacts with servants, as Sarah did.

Rebekah has not received a good press. Biblical scholars and others have often focused only on the negative. But alongside Sarah and Rachel, to say nothing of Abraham, Lot, Isaac, Jacob, and Joseph, her dishonesty does not stand out. She is determined to give her younger son the perks of older-son status (as God had foretold) even if it involves a crazy scheme of dressing him in smelly clothes and goatskins. But compared to Abraham's deception in dealing with the Pharaoh, her ploy seems far less serious.

To even begin to understand Rebekah, we first need an awareness of the culture in which she was born. Women under patriarchy were typically denied power or authority because of their gender. The sister might be more intelligent and conscientious than the brother, but she was not offered the option of taking over the family business. She might easily perceive that her power came through manipulation. But was Rebekah a master manipulator as some have assumed? We have one incident alone to go on. Perhaps, in comparison to our own flaws and failures, it's time to give her some slack.

If we were to censure her, perhaps her favoritism for one son over another is the one fault we should point to first. Like Sarah, she blatantly favored one son over another—though in Sarah's case it was a stepson. God had a clear plan for Jacob, but did that require Rebekah's deceit and her obvious favoritism? Who knows? Maybe so. God works in mysterious ways.

Perhaps the words that most painfully distinguish Rebekah are "let the curse fall on me."[10] Her beloved son departs, and she never sees him again, never meets her daughters-in-law, Leah and Rachel, never bounces her grandchildren on her knee. And upon Esau, at least in her lifetime, will fall the benefits and responsibilities of the firstborn son, a supreme irony.

Questions to Think About

Do *good* girls like Rebekah become *bad* and vice versa, or do we assume that the bad was always there, at least underneath the surface? Are there people in your circle of acquaintances who have followed Rebekah's path of deception and betrayal?

Can we imagine that Rebekah may have been disappointed with her new husband? What options might she have had in such a situation? Although her marriage was arranged prior to their meeting, do you know of similar disappointments in marriages today?

How important in Rebekah's journey is the transition from mere daughter and sister to wealthy matriarch? Is that transition one we can relate to today?

How should we assess favoritism of one child over another, other than the fact that it is a common element among families in Genesis? Is this phenomenon common today? Is it especially common when stepchildren are involved?

How *bad* is Rebekah? Does she deserve the negative reputation that has fallen upon her? How does she rank alongside Sarah, her mother-in-law?

Can you in any way relate to Rebekah's ominous words, "Let the curse fall on me"? Have you ever felt that a curse was on your life or on your family?

If you were stuck in a tent for a day with one of two women, would you choose Sarah or Rebekah?

5

Rachel and Leah

Rival Sisters

o the young man goes to his doctor. His symptoms are ominous:
shortness of breath, irregular heartbeat, hyperventilation, insom-
nia, inability to concentrate, and more. After taking some initial
readings, the doctor shrugs and tells him he's in love. It's the story of a
1990s country hit, but most of us don't need song lyrics to remind us of
the incapacitating nature of *falling in love*. Such was the case with Jacob,
son of Rebekah and Isaac, thousands of years ago.

Scientific studies in the twenty-first century tell us all kinds of things
about love that would have meant nothing to Jacob. And even with our
scientific knowledge today, understanding how our brains work when we
fall in love makes no difference. We love falling in love. Despite our sleepless
nights and obsessive daydreams, we would have it no other way. Researchers
tell us that this condition of being *madly in love* causes a drop in serotonin
levels in the brain. It also increases the production of cortisol, a stress-
response hormone that causes elevated blood pressure.

If that is not enough, it turns out that ordinarily reasonable and rational
individuals who suddenly fall head-over-heels in love are transformed into

dithering ninnies. Their neural circuits go haywire, and the ability to make social judgments and to carry on with normal decision making escapes right through the top of their heads. Scientific fact, though perhaps sometimes worded more scientifically.

Jacob is the Bible's *Exhibit A*. And Rachel is the object of his ardor—the one responsible for his sudden brain paralysis. Other women do not deprive him of serotonin and throw buckets of cortisol at him, nor do they mess with his neural circuits. Leah has no such effect on him. Even when she crawls under the covers with him, all he can think about is Rachel. What's wrong with him?

Rachel, of course, is where we place the blame. She's got beauty and personality. And poor Leah. She is the stuff of the fairy tales, the ugly duckling, and often-evil sister. The other is pure loveliness. Actually, the only immediately obvious defect with Leah is her apparent weak eye. A pair of stylish glasses would have done the trick. But perhaps the text fails to tell us about her stringy hair and her crooked teeth. At any rate, most of us identify more with the *Leahs* than with the *Rachels* of this world. The account is fascinating, if for no other reason than the heated rivalry between sisters. Indeed, so intertwined are they that we tell their story as one.

Rachel and Leah

Rachel is the only woman in the scriptural text whose beauty and seductive powers elicited head-over-heels, love-at-first-sight, heart-pounding passion. We are sometimes led to believe that people didn't *fall in love* until the late eighteenth and early nineteenth centuries. Romanticism, so it goes, celebrated romantic love and brought it into the modern era. When marriages were arranged and women were covered, romance was not part of the picture. For sexual pleasure, men sought out prostitutes and perhaps exotic dancers, but marriages were business transactions, determined by wealth and kin and social status. If love developed, well and good, but procreation was the goal.

Were all the young men smitten by Rachel? Or was it just Jacob? She is the Bible's ultimate heartthrob. Sarah and Rebekah are both beautiful women, but there is no evidence that they trigger such unquenched ardor.

I picture Rachel as a 1960s country music star. She's no fairy princess in a flowing gown. Rather she's muscular and tanned, sleeves rolled up, wind-blown hair, boots visible as a breeze lifts her skirt. Her natural friendliness belies her determined *don't-you-dare-touch-me* demeanor as she interacts with the hired hands.

It's a routine day of work for her. She is a shepherd, herding the family flock as she normally does. As she approaches the well, she sees not only the usual bunch of rough and rowdy shepherds but also a stranger. Her curiosity is piqued when he single-handedly moves the huge boulder from the well—an effort that typically requires all the strength of the guys combined. It is obvious that the stranger has noticed her. With this feat accomplished, he heads for her. Before she realizes what is happening, he is kissing her. Only after breaking down in sobs does he introduce himself. He is Jacob, son of her father's sister, whom she has never met.

Rachel has grown up in Paddan Aram. It's a region in northern Meso-potamia that had biblical significance ever since her great uncle Abraham had settled there, having journeyed from his home in Ur of the Chaldeans. Abraham had been called by God to move on to Canaan, while her great-grandfather Nahor remained settled in the region. Many years later, her grandfather Bethuel had welcomed Eliezer (Abraham's servant) when he showed up shopping for a bride for Isaac. Now Isaac's own son Jacob has shown up on a similar mission—though this time seeking a bride for himself.

We easily imagine that the life of a shepherd might be romantic, albeit a tad tedious. The *Shepherd Psalm* (Ps. 23) speaks of green pastures and still waters. Paintings depict hillsides blanketed in nibbled grass and color-ful wildflowers. A rippling waterfall breaks the easy flow of an otherwise meandering stream. The sun shines amid puffy clouds. The robed shepherd sits on a rock, staff in hand, surrounded by docile sheep. But in Paddan Aram, green pastures quickly turn to arid, windswept plains, and still waters are at the bottom of deep wells, often fought over by competing bands of herdsmen.

Rachel is identified as a shepherd. When Jacob first meets her, there is no reference to her brothers; they are mentioned as shepherds themselves some fourteen years later and may have been small boys when she was herding sheep on that unforgettable day. So this vocation may have fallen to her as the second-oldest daughter, but why hadn't her father secured hired hands as was a common practice? The text does not say.

It is not difficult to imagine that Rachel embraces this work, indeed, that she much prefers herding sheep out in the open fields to that of hovering among the servants over the cooking pots. Far better to be out where the wind blows and where she can banter with other shepherds. She's young and free and easily imagined as the tomboy of the Old Testament.

But she's far more than that. So alluring is she that Jacob, after spending a month on Laban's spread, makes an extraordinary offer: "I'll work for you seven years in return for your younger daughter Rachel."[1] In ancient Palestinian culture, as in many African cultures today, marriages are negotiated with a "bride-price." But seven years of labor? The best years of his youth? There is no offer like this in all the pages of Scripture. But so in love is Jacob that eighty-four months seem like "only a few days."[2]

What Rachel knows of the negotiations is not revealed. Perhaps for her the seven years drag on; after all, she is aware that most marriages are arranged much more quickly. Does she continue to herd sheep during this time—or does Jacob take her place? Is she now required to act like a lady? If only the text were more forthcoming.

Alas, the day finally comes. The servants have been up all night preparing for the grand marriage feast, and everyone is invited. There's music and dancing, tasty hors d'oeuvres, steaming bowls of mutton stew, and prime rib on the spit medium rare. The guests linger over their wine and sweets as the sun sets in the west.

Then everything falls apart. Sad stories featuring a flight of the groom (or bride) abound in literature and in real life. There is no chance of this, however. Jacob surely is not going to work seven years for nothing. What happens next is mind-boggling. It is the most stunning bride-switching story in all history. Think of it. What a shock to Jacob on discovering that he's consummated a marriage with the wrong sister. But this account is not about Jacob.

Imagine having your heart set on a good-looking young guy who absolutely adores you only to discover that your father has gone behind your back and surreptitiously arranged for your sister to be veiled and sent to the marriage bed. What a bummer.

61

Is Rachel outraged with her father, or has he so toyed with her emotions that she thinks that she is the one who has misunderstood all along? Of course, Leah is her older sister, and it is customary that the oldest marries first. But how is it that all along she's been thinking this wedding feast will be in her honor? Stuff happens. She'll somehow just have to carry on.

And what about Leah? Imagine always being compared with a dazzlingly beautiful sister. It would be okay if one were described as the Rhodes scholar alongside the beauty-pageant sister. But in this case they are both described by appearance only, and Leah comes out on the very short end. Had she been chubby or her hair been matted, she might have gone on a diet or visited a salon. But the issue relates to her eyes. Most likely Leah, no fault of her own, is cross-eyed. And with no apparent scheming on her part, she is suddenly Jacob's wife.

But then one week later, with no fanfare, Rachel becomes Jacob's second wife. She's waited seven years and seven days. The text says nothing about her awareness of these most recent negotiations. We would not blame her for utter disillusionment with this whole patriarchal system in which she is embedded. And, for all she has endured, we can't help but wish her well. But anyone who is familiar with the story of Rachel and Jacob knows that this is hardly a *happily-ever-after* scenario.

Marriage brings not only a new husband but also a new servant for Rachel. Now she's a lady of the house. Her mother? We know nothing of her at all. The wife of Laban is never mentioned in the text and is perhaps deceased by the time Jacob has settled in with the family. Rachel, however, has a new status, now with Bilhah, a servant of her own. She's a hausfrau, ordering her servant around. Gone are the carefree days of herding sheep. Her most important role, however, will be that of mother. Apart from her inherent maternal instincts, she has a duty to perform in bearing children. So also does her sister.

The sport of polygamy in the Bible has at least one common thread: it is fraught with fierce competition. So it is with Rachel and her sister, Leah. True, Rachel is the one Jacob loves, but what does it matter if her sister has babies and she does not? In fact, the text reveals that the matter of conceiving and not being loved by Jacob are directly related: "When the

LORD saw that Leah was not loved, he enabled her to conceive, but Rachel remained childless."[3]

Leah, it seems, is scoring a goal every time she competes in this cutthroat baby-making game. Finally Rachel is down 4-0, and she's furious. *Babies or bust* is her motto. "Give me children, or I'll die!"[4] she rages at Jacob. He comes right back at her, though interestingly, he doesn't blame her as might be a logical reaction. He places the matter squarely with God. Does Rachel finally respond appropriately? Does she pray for forgiveness and plead with God to open her womb? No. This is not Rachel's way. Like her mother-in-law and grandmother-in-law, she takes matters into her own hands. She sends in a substitute, her servant Bilhah.

One might wonder at this point how poor Bilhah feels about being a pawn in this game of polygamy. Is she aware of the behind-the-scenes maneuvers? Is she young, only fourteen or fifteen years old? She obviously has no say in the matter, but she might have been pleased by the thought of having a baby of her own—maybe thinking it would be like having a doll to diaper and cuddle, not fully aware that she is essentially a disposable surrogate.

A son is born, and Rachel names him Dan; then a second son, whom Rachel names Naphtali. By now Bilhah surely knows that she is more than a mere baby-making machine for Rachel. She is Rachel's servant and as such has primary care for these boys. Likewise, she knows that these very sons of hers are Jacob's own sons, thus enjoying far greater status than any child she might bear to, for example, an unrelated herdsman.

As for Rachel, bottom line, she's still barren, and the sisterly rivalry continues. The score now 4-2, Leah gets back into the game by sending in her own sub, her servant Zilpah, who scores twice more with Gad and Asher. Rachel is down by four. Now the game is 6-2. There are no screaming crowds, but the winning team is smug. True, the game is not over. Rachel is yet to score, Joseph first and then Benjamin, a goal that takes her life.

But before then the family saga will undergo many twists and turns, never devoid of drama. Leah's oldest son, Reuben, happens to find a patch of mandrakes during the wheat harvest. A smart kid, he knows that these bulbous roots hold magical powers for women and are referred to as *love* plants, the most potent fertility drug on the market. Leah is delighted—the ultimate Mother's Day gift from a son.

There's a major obstacle, however. Jacob no longer sleeps with her. Nothing she does is enough to entice him for a night of lovemaking. She blames her evil sister. She knows Rachel is behind it. So, it would not surprise us if she purposely flaunts her precious find when her infertile sister happens by. Rachel's eyes pop. She wants them, and she begs, fully aware of what Leah wants.

And Leah doesn't let her forget it. In essence: *You stole my husband, how dare you ask for my mandrakes!* The solution is obvious: husband for mandrakes. This is no doubt what Leah has in mind all along, but Rachel makes the proposal and arranges for Jacob, if not to welcome her, at least to allow Leah to spend the night with him. In the end, the mandrake investment pays well for Leah. There will be more than one rendezvous, during which time she scores another goal with a little hockey puck she names Issachar. Then Zebulun is conceived. The score now stands at 8-2 (or 9-2, if baby girl Dinah is counted).

Rachel is heartsick. The mandrakes are worthless. What a crock! She might as well curl up and die. But then, amid her grief, God *remembers* her. Had she thought God had forgotten her amid her pleas for a son? Now she conceives and bears Joseph, declaring, "God has taken away my disgrace."[5] *Disgrace* is an interesting emotion at this point. Had she used the term *sorrow*, we would readily understand. But we cannot forget that she is playing a competitive sport. With Leah alone, she is still down 6-1 (in sons), but scoring once is certainly a lot better than not scoring at all.

The next words out of her mouth are not ones of profound gratitude. Rather, "May the LORD add to me another son."[6] She is still in a competitive mode. Before she will give birth again, however, she is packing up her entire household to make a major move. Jacob is chomping at the bit to get back home to Canaan, where years earlier he had escaped the wrath of his brother, Esau.

Rachel's father, Laban, is not eager for Jacob and his household to move away. If we imagine that his rationale relates to the sadness of not seeing his daughters and grandchildren again, such is not specified in the text. Rather, his motivation is blatantly materialistic: "I have learned by divination that the LORD has blessed me because of you."[7]

They do not depart, however, until Jacob, through his own trickery and divination (relating to the speckled, striped, and spotted among the sheep and goats), obtains great wealth in flocks, camels, donkeys, and servants. Laban and his sons are not exactly pleased by this turn of events, and Jacob knows it. In fact, he overhears his brothers-in-law claiming that he's cheated their father. Before he can get his wits about him, he hears the voice of God ordering him to get out of there ASAP. This is insane. Laban will never permit him to get away with his massive wealth. And how do you sneak off with a whole caravan—a train of animals, kids, wives, and all your household possessions?

Jacob is willing to trust God, but first he must have his wives on board. How will they feel about packing up everything and going to a strange land? He could simply order them to make ready and come along, but they aren't always exactly compliant. Besides, their father and brothers are ready to do battle to protect them if need be. So he sends word for them to meet him way out in the pasture where he's herding sheep. That one of them would go out with a little wine and cheese for a picnic lunch would not necessarily raise eyebrows, but that they would go together might have created suspicion.

Nevertheless, Jacob, alone with Rachel and Leah, lays out his plan based on his observation that their father has not been treating him well lately. He reminds them how hard he has worked these past two decades even though their father has cheated him at every turn. He emphasizes to them that the incredible wealth he has accumulated has been fair and square, albeit a rich blessing from God. They listen as he offers them an abbreviated version of how God has seen to it that his speckled, striped, and spotted sheep among the flock have flourished.

What transpires next is amazing. Rachel and Leah speak in unison, agreeing that they also have not been done right by their father and affirming Jacob's plan to escape. Like Jacob's, their concerns appear to be primarily with material wealth:

> Do we still have any share in the inheritance of our father's estate? Does he not regard us as foreigners? Not only has he sold us, but he has used up what was paid for us. Surely all the wealth that God took away from our father belongs to us and our children. So do whatever God has told you.[8]

They pack up all their belongings and flee while Laban is on a three-day trip. This is a major undertaking. Even if we assume that such things as clothing, jewelry, and cookware are ordinarily stored in trunks or leather bags, there would be rugs to roll and tents to take down and wrap. While everyone is scurrying around, Rachel sneaks into her father's tent and steals his idols. Apparently Laban has a stash of household gods that Rachel believes will bring her family good luck. She may also fear that the gods, if they are under her father's control, will retaliate. And she no doubt wants to cover her bases. If Yahweh fails them, maybe the idols will come through. Rachel, keep in mind, has not been raised as a pious little Sunday school girl.

Day after day, they travel until their weary flocks can go no more. It's a strain on all of them, and it cannot be a surprise for Rachel or Leah or any of the others when word arrives seven days into their escape that Laban is on his way and will overtake them by nightfall. If they expect him to show up with swords drawn, however, they must be surprised to discover him to be amazingly calm. He's the aggrieved father and grandfather. Why, the wily Laban wonders aloud, did Jacob and the rest of them not leave in plain sight and properly kiss him good-bye? He feels sad and betrayed. He would have gladly sent them on their way with his blessing. Sure.

He has one huge issue, however: the theft of his idols. It's one thing to run off while he's away from home, quite another to maliciously infringe upon his family rituals. What's he talking about? Jacob is incredulous. Yahweh is the one they trust. He didn't steal any idols, nor did anyone else in his household. Why would they? The whole idea is insane. Indeed, so insane that he'll prove it. Laban can go through every tent and all their belongings and if he finds the idols and the thief, he can execute the individual on the spot.

Rachel overhears what is transpiring outside her tent. Might she actually be executed? She panics. There's no place to bury them, and he will go through every traveling bag she owns. Then she has an idea. She hides the idols beneath her camel's saddle and sits on it. Then she waits. Fortunately her father does not come to her tent first. After going through everyone else's possessions, he steps inside her tent. She's ready. "Don't be angry, my lord, that I cannot stand up in your presence." Boohoo! "I'm having my period."[9] She's a clever lady, a chip off the old block.

Having found no idols, Jacob takes Laban to task. How could anyone ever accuse him of theft? So they agree to let bygones be bygones. They make a covenant and share a meal, and Laban, having kissed and blessed his grandchildren and daughters, takes his leave and returns home.

The caravan moves on toward Canaan until they are approaching the territory of Jacob's twin brother, Esau. Jacob is nervous as a cat, fearing Esau may settle an old score and slay every one of them. The text does not reveal whether Jacob consults with Rachel and Leah before sending servants on ahead with gifts, nor is there any reason to believe that he shared with them his long night of wrestling with an angel. But the next day he is limping, and word is out that Esau is on his way with four hundred men. Jacob quickly lines up his people in formation behind him as though he were a drum major leading a marching band. First come the female servants, children behind them. Leah follows with her brood, and bringing up the rear are Rachel and Joseph.

If Esau thinks this odd when he peacefully arrives, he doesn't say so. He simply asks who they are. Jacob introduces them as his children. They all step up to bow before him. It is a grand reunion. Esau returns home, and Jacob lingers for a time and then sets up camp near Shechem. It is not until they have moved again, this time to Bethel, that God tells Jacob to get rid of idols—the idols Rachel had stolen from her father. The text

Laban's Family Legacy

All families have strengths and all families have struggles. Threads of both can be clearly seen woven through the tapestry of any family's history. Some families pass on a legacy of strengths. Sometimes character flaws flow across generations, such as abuse and violence, cheating, or promiscuity. In the family tapestry of Abraham, the lineage of Isaac, a common thread—deception—turns up again and again. . . . This thread of deception is evident also in the family of Nahor (Abraham's brother), the lineage of Rebekah. Laban (Rebekah's brother) eventually deceived Jacob on his wedding day, giving him Leah instead of Rachel, the intended bride (Gen. 29:23–24). Rachel would later steal the religious figurines from her childhood home, hide them under her skirts and lie to her father about them, "Don't be angry, my lord, that I cannot stand up in your presence; I'm having my period" (Gen. 31:35).

Karen and Ron Flowers, "If the Twins Could Talk to Us"

records no surprise on Jacob's part, only the response: "So they gave Jacob all the foreign gods they had and the rings in their ears."[10] Who is included in *they* besides Rachel, and how much Jacob may have known about these foreign gods, is anyone's guess.

From Bethel, Rachel and Leah move on with their entire household, Jacob at the helm. Did they wonder why the people in the towns they pass through seem to be terrorized by their very presence? Are they relieved to have gotten rid of the idols?

The account of the sisters at this point seems to fade away but for the mention of two deaths. Deborah, Rachel's nurse, dies and is buried along the way. As they continue on their journey, Jacob again hears the voice of God, this time blessing him as he had his father and grandfather. If this is a heady time for him, it does not last. Rachel goes into labor and dies in childbirth, naming her son Ben-Oni with her last breath. Jacob, however, will name him Benjamin.

Rachel is buried on the road to Bethlehem.

Concluding Observations

Both Rachel and Leah are complicated individuals, though Leah will forever stand in the shadow of her beautiful and more prominent sister. For most of us, the course of our lives depends to a large extent on our birth surroundings—our nationality, our neighborhood, and of course parental care and discipline. Our own particular genetic endowment is inherited from our parents, but not all endowments are equal. Leah, like many of us, appears to have come out on the short end.

Leah, of course, has more children than Rachel, but she never wins the love of her husband. Yet she may have possessed the strength of character that eluded Rachel. I'm inclined to think that the answer they gave Jacob in their speaking duet may have been the words of Leah, while younger sister Rachel nodded in assent. I doubt the text means to say that both said the exact same words in unison as if they were reading this unanticipated question from a script. And they weren't, after all, identical twins.

Leah may have been altogether flattered that Jacob had asked her opinion as though he were treating her—for the first time—as an equal wife. It is not difficult to imagine her desperately wanting to please him. It's possible Rachel went along with her older sister's response, assuming Jacob had already made up his mind; she surely didn't want Leah going off with him, leaving her behind.

The protracted struggle between these two women is not wrongly cast within a sports analogy—an analogy not so unlike that used for their husband, Jacob, who *wrestles* with an angel. It is unfortunate when such conflicts (among women) are referred to as a *catfight*, with the underlying assumption that women's conflicts, unlike men's, don't really matter. The intense competition between Rachel and Leah was serious; their very lives and legacies were at stake. A woman's place in this patriarchal era was primarily that of wife and mother. Leah fought for her place in the former realm, Rachel in the latter. They *wrestled* and *ran the race* (as did the apostle Paul) and scored with hockey pucks as competitively as seasoned athletes. At the end of the game, when Dinah is included, the scoreboard shows a 9-4 win for Leah, but, as is sometimes true in sports, the loser goes down in history with one unforgettable goal, in this case Rachel scoring. The result: a real puck. Joseph.

But that's another story. It is surely not entirely unrelated, however. Joseph, son of Jacob and his most favored and beautiful wife, Rachel, becomes the favorite son of his father and in the eyes of his half brothers (particularly the sons of Leah), the object of jealousy and hatred. In the end, however, the line of Abraham, Isaac, and Jacob will be carried on primarily through Leah, and her son Judah will not only have his name emblazoned on a very significant tribe of Israel, but he will also be Leah's link in the ancestral line of Jesus.

Questions to Think About

How do you relate to the *pretty-sister syndrome*? (I choose to use that term instead of the *ugly-sister syndrome*, which actually gets four times as many results on Google.) Have you, or anyone you've known, been on either side of the divide? What lasting issues are involved?

What does the account of Leah tell us about God, about her, and about ourselves? Do we all see a fleeting glance of Leah in the mirror, at least in her moments of brooding jealousy?

Is Rachel actually an enviable character? How does she rank, in your rating system, alongside other biblical women we've met thus far?

Can you relate to the experience of having someone fall head-over-heels in love with you? Can you relate to a long—very long—engagement?

Is the baby-making competition between Rachel and Leah properly represented in sports terminology? Are there better metaphors or ways of describing their intense rivalry?

What do you make of Rachel stealing her father's idols? Can you relate to that in your own spiritual pilgrimage?

When we consider how history has dealt with these two women, which one grabs our attention? Does the pretty girl win in the end?

6

Dinah and Tamar

Shameful Stories of Pain and Complicity

Even today, after the 2012 election fiasco involving a Republican congressman's use of the term *legitimate rape*, rape is sometimes difficult to define. There are many scenarios that leave the matter less than clear. As horrific as rape is, I hesitate to use the term for a deplorable and disgusting incident in my own life. Should the term *rape* be used for a married woman who has repeatedly been physically abused by her husband, and then one day as she is packing to leave for a speaking engagement is interrupted and forced to have sex? Let's say there is no physical violence, only a demand and a threat: no getting out of the house until the sex act has been accomplished.

What are the woman's choices? Calling the police? To report that her husband is telling her she must have sex before traveling? I'm not sure about today, but three decades ago that probably would have made the list of silly police reports. Does the woman call the conference organizer and say she's sick? Does she endure the awful nonconsensual sex with her husband, fulfill her speaking engagement, contact an attorney as soon as

71

she returns home, and file for separate maintenance? Does she call this appalling incident in her life *rape*?

It should be no surprise that the violence of rape emerges in the biblical narrative, alongside every other form of evil. But how the ancient world regarded rape is very different from our present-day understanding. For example, Lot's daughters' premeditated *seduction* of their drunken father would surely fall under the definition of rape today. Sending a young servant to bed with an old patriarch for the purpose of procreation would at least in the Western world be regarded as rape. In light of such stories, we seek to understand the narrative featuring the beautiful and seemingly carefree Dinah.

Tamar's story is very different—that is, the first Tamar, Canaanite daughter-in-law of Jacob's son Judah. (The second Tamar, beautiful daughter of David, was brutally raped by her own half brother Amnon. Her story appears in chap. 13.) In the case of the first Tamar, however, the issue also relates to sex and violence. Accusing her of plying the trade of prostitution, her father-in-law, Judah, wants her dead, but she cleverly outsmarts him.

The accounts of Dinah and Tamar further illustrate the pervasiveness of sex and sexual abuse in the Hebrew Bible. There are no obvious negative sexual overtones with the story of Adam and Eve (though some have sought to create a scandal between Eve and the serpent). But the awful side of sex comes into play in a major way only eight chapters later when Abraham is sending his wife into the Pharaoh's harem. Isaac attempts a similar ploy, and long before that his father is engaging in sex with his wife's servant. Jacob has sex with the wrong sister on his wedding night, and Reuben brings mandrakes to his mother to be used as a love potion.

It is interesting, in light of our puritanical Western heritage, how non-puritanical these accounts are. The biblical writers certainly did not shy away from the topic of sex.

Dinah

Adam had sons. Abraham and Isaac had sons. Jacob had sons and one daughter, Dinah. In one narrative after another, the Hebrew Bible highlights sons. The wives of these patriarchal giants are most remarkable, but not their daughters. Lot, a key figure though hardly a patriarch, has daughters, albeit unnamed and known only for their shocking incest with their father.

Dinah, daughter of Leah and Jacob, is also identified by one awful episode, but unlike the daughters of Lot, she at least has a geographical birthplace, a household, and a mother already known to us. She is the seventh and youngest child born to Leah. It would not be difficult to imagine that she quickly became the little doll of the household. Does Mom dress her up like a princess? Do brothers Reuben, Simeon, Levi, Judah, Issachar, and Zebulun watch over her almost like a priceless porcelain figurine? Do they smother her—and nearly spoil her to death?

Life for her, however, is anything but a fairy tale. She understands early that there is bad blood between her mother and Aunt Rachel—bad blood that extends to her aunt's servant Bilhah and her children. There is suppressed anger and backbiting that never seems to go away. And there's work to do. She might easily envy her brothers always at play or out in the pastures with the flocks. She has no sister to whom she can tell her secrets and play dress-up. With all the mouths to feed, she assumes she wouldn't have time for such carefree idleness anyway.

Her whole world is a desert town, hardly more than a bustling sheep ranch. During her early childhood, her father is focused on breeding the flock and may seem too busy to dote on her. But we imagine her waiting at the entrance of the tent for him to call her over and pat her on the head before he enters Aunt Rachel's living quarters. He's her *father*. She worships the man.

The years pass, marked by feasts and festivals and the ever-present tension that hovers like smog over the encampment. Then one day in a sudden flurry of activity, she is ordered to help her mother pack up all the household belongings and be ready by morning for a long journey. What about Grandpa? Is he coming too? What about all the others? Is Aunt Rachel coming? Is Zebulun coming, her dear brother nearest her age?

The following days are hectic as they are putting as many miles as they can between themselves and the home place. Then her grandfather and uncles and cousins show up; the men talk and argue, but before he leaves, Grandpa gives her a kiss and a blessing. After that they continue on their journey toward Canaan. Everything seems to be going well until

73

they suddenly get word that her mysterious uncle Esau is on his way with four thousand men—or maybe it's only four hundred. She's not sure. But she's heard stories from her brothers about this fierce uncle. He's probably a giant. She knows for sure that he's a wild man with hair all over his body, and he's a hunter, stalks his game, and kills it every time.

These are the scariest hours she's ever endured. She wishes her father were a hunter or a commander of an army like Uncle Esau is. Sure, he's handsome, but what does that matter now? But her father has a plan. She gets word that he is sending gifts on ahead—not just a few goats, but servants and donkeys and camels and sheep, some of the best of their flocks. He really must be scared.

Finally the time has come for the encounter with her ferocious uncle. She's lined up with her mother and her brothers from youngest to oldest. There are aunts and cousins ahead of her and Aunt Rachel and her cousin Joseph behind. Is she aware of this positioning—that if there's an attack her mother will get the brunt of it before Aunt Rachel? But as it turns out, there is no army attacking them at all. In fact, her father and Uncle Esau are kissing each other. Now he's heading over to where they're all standing. He's no giant, and he doesn't look scary at all. Her father begins making all the introductions, and, like her mother, she bows low when he comes to her.

Once again the caravan is on its way, but not for long. She overhears her brothers talking. It seems that their father has purchased land. They will all be settling down. She wonders how life in this place is any better than it was back home. Maybe someday she'll figure things out for herself. She wishes someone would ask for her opinion, though she can't even imagine the likelihood of that. Her brothers are being consulted, and less and less often do they pass their secrets on to her.

If only she had some sisters—or some friends to do some serious girl-talk with. She's sick of the same old drudgery every day, of being expected to do an adult's share of work but never asked her opinion on anything. Time drags on. All the unpacking is done; everything in the tent is in its place. She works with her mother and aunts, but how utterly boring is their chatter. She misses home. At least there were extended families and more excitement, such as it was. Here they're out in the middle of nowhere, except for the nearby town of Shechem.

Sometimes she looks across the fields and fantasizes about that little town. Are there any girls her age? There must be. It's actually a good-sized village compared to what's she's used to. It sure would be nice to make some friends. She is also intrigued by the fact, as she's overheard from her brothers, that the town is actually named not for the father of the household, Hamor, but for his son. Strange. She wonders who this young man might be. She can't imagine living in a village named Reuben or Levi or even Joseph—not even a town named Jacob for her father.

She's curious about so many things. So, having heard her brothers are heading out with their flocks in the other direction, she decides early one morning to dress up in her best clothes, sneak out of the tent unnoticed, and take a jaunt over to check out the village. The text simply states matter-of-factly that she "went out to visit the women of the land."[1] (Up to this point any details of Dinah's life are largely conjecture.) She barely gets into town when a man grabs her, pulls her into an open doorway, and rapes her. Hadn't she realized that walking into a strange town alone would be risky? And to assume that the girls would be as eager as she is to make friends is unwarranted. She knows her mother all too well and her jealousy of pretty Aunt Rachel. Might these girls resent her prancing into town wearing her best clothes?

The action taken by Shechem is unambiguous. No translation of the text allows the reader to imagine that this was consensual sex. And we surely cannot ask whether this was *legitimate* rape. Was it a form of date rape, someone may ask? Did she flirt with him? Did she lead him on? Rape is rape. There is no doubt about that. But cultures differ significantly on

> **In Search of Green Pastures**
>
> The land in the fertile crescent [was inhabited by] peoples who watched over their sheep, gathered the fruits from the trees, wove cloth from wool they sheared, and slept on mats in tents made from hides of their animals. . . . In the late summer they harvested grapes and olives. In the early fall, when the rains began, they planted seeds. Then came two months of cutting flax. Late winter they gathered seeds to eat or press into oil. Then they harvested the barley. . . . The wandering clans brought their harvests to the city gates and sold them. They moved with the changing seasons in search of green grass, protection from fierce wind, and always they were looking for water.
>
> Anne Roiphe, *Water from the Well*

what constitutes date rape. Sexual mores are very difficult to define across the culture-laden millennia.

In some cultures and in some eras, a man who engages in nonconsensual sex with a woman (or even consensual sex) is required to marry her. In Shechem's case, demanding that he marry her was hardly an issue. In fact, the text says: "His heart was drawn to Dinah" and "he loved" her and "spoke tenderly to her."[2] This seems like an odd reversal of emotions—especially in the biblical text. It is true that a rapist can suddenly appear to be very tender, but it is entirely possible that the text is telling us more than what our minds are able to absorb. Here, as in many instances, we so wish for details.

We may have seen a clip from an old movie, the handsome leading man seizing the leading lady and planting an unexpected kiss on her lips. He's forceful; she's startled, and they fade into the darkness behind the doorway. Is it possible that Shechem seized Dinah in such a way—that she was ravaged more than raped? The meaning of the word *rape* is to seize or to take by force, with, of course, sexual implications. There is nothing in the text, however, that indicates Dinah was distraught. Even in a twenty-first-century court of law, it is difficult to bring charges against a rapist whose victim has fallen in love with him and will not testify.

> ### Dinah in Fiction
>
> In 1997, novelist Anita Diamant re-imagined Dinah's story in her book, *The Red Tent*, a *New York Times* best-seller. In this novel, Dinah is the first-person narrator, and her encounter with Shechem is not rape but consensual sex in anticipation of marriage. Dinah willingly marries the Canaanite prince and is horrified and grieved by her brothers' vengeful actions. She flees to Egypt to bear Shechem's son and is reunited with her brother Joseph, now Egypt's prime minister.
>
> Cynthia Astle, "Giving Voice to Dinah"

The record shows Dinah silent. She does not testify. The text states that she was now considered "defiled." The brothers are "shocked and furious, because Shechem had done an outrageous thing in Israel by sleeping with Jacob's daughter—a thing that should not be done."[3] There is no indication that Dinah's feelings—or testimony—count for anything.

In fact, this is essentially where Dinah's story ends. Her brothers now take over. Jacob himself has only a bit part when he is sought out by Shechem and Hamor, who asks permission for his son to marry Dinah.

Dinah's brothers, who were also consulted, deceitfully consent, but only if Shechem, his father, and all the men of the town agree to be circumcised. So in love is Shechem that he and his father consent, and everyone is happy. "These men are friendly toward us," they say. "Let them live in our land and trade in it; the land has plenty of room for them. We can marry their daughters and they can marry ours."[4]

Then, a few days later, after the circumcision ceremony is over, when the men are still writhing in pain, Simeon and Levi come into the town and kill Shechem and his father and loot the city. Only then does the text say that they "took Dinah from Shechem's house and left."[5] What, we may wonder, was she doing at Shechem's house all this time? She didn't *flee* Shechem's house; she was *taken*.

The entire account ends with a most unusual question. Dinah's brothers, in attempting to excuse their murderous rampage, pose this rhetorical question to their father: "Should he [Shechem] have treated our sister like a prostitute?"[6] A *prostitute*? A prostitute makes herself readily available. Has Dinah said something to her brothers in the meantime that would cause them to change their tune? Being treated like a prostitute is quite different from being raped. Prostitution was not unusual in the biblical world. While no upstanding patriarch would have wanted his daughter to be labeled a prostitute, the profession was both common and consensual, surely not equated with rape.

> **A Fictionalized Footnote**
>
> We have been lost to each other for so long.
>
> My name means nothing to you. My memory is dust.
>
> This is not your fault, or mine. The chain connecting mother to daughter was broken and the word passed to the keeping of men, who had no way of knowing. That is why I became a footnote, my story a brief detour between the well-known history of my father, Jacob, and the celebrated chronicle of Joseph, my brother. On those rare occasions when I was remembered, it was as a victim.
>
> Anita Diamant, *The Red Tent*

Tamar

In the biblical worldview, prostitution truly is consensual sex. The story of Tamar bears this out. In fact, the account begins with the next generation, Jacob's grandchildren. Following the narrative relating to Dinah, Tamar becomes entangled with Dinah's brother Judah and his two sons, Dinah's nephews. Assuming Dinah is still alive, and there's no reason to believe she was not, Tamar and Dinah might have known each other, and Tamar may have heard about the bloody rampage triggered by Dinah's going off to see the girls in the town of Shechem.

Tamar's story is fascinating if for no other reason than that she is the first female *outsider* whose story is picked up in the biblical text. She is a Canaanite, and for that reason alone Dinah might have befriended her. After all, Dinah did go to Shechem to try to make friends with the Canaanite girls of that town. Geography, however, would have been their greatest obstacle to friendship. Judah has moved away from this family (after his complicity with his brothers in selling Joseph into slavery) and has taken a Canaanite wife. Thus Tamar is fully accepted into his family as a daughter-in-law despite her Canaanite ethnicity.

Tamar enters the picture when Judah's oldest son, Er, is of age. That she is anything other than a local Canaanite girl is highly unlikely, though nothing is revealed of her hometown or parents. With not even a sentence in between about her relationship with her husband or her mother-in-law, we learn that Er has died. And not of natural causes or military exploits, the plague, or a barroom brawl. He has been struck down by God. The reason? He had done something so wicked that the text dare not even disclose what it was.

It is no surprise that Tamar is childless. So Judah orders Onan, his second son: "Sleep with your brother's wife and fulfill your duty to her as

Judah and the Sin of Shechem

While with Hirah at Adullam, Judah saw a certain Canaanite woman whose name is never given. She is only referred to as "Shua's daughter." . . . I could not help but look back to chap. 34 where we are told of Shechem taking Dinah. It is said of him that he "saw her, he took her and lay with her" (34:2). There is very little difference between those words and the description we have in v. 2 of chap. 38. Judah "saw" this woman and "took her" and "went in to her." Only the last expression differs, but both describe a physical union. The act which angered Israel's [Jacob's] sons to the point of murder is very much the same as Judah's taking of a wife.

Bob Deffinbaugh, "The Skeleton in Judah's Closet"

a brother-in-law to raise up offspring for your brother."[7] *Do I have to?* We can almost hear the whiny voice of the adolescent. *Yes* is Judah's unequivocal response. But knowing that any child born to this union would not be his own, Onan *spills his seed.* For such a wicked act, he also receives the death penalty from God.

Tamar shows no sign of being a grieving widow. But if not sorrowful, surely she must be terrified—and perhaps mortified. Two dead husbands, both struck down without warning. Will she be the next to die? Are people blaming her for being an awful wife? What about her father-in-law? Is he nervous about being around her? He tells her to go back home, live in her parents' house, behave like a widow, and wait for Shelah, his youngest son, to come of age.

She sees no other choice than to return home, which she does. The years pass. Nothing. No word at all from Judah. Shelah is now a young man. True, she's a lot older than he, but it's more than that. She is no fool. She knows Judah thinks she's jinxed and fears Shelah will die as well. But if Shelah's out of the picture, that will leave her childless with no means of carrying on the line of Judah. Then an idea strikes her. Her mother-in-law is recently deceased. So she could carry on the family line through Judah himself. He of course would shun the idea—almost like having sex with his own daughter. She needs a plan. How can she get him in bed with her?

She has her ear to the ground and learns that his time of grief is now over and that he will be heading out with his buddy Hirah to enjoy the sheep-shearing celebrations. She immediately hits the road herself, leaving behind her widow's attire. Donning a purple gown with a pink sash (or something similar), she sits alongside the road at Enaim as a prostitute would. When she sees him coming, she covers her head with a veil so that he won't recognize her.

Sure enough, he takes the bait. He asks her for her services, promising a young goat as payment. She's a clever lady. Though she's never plied the trade of prostitution, she knows a promise is worth nothing. But monetary payment isn't what she wants. She asks him for a token of his pledge. *Give me something important to you, and you've got a deal.* So what does she want? She looks him over as though she is weighing her options and then says casually, *How about your seal and staff?* He knows such things are of no value to her, but they are to him, so he hands them over. Later he'll trade them up for the goat.

Judah impregnates the veiled prostitute, catches up with Hirah, and joins the merrymaking of sheep shearing. Soon after that, he asks his friend to return with a goat for the prostitute whom he'd met by the road and to retrieve his seal and staff. Hirah, however, cannot locate her. He asks around only to learn that there hasn't been a prostitute on that crossroad, perhaps for quite some time. The people have no clue whom he is talking about.

When Judah hears the news, he realizes that he's going to have to go out and get a new seal and staff. Sure, he could probably track her down, but wisdom prevails: "Let her keep what she has, or we will become a laughingstock."[8]

Some months later Judah learns that Tamar has become pregnant. But that's not the half of it. He hears she's been moonlighting as a prostitute. He's livid. *Bring her here*, he thunders. *I'll see that she is torched at the stake.* So the thugs head over to her village to fetch her for her execution. But she's hardly out of her tent when she insists that a messenger take a gift on ahead to her father-in-law. No surprise, his seal and staff, along with a cryptic sentence: "I am pregnant by the man who owns these." For good measure, just to rub it in, she adds: "See if you recognize whose seal and cord and staff these are."[9]

If Judah were like a lot of people caught in such an embarrassing scenario, he would have denied culpability, insisting someone had stolen his identity. But his response is stunning, accustomed as we are to hearing lies in such situations: "She is more righteous than I, since I wouldn't give her to my son Shelah."[10]

Tamar gives birth to twin boys. No fighting in the womb as was the case with Rebekah, but in other respects strikingly similar. When the apparent firstborn starts to come out hand first, the midwife ties a red string to his wrist to ensure that the two won't be mixed up after birth. But then the infant with the red string pulls back his hand, and his brother overtakes him on the journey through the birth canal. He is named Perez (meaning "breaking out"), his brother clad only in a red string is named Zerah (meaning "scarlet").

It would be left to Perez to carry his mother's line eventually on to King David and many generations later to Jesus of Nazareth. How strange, life's twists and turns. Jacob's son Judah, who negotiates the services of a prostitute, and Tamar, a Canaanite woman (and his daughter-in-law) playing the part of a prostitute, have a child whose lineage leads to the Messiah.

Concluding Observations

Dinah and Tamar are two of the most fascinating women in the Bible. Their stories are less familiar than the patriarchal wives who preceded them, but their breaking of patriarchal rules makes them stand out. Sarah, Rebekah, Rachel, and Leah all worked within the system through manipulation. Even Rachel's herding sheep, we have every reason to believe, is sanctioned by her father.

But both Dinah and Tamar are working entirely outside the system. Dinah, bless her heart, goes off to the neighboring town to seek out some girlfriends. That fits right into my own 1960s teenage worldview. I grew up on a rather isolated farm, and I would sometimes go off on my bike and find girlfriends. Sure, we all went to the same country church, but on Saturdays we'd often meet, some of us riding several miles from our own homes. Dinah would have fit right in.

Unfortunately for Dinah, the male-dominated system, both Canaanite and Israelite, betrayed her. Whether or not she welcomed the advances of Shechem (since her brothers accused her of being treated like a prostitute), she may have grieved his death. And she paid dearly for breaking the rules. No decent woman was supposed to go off on her own to begin with.

Tamar would not have fit into our 1960s unofficial girls club. But we would have admired her cleverness. She turns the tables on Judah and the whole system. Men can take women or seize them and have sex with them. Why can't she do her own version of the same thing? Like Dinah, she leaves her father's home and goes off on her own. She tricks Judah by taking his seal, along with the cord, and his staff. He can easily get another staff, but his seal is his very identity, though that too can be replaced. Besides confirming his identity, she has no use for it. She would have had a tough time buying a tract of land with his seal.

But whether intentional or not, there is wonderful biblical symbolism in the seal and the staff. Both are metaphors with deep spiritual meaning—God's care for his people. And it is not a stretch to imagine that they therefore have symbolic significance in this story.

Questions to Think About

How do you assess Dinah's going off to the neighboring town? Have you ever wanted to just get away from it all and leave your family behind?

Was Dinah raped, or is the account less than conclusive? What constitutes rape, date rape, marital rape? Do you know anyone who has been raped?

If you were making a movie or writing a novel about Dinah, how would you embellish and finish her story?

Do you see Dinah as a more modern woman than Tamar? Who would you most like to have as a Facebook friend?

Does it seem odd that marrying one's brother-in-law would be expected in the case of a widowed woman but that marrying one's widowed father-in-law would be absolutely forbidden? How would we regard such marriages today?

Do you admire Tamar for her sting operation, or do you think she was dishonest? Did Judah deserve exactly what he got? Do you know of any situations of similar trickery today?

As we reflect on a daughter of a great patriarch and a Canaanite woman named in Jesus's genealogy, should we be surprised that neither appears to have even a perfunctory relationship with God?

7

Jochebed, Miriam, and Zipporah

Moses's Mother, Sister, and Wife

When my son was in high school, he encountered a vicious form of racism. How could that possibly be? He was a tall, nice-looking, Caucasian kid, complete with short sandy-blonde hair. A claim of racism seems ludicrous. Maybe the boy had an over-protective mother fretting about a nonincident. Maybe not.

We lived at that time in a mixed urban neighborhood; his friends down the street and in public school were both black and white. He often went to a movie with a group of them, whoever was not tied up with family or a weekend job. On a few occasions, the only other one available in the group was a neighbor girl. He told me some years later how that in more than one instance while they were grabbing a burger at a fast-food joint they were the objects of racial slurs. How his friend must have felt one shudders to imagine. How my son felt, I heard firsthand: calling him an *n-word lover* was their way of somehow seeking to bolster their own pitiful egos.

Moses heard something similar from Miriam regarding his *Cushite* wife.

For the first time in the biblical text, we meet women who identify Africa as their home, three of them directly related to Moses (another, the wife of

Potiphar, a high African official). All four are born there, though Miriam, and most likely her mother, Jochebed, will leave and wander in the Sinai Desert for forty years. Zipporah is believed to be from Cush, south of Egypt in the région of present-day Sudan or Ethiopia.

Moses is the common denominator. Born in Egypt himself, he will flee to Midian and then return under the orders of God. In any movie starring Moses, these three women would play bit parts. Here we reverse the roles, and it is Moses who plays the bit part.

Jochebed plays a critical but small role in the story. Yet she sets the stage for this man who will for millennia to follow be elevated to near-divine status. In Judaism he occupies a place almost next to God himself; and in Christianity he is a symbolic figure for God in the words of Jesus: "As Moses lifted up the serpent in the wilderness, even so must the Son of man be lifted up."[1] The mother of Jesus is prominently featured in the biblical text. Not so the mother of Moses.

Miriam, the sister of Moses, becomes a powerhouse in her own right. But, except for a brief interlude in his infancy, she is always playing second fiddle to her famous brother. In fact, she plays third fiddle, having soon been overtaken by brother Aaron, whose gender serves him well.

Zipporah is the mystery woman. No blood relative of Moses, not even distant kin, she is an outsider. In fact, we see in the treatment of her the first real signs of racism recorded in Scripture. Ethnocentrism is prevalent much earlier, but in her case it is likely she is vilified due to her dark skin alone. But perhaps the Cushite wife is not Zipporah at all. Is she, as some suggest, another wife of Moses?

Potiphar's wife holds significance not only because of her attempt to seduce Joseph (and the resulting fallout) but also because she is the first woman singled out in the text who is clearly identified as African, albeit Egyptian.

Jochebed

In order to better understand the mother of Moses, we pause for some biblical context. Tamar has just tricked Judah, and he becomes the father of twins. Judah, we recall, was one of six sons of Leah and Jacob. Prior to his move away from his father and brothers (and prior to his fathering three sons by his Canaanite wife and two by his Canaanite daughter-in-law), he was a key figure in an act of treachery. He and his ten brothers were jealous of their much-coddled brother Joseph, favorite son of Jacob by his late wife Rachel. In fact, it was Judah who suggested to his brothers that they not kill Joseph but rather sell him to traders who were on their way to Egypt. Judah may have moved away because he felt tremendous guilt for not shouting down the brothers, insisting he would have no part at all in bringing harm to his half brother. Or perhaps for other reasons. But whether he feels guilt or not, his suggestion changes the course of history.

Joseph, unbeknown to his family, does well in Egypt and becomes a high-ranking official under the Pharaoh, after having spent time in a dungeon on a false charge by Potiphar's wife. When famine strikes Canaan, Jacob sends his sons there for food. One thing leads to another, and Jacob's entire family moves to Egypt. We assume this caravan includes Dinah and even Tamar since Judah is among them. (In fact, it is an amusing digression to imagine these two women talking and laughing and whispering about this weird—and often wicked—family in which they are enmeshed.) The whole clan of Jacob remains in Egypt and reproduces for some four hundred years, during which time they have become slaves to the Pharaoh and his brutal overseers. They are numbered by now into the hundreds of thousands and are known as the Israelites (taken from Jacob's name change to Israel).

The current Pharaoh is not friendly to these outsiders. In fact, he greatly fears the Israelites, who are multiplying rapidly. He calls in the Israelite midwives Shiphrah and Puah, who are busy day and night delivering babies. *What could the king possibly want with us?* they're thinking. But they quickly find out. His words are unambiguous: "When you are helping the Hebrew women during childbirth on the delivery stool, if you see that the baby is a boy, kill him; but if it is a girl, let her live."[2] They agree and exit his presence shell-shocked. Did they hear him right? They're used to taking orders, but this is not like being forced to work an extra two hours a day. This is outright murder. Their fear of God prevails, and they ignore the order.

The king summons them back, demanding to know why the Israelite women are still knitting blue booties for their babies. They are ready with a joint response. It's an old midwives' tale, but he will never know the difference: "Hebrew women are not like Egyptian women; they are vigorous and give birth before the midwives arrive."[3]

The Pharaoh doesn't check the facts, and the Hebrew women just keep birthing babies, presumably as though they are canteloupes popping right out, with no painful hours of labor. And the midwives are themselves rewarded by God, who gives them babies of their own.

So exasperated is the Pharaoh that he brazenly takes matters into his own hands and orders that every baby boy born to an Israelite woman be kidnapped and thrown into the Nile River. Is he serious? This guy is a madman. The people are horrified. Pregnant women, praying for baby girls, hide in their closets when the time comes—no midwife at all in order to avoid suspicion. But now what? How do you stop your baby boy from crying, and how do you avoid being out in public yourself when your work is slave labor? It is a collective nightmare for all the descendants—male and female—of Sarah, Rebekah, Rachel, Leah, Bilhah, and Zilpah. Everyone is wailing at the prospect of losing their little boys.

This is where we find Jochebed and her husband, Amram, both from the tribe of Levi. They are under the stranglehold of the Egyptian ruler, fearing for the life of their newborn son, Moses.

Jochebed is the daughter of Levi, and Amram is her nephew, the grandson of Levi. If it sounds confusing, it is not out of the ordinary in ancient times. We learn in Exodus 6:20 that "Amram married his father's sister Jochebed, who bore him Aaron and Moses. Amram lived 137 years." How long Jochebed lived is not revealed. (The perplexing issue relating to this three-generation genealogy found in Exodus 6 and elsewhere, and the Exodus 12 reference to the 430-year sojourn of the Israelites in Egypt, is a matter we leave to biblical scholars.)

We can more easily shrug off the news that Jochebed marries her nephew than the news of how she reacts to the Pharaoh's edict. After all, Sarah was married to her half brother, and Rebekah, Rachel, and Leah were married to cousins, though more distant than first cousins. But who can believe that she would set her baby afloat in the Nile when that's the very river decreed to be his tomb? True, the Nile is a huge river, but she's not journeying upstream a hundred miles. She puts him in a floating basket, shaded by reeds, in the water right under the Pharaoh's nose.

Jochebed, however, is no fool. She reasons that there is no way she can keep a lively baby boy alive under the piercing eyes of the Pharaoh's henchmen. So she turns the tables and hides him in plain sight—plain sight not of the Pharaoh himself, but of his daughter who comes to the river to bathe. In one sense this is the safest place in all of Egypt. The Pharaoh's gestapo would have no qualms about breaking down a door and grabbing a baby boy out of his mother's arms. But to hang around where the princess is bathing? They surely know better than that.

And Jochebed knows from experience the muscular might of maternal instincts. Not only the *she-bear* protectiveness that a mother possesses after she has given birth to a baby. Of course, it's that. But it's also something she possessed at an early age: that instant baby talk and affection that arose whenever she saw an infant. Surely the Pharaoh's daughter knows this feeling as well. Her heart will swell the moment she lays eyes on him. And so it does.

We can imagine Jochebed's very careful instructions to her daughter. When the princess does approach the basket, the infant's sister is ready to offer a solution to the princess's unspoken dilemma: how to care for a Hebrew baby boy in the midst of her father's murderous policy. Her words are exactly those that her mother had coached her to say: "Shall I go and get one of the Hebrew women to nurse the baby for you?"[4] Note, she does not say: Shall I go and get *my mother* to nurse the baby? When the princess agrees, the girl runs home for her mother.

It is difficult to comprehend the sheer terror that Jochebed must have experienced during those fateful hours. Sure, she had thought through this scheme, but it was fraught with danger every step of the way. Even as she is leaving her house to meet the princess, one false move could blow the whole thing to bits. If the princess notices her nervousness, however, she

> ### A Mother, a Father, and Child Abandonment
>
> Not all interpreters . . . have considered the actions of Moses' parents to be commendable. John Calvin found it hard to excuse their timidity and fear, which led them to desert their child. The parents did well to trust God to protect them. Nonetheless, Calvin recognized the pain they must have felt and concluded that Amram was too stricken with grief to help hide Moses.
>
> Scott M. Langston, *Exodus through the Centuries*

quickly puts her at ease when she offers to pay her for her services. Has anyone in all history been paid for such a glorious task?

Was the princess really so dense that she wasn't onto the ruse? Even her attendants, we presume, were smart enough to figure it out—each and every one of them endowed with their own maternal instincts.

For Jochebed, however, the rescue of her son is only temporary, maybe only two or three years. During this time, she is apparently living in her own home under security by order of the princess. But she knows that this boy is not hers. He must be handed over to the palace before she can even instruct him in the ways of her people. How can a mother, with all her instincts intact, hand over her three-year-old to another mother? The text leaves us bewildered. And, one might ask, how did little Moses deal with this shocking handover?

This is our last glimpse of Jochebed—a mother, now home, weeping uncontrollably. The text does not confirm any such episode. But we quickly learn that Moses is being raised as the son of Pharaoh's daughter. Did he miss his mom? Did he ever see her again? Those questions and many more will forever go unanswered.

Potiphar's Wife

This story takes us back into Genesis, but sets the stage for the long exile in Egypt that ends with the account of Moses and the three women in his life. Having lived generations earlier, Potiphar's wife has no connection at all to Moses. In fact, it is unlikely that he had ever heard of her while growing up in the palace. As an adult when he returned to lead his people out of Egypt, Moses would certainly have learned about his ancestor, the great statesman Joseph. Indeed, he would have resonated with him— the only one of his ancestors who would have understood palace life. He would have also understood the suddenness of disfavor. In fact, the story of Joseph's imprisonment due to false charges might have brought Moses solace during his own episodes of despair and despondency.

It is difficult to be sympathetic at all to Potiphar's wife unless perhaps we imagine a characteristically brash Joseph strutting around and maybe even flirting with her. But the text gives no cause for us to make such a leap.

Joseph has worked his way up, now top dog in Potiphar's household. He's an expert money manager, and Potiphar is impressed with the growth of his financial portfolio.

Potiphar's wife, unnamed in the biblical text, is also enjoying the life of the nouveau riche. She lives in a palatial home and gets everything she wants. She has eyes for the handsome young man who is now administrator of her husband's entire estate. She would naturally discuss household matters with him and make various requests. One day she casually slips in a more intimate request, perhaps something like, *I just got a new mattress. Why don't you come try it out?* He might have come back at her, *What on earth are you talking about? You're old enough to be my mother!* Instead he respectfully lets her know that he's rejecting her offer because of his faithfulness both to her husband and to God.

She doesn't give up. Day after day, she corners him with the same line. Then the perfect moment arises. The servants are out. The two of them are alone. Perhaps she chases him around the bed as if it were a scene in a movie. The text is straightforward. She grabs hold of him; he pulls away and runs, his garment left behind in her hands. It would seem that he would want to take his cloak with him so as to not be seen running half naked out of the house. But that's not what happened. She has both his garment and a scandalous story, spread by way of social media—her servants.

Her version has him coming on to her, entering her private boudoir for sex; her frantic screaming causes him to run away without his outer garment. We can only imagine the embellishments that are added as the tale flies through the palace and beyond. *Did he really try to rape her? . . . He did what? . . . You say he raped her? . . . She was raped.*

When Potiphar hears the vile account, he is understandably irate and immediately sends Joseph to prison. But Joseph is the kind of guy who can quickly turn bad fortune around—with God's help, that is. A few

> **Leaving Potiphar's Wife to Her Own Conscience**
>
> It is easy to talk, comparatively easy to talk well, but to be quiet is the difficulty! [Joseph] never said a word, that I can learn, about Potiphar's wife. It seemed necessary to his own defense, but he would not accuse the woman. He let judgment go by default and left her to her own conscience and her husband's cooler consideration.
>
> C. H. Spurgeon, "A Miniature Portrait of Joseph"

chapters later, we find him in charge of all of Egypt. When Genesis ends (just before Joseph dies at 110), he is promising his brothers (with Dinah and Tamar in the background), who are with him in Egypt, royal protection and provision. He could not have imagined future generations of harsh slavery under the callous rule of one Pharaoh after another. Nor could he have fathomed the astonishing events surrounding Jochebed and her baby in a basket—a baby who would become an illustrious liberator and leader.

Zipporah

If Joseph, son of Jacob, finds his way to the top of the heap among eleven brothers, why should not Zipporah, daughter of Jethro (priest of Midian), do the same among her six sisters? Other sisters may have far exceeded her in many ways, but only her name is written in indelible ink as the wife of Moses. There is no mention of brothers, at least while the family is living in Midian. Much later, however, we find Hobab, son of Jethro, in the wilderness telling Moses he plans to return home, despite Moses's pleas that he join the Israelite venture into the Promised Land.

As with Rebekah and Rachel previously, watering sheep leads to an arranged marriage. What is it with those Hebrew men? Why are they always marrying women who water sheep? And the well? In biblical parlance, perhaps akin to a singles bar of today where men brawl and pick up women. (We will be reminded in chap. 20 of the disciples' displeasure on seeing Jesus alone with a woman at a well.)

Zipporah, like Rebekah and Rachel, lives way out in the middle of nowhere. Nothing happens in Midian. That is until one day Moses comes hiking in from Egypt. Off in the distance, he has seen and heard a commotion. As he nears, he realizes that there is conflict over water rights. There he finds seven sisters who are simply trying to lower their buckets into the well and water their sheep as they usually do. They had been first in line, but then other shepherds arrived and bullied their way in front of them.

Moses to the rescue. Unlike Jacob, who lifts a boulder from the top of the well, Moses goes straight to the well, his violent demeanor speaking volumes, and drives the boorish jackasses away. Shortly before this incident, he had killed an Egyptian, and now his temper has flared again. Spurred by an adrenalin rush, he draws bucket after bucket from the well and waters all the sheep. The seven sisters race home to their father, who is surprised that they have returned so early. No doubt they had been pushed to the end of the line before.

Satisfied with his chivalrous gesture, Moses apparently expects no reward. But the moment Jethro hears the story he asks why in heaven's name they didn't invite the stranger for a meal. With a proper invitation, Moses eats, overnights, and marries Zipporah all in one verse—Exodus 2:21. In the next verse she gives birth to a son whom Moses names Gershom, a name signifying that he is a stranger in a foreign land. A second is born, Eliezer.

During her long marriage does Zipporah realize how well educated and highly cultured this hotheaded husband of hers is? Does he tell her about his life in the Pharaoh's palace? About his *mother*, the princess? About his killing an Egyptian man? Does he consult her in his decision to remain in the household and herd sheep for her father for forty years, or does this cause her to question his independence and initiative? Does he tell her about God speaking to him from a burning bush? Does he tell her how he, on God's orders, threw his staff on the ground and it became a snake and that God made his hand temporarily leprous? Does he discuss with her the plan to move back to Egypt, or is she informed only days ahead of time? These are secrets the text holds tight.

The next time Zipporah is mentioned we learn that Moses took and put her on a donkey, and with their two sons they set out for Egypt. But Zipporah is not merely being acted upon. In fact, she takes action herself in one of the most mystifying episodes in the entire Bible. The family has secured lodging along the way. During this stay, we learn that God was on the verge of killing Moses. Only one verse earlier, God had been assuring Moses that he and the enslaved Israelites would prevail over the Pharaoh. Now this. Had Moses cursed God? Did he stomp away in a fit of anger? We have no clue but perhaps for the bewildering passage that follows:

But Zipporah took a flint knife, cut off her son's foreskin and touched Moses' feet with it. "Surely you are a bridegroom of blood to me," she said. So the LORD let him alone. (At that time she said "bridegroom of blood," referring to circumcision.)[5]

91

There are several aspects of this brief episode that leave biblical scholars scratching their heads. Apparently God's indignation with Moses has something to do with the circumcision of his sons, who are now presumably well into their thirties. Had Moses, raised in Egypt, not known about this command given to Father Abraham and thus had not conducted the ritual when his sons were infants? Had God given him orders to do so after the burning bush experience? When Moses informed Zipporah, had she said, *Are you stark raving mad?* Did Moses give in to her and thus ignite God's burning anger? And is this why Zipporah is carrying out this male-only ritual instead of Moses himself? Is she staying God's hand from slaying her husband?

Zipporah apparently continues on the road to Egypt with her husband, who is soon joined by his brother, Aaron. She is a stranger there to both the Egyptians and the Israelites. It would not have been easy for her to make friends with other women. She and her sons are with Moses during the nerve-wracking days of the plagues and the harrowing trip through the Red Sea and later on the sidelines of the tense battle against Amalek and his fighting men. But then he sends her and the boys back to Midian to live in Jethro's household.

Sometime after that, however, Jethro returns with Zipporah and his grandsons Gershom and Eliezer. Moses welcomes Jethro and invites him into his tent. Whether he welcomed Zipporah is unclear. He accepts wise advice from his father-in-law and then gives him a send-off. But does he send Zipporah away as well? Many commentators say he did; others believe that only Jethro, and perhaps servants, departed.

Zipporah truly is one of the leading mystery women of the Bible. Because she is the wife of Moses, we naturally assume we deserve to know more about her, but alas we take what we get. Whether she returned to Midian has more significance than merely her geographical location at any particular time. If she had not been sent back to live with her father in Midian, we presume rightly that she is the one who is the object of Miriam and Aaron's racial slurs when they harangue their brother Moses for having a *Cushite* wife. Some scholars maintain that people from Cush had migrated east to Midian.

So, the sixty-four-thousand-dollar question remains: Is Zipporah a Cushite, or does Moses take another wife, a Cushite?

Miriam

We very much want Miriam, sister of Moses, to be the same sister who watches his floating basket as it rocks in the Nile. The text does not say, but Miriam is the only named sister of Moses in the Bible.

She is a mature young girl. She does exactly as her mother has instructed and casually steps from behind the bushes and offers to fetch a nursemaid for the Pharaoh's daughter. She does so in a way that avoids creating suspicion. It's a lot to ask of a young girl; she plays a critical role in saving her brother.

Time flies. Miriam is in her eighties. (She is older than Moses, who spends his first forty years in Egypt, his second forty in Midian, and his third forty in the wilderness.) She is part of the massive exodus from Egypt. She has heard from her brothers, Moses and Aaron, about the demands they have made of the Pharaoh—their plea directly from God: *Let my people go!* And she has witnessed all the plagues firsthand, beginning with the Nile River turning to blood, the very river where she had watched over her baby brother. Then frogs had overrun the land, followed by gnats, swarms of flies, plagues on livestock, boils on both people and animals, destructive hailstorms, locusts, darkness, and finally the most terrible of all, the death of firstborn sons. Imagine living through all that trauma. Though you yourself are spared, neighbors and people across town are suffering overwhelming hardship and grief.

Finally Pharaoh relents, and all of the Israelites with loads of loot are on their way back to the Promised Land, the land of her mothers: Sarah, Rebekah, Rachel, Leah, Dinah, and others. But she dare not fantasize too long. There are dangers ahead—and behind. Do her brothers really know where they are going? Seems like they're leading everyone around in circles. Pharaoh and his men will overtake them in no time. But Moses, without the benefit of GPS, has gotten the right directions from God, and soon they are heading north again. But it's too late. The enemy is bearing down on them from the west, and they are trapped between the Egyptians and the Red Sea. She's ready to give up—all those plagues and the rush to escape and now this. Is it all for nothing? Far better to have died a slave in Egypt than to spend the last hours of her life in a desperate flight that will end in agony by the sword—or worse, by rape.

Then suddenly, at her younger brother's command, the sea splits apart with a wide swath of dry ground leading to the other side. She's stunned. The water stands on either side like walls of a canyon. Everyone moves through in a more orderly fashion than she could have imagined. Only after she's on the opposite side of the sea does she realize that at the end of the seemingly endless line the walls of water are crashing down—crashing down and drowning the enemy troops.

What follows is a majestic choir of voices, led by Moses, beginning with the chorus and continuing to tell the story of victory:

> I will sing to the LORD,
>   for he is highly exalted.
> Both horse and driver
>   he has hurled into the sea.[6]

The hymn continues on with sixty more lines and ends with a short coda: "The LORD reigns for ever and ever."[7] At that point Miriam, now identified as a prophet, grabs a tambourine and leads all the women in a festive dance. She's in her eighties, but she can still kick up her heels, and her voice is loud and clear as all the women and girls join in. They dance and sing again and again the catchy chorus:

> I will sing to the LORD,
>   for he is highly exalted.
> Both horse and driver
>   he has hurled into the sea.

This celebration is followed by forty years in the wilderness. There is only one recorded episode during this time that relates directly to Miriam. She is not mentioned when her brother Aaron leads the Israelites in golden-calf worship while Moses is on Mount Sinai receiving the Ten Commandments. But sometime later (before the spies are commissioned to scope out the Promised Land), she and Aaron begin challenging their younger brother's place as CEO on the organizational chart. They want an equal role in decision making. Three heads, they reason, are better than one. Indeed, Miriam might have a calming effect on the hot-tempered Moses.

Besides, there's another matter. He's married to a *Cushite*—an Ethiopian or Sudanese—woman. What that could possibly have to do with the matter of his sole leadership is inexplicable apart from bald-faced racism. Even if his wife is playing an important role behind the scenes, the fact that she is African is entirely extraneous. It thus besmirches Miriam's otherwise untarnished character.

She is to be faulted less, it would seem, for her challenge of her hothead younger brother, Moses. From her standpoint, he has been making some less than stellar decisions. But God sees the matter differently. He calls her and Aaron to come before him for a special cloud-covered meeting—in reality, taking them to the woodshed. He makes it clear to them that Moses is like none other, for God speaks to Moses face-to-face.

They are both, we can imagine, scared witless by this dressing-down by none other than God himself. Then the cloud lifts, and Miriam is stunned when she realizes that in a snap of a finger she has become a leper—her skin white and eaten away by this defiling disease. Aaron sees her and is horrified; he begs Moses not to hold their sin against them.

Moses is in shock. He cries out to God to heal her. God does, but not until she has suffered outside the camp for seven days. Only then, after this one-week delay, are she and the whole encampment permitted to move on toward the Promised Land. She dies sometime later, never even glimpsing that land of milk and honey.

One might wonder why the idol-worshiping Aaron wasn't also struck with leprosy, but that would be to question God's judgment. Despite this negative side of Miriam, she was highly regarded by succeeding generations. Micah the prophet, speaking for God, declared:

> I brought you up out of Egypt
> and redeemed you from the land of slavery.
> I sent Moses to lead you,
> also Aaron and Miriam.[8]

Concluding Observations

Perhaps we should label the women featured in this chapter *the African Quartet*. They all walk out of the pages of Scripture from Africa. This represents a significant geographical and cultural rotation away from Mesopotamia and Palestine. Sarah, of course, had sojourned in Egypt, but only to participate in an unfortunate episode that forever sullied her husband's reputation. These women by their ancestry or adopted homeland are actual Africans.

Chronologically, Potiphar's wife comes first in this line of Africans. She is known for one incident only, her attempted seduction of Joseph. In ancient times—and even today, to a lesser extent—it was perceived as the male prerogative to seduce a woman. The Pharaoh, with no discredit to his reputation, added Sarah to his harem, albeit thinking she was unmarried. While Potiphar may not have had a harem, it is not difficult to imagine his being unfaithful to his wife, considering the environment in which he lived. That his wife might have wished to engage in a comparable dalliance with a handsome, unmarried man in her service should not shock us. That she turned the tables and had him sent off to prison, however, secures her a place among the world's wicked women.

Jochebed's claim to fame is giving birth, saving, and giving away her son—and not just any son. Her sacrificial role opened the life-gate for the most heralded figure of the Hebrew Bible. Sister Miriam plays a leading role in saving Moses as well, and unlike her mother goes on to play an important part in leading the Israelites in their forty years of wandering. She is the first of many women prophets in both the Old and the New Testaments.

Zipporah was the lucky one of seven sisters. Or maybe she wasn't so lucky. Moses, we can imagine, was not an easy person to live with. That the marriage was one long romance is not warranted by the text.

Questions to Think About

Is there anything favorable at all—apart perhaps from her good taste in men—to be said about Potiphar's wife? Have you ever known anyone who reminds you of her?

If you were Jochebed, how might you have taken a different course in attempting to save your son from the wrath of the Pharaoh? Is there any life experience that allows you to comprehend the anguish of handing him over to another *mother*?

Is Miriam's task of guarding the infant too great a responsibility to ask of a child? Do you know children who have been put in this kind of position?

Do Miriam's strengths outweigh her shortcomings? Is there a place for women to challenge authority—especially male authority?

Do you know any women in their eighties who can kick up their heals like Miriam? How do you assess Aaron's getting off scot-free while Miriam suffers the effects of leprosy?

How do you size up Zipporah? Do you prefer to imagine her as a Cushite and the only wife of Moses or as one of two wives?

Have you ever endured racial slurs or known anyone who has?

8

Rahab and the Five Daughters of Zelophehad

Reward and Justice

Prostitution is illegal in all fifty states except Nevada. As was true in biblical times, however, it is a common phenomenon in cities throughout the country. On Division Street in Grand Rapids, considered a very religious community, prostitutes have openly plied their trade. If I sometimes saw them as I drove by, I essentially ignored them. In fact, I never gave them much thought at all until my son's beloved high school economics teacher was put on trial for stabbing to death a prostitute.

Without my permission, Carlton had skipped school with a friend to be at the arraignment. He spoke to the media. There he was—on the evening news of a local television station, telling a reporter how he (son of a single mom and a deserter dad) had looked to Mr. Jenson as a father figure. He stated that he couldn't believe his teacher would do such a thing. In the end, Richard Jenson, forty-four, was convicted of the murder. That my son continued to defend his innocence should not have shocked me. I knew how much he had idolized his teacher. But when he made the comment *she was just a prostitute*, I was suddenly shaken into the realization that a critical aspect of my parenting had horribly slipped through the cracks.

This murdered prostitute, stabbed fifty-five times on March 17, 1991, was not *just a prostitute*, a nameless piece of human flesh whose body belonged in a dumpster or a rural wetland. She was a young woman who had needs and aspirations that led to a series of very unfortunate decisions. She was Kerry Mansfield, sister of Kimberly, only twenty-three years old, young enough to be my own daughter, big sister to Carlton.

She was *Rahab*.

Rahab is the only woman in Scripture involved openly in prostitution who then becomes a hero. Her role is critical, some would argue, to Israel's taking of the Promised Land. Whatever the nature of that role, however, it is important to see her as a woman not so different from any one of us. She is a neighbor, the woman waiting in line for coffee, the driver we rear-ended on slippery pavement. She is more than simply the lowlife we snub as the Jericho prostitute. Though we may easily look down on her, she has her dignity and her own underground rules for survival.

But Rahab, by demanding an oath from the spies, uses society's rules to ensure her ultimate survival when she is facing sure death. And she is rewarded. In another instance in Scripture, women also take a risk. Five sisters demand justice, and they too receive their reward. These daughters of Zelophehad approach Moses and the Israelite elders who handle such matters. Their legal issue arises while the Israelites are wandering for forty years in the desert. Rahab's story is part of the actual conquering of the Promised Land.

The Daughters of Zelophehad

The seven daughters of Jethro. And now the five daughters of Zelophehad (pronounced Zel-loaf'-ĕ-had). Soon to come are the three daughters of Job, and later the four daughters of Philip. Apart from one episode in their lives, we know nothing about these five daughters, each of whom is named. Nor is their deceased father known apart from them. We could only wish for additional chapters in the book of Numbers to turn up in an ancient cave—chapters that would give us personal details of their lives.

It is most interesting that they are without a guardian when they approach Moses and the elders. Such circumstances would lead us to believe that they may have been well into their adult years. They are descendants of Rachel through her son Joseph, who lived six generations before them. Like Miriam, they may very well have grown up in Egypt as children of slaves. Do they look back on those days when the Pharaoh ordered the overseers not to provide any more straw for brick making? How they as young children had to work twice as hard—going into the fields, gathering straw, and still forced to make as many bricks as before?

Do they remember the terrifying sight of the Nile River blood red, and the awful smell of dead frogs piled up? And, oh, those millions of flies and gnats and locusts stinging and getting in their hair and under their skirts. Everything, it seemed, was happening at once—now, looking back, a blur of destruction. Then, without realizing what was happening, they're helping their folks pack, not just their own things but silver and gold and jewelry from their Egyptian overseers. Next thing they know they're on the road out of the only land they've ever known.

With hundreds of thousands of others, they would have hurried along the path through the Red Sea lined by canyon walls of water. Imagine them school-age girls, all holding hands, prodded on by their father, Zelophehad (and perhaps their mother). They're safe at last. What a relief! And how can they ever forget the great prophet Miriam. She's an old lady but young at heart. They join with all the women dancing and singing the victory chorus of Moses—a praise song to God.

If they were children during the exodus from Egypt, they come of age while wandering in the vast desert, following a pillar of cloud by day and a pillar of fire by night, and eating manna for every meal. Those years of manna eating became a trial for the wandering Israelites. We know from earlier times that appetizing meals were relished. Abraham sends a servant to prepare the best calf in the herd for visitors. Later, Rebekah orders Jacob: "Go out to the flock and bring me two choice young goats, so I can prepare some tasty food for your father, just the way he likes it."[1]

Though food preparation in ancient Israel was not exclusively women's work, the women in the camp must have missed that creative diversion of sharing recipes, gathering herbs, and joining together to prepare grand feasts. Now their only meal preparation is collecting the manna that falls to the ground day after day. True, it tastes just fine, like wafers made from honey. But every day, with no variety? How tiresome.

If food preparation does not break the long days of wandering, troubles and tensions often do. People are particularly upset with Moses's leadership. The sisters would have known of Miriam and Aaron's rebellion and Miriam's leprous punishment. They are also familiar with a later incident instigated by Korah, Dathan, and Abiram. Some 250 leaders of the camp come as a delegation to Moses and Aaron, complaining that the two of them have set themselves above all the rest of the people, treating them as slaves—as bad as it was in Egypt.

So Moses tells Korah to come the next day with all his followers and stand before God. It will be God's decision whose side stands or falls: Moses's or Korah's. The next day, all the families who had supported Korah are separated from the rest of the camp, and a massive sinkhole swallows them up. This terrifying incident is on the minds of the five daughters of Zelophehad when they come to bring their case before Moses.

So significant is their case and audacious their approach that each of them is named: Mahlah, Noah, Hoglah, Milkah, and Tirzah. Such beautiful names that it is surprising they have not become more popular choices for baby girls in the millennia since. The sisters have come to the entrance of the tabernacle (tent of meeting), where all domestic and civic disputes are brought.

They are technically orphans, with no mother and their father having died only recently. They want Moses to know right off the bat that their father was not among the followers of Korah, "who banded together against the LORD." He was not, they make clear, a rebel. But what they say next is most curious: "he died for his own sin."[2] Had he committed a sin for which God struck him down? Or might he have died of natural causes? Or was his death accidental or something else? The text does not say.

All we know of the now-deceased Zelophehad (besides his ancestors) is that he apparently was a man of means, and he had not secured an estate planner, did not even have a will. His brothers are anxious that they be deeded the property. This may have been how estates in such instances were divvied up in Egypt, perhaps even among the patriarchs, though Abraham, if he had had no sons, would have deeded his estate to his trusted servant Eliezer.

The five sisters have prepared their argument, and they make clear that it is not material interest alone that drives them. As property owners, they wish to carry on their father's name. "Why," they ask, "should our father's name disappear from his clan because he had no son?"[3] Carrying on a name in this culture was more important than inheriting wealth.

Moses prays, and God gives the answer. Their request is granted. What is most significant about their story, however, is that this precedent-setting legal case establishes property rights never before enjoyed by women. Now, under the law of Moses—the law of the land—daughters' property rights come before those of their uncles when their father dies.

As to the sisters themselves, we must assume that at least one of them, if not all five, is either married and has children or intends to marry. How else would their father's name be carried on? It would be similar to circumstances today when a daughter inherits the family business, keeps the family name, and passes it on to her children—both daughters and sons.

Rahab

Rahab also receives an inheritance, though in a very different form. She is promised by Israelite spies that she and her family will not be slaughtered. Rather, they will be permitted to become part of God's people as they settle the Promised Land.

Moses is now dead, so also Aaron, both on the verge of entering Canaan. Miriam had died not long before while the Israelites were still wandering in the desert. Joshua is in charge, having been commissioned by God to actually move into Canaan. He sounds almost foolhardy when he gives orders to his leading lieutenants: "Get your provisions ready. Three days from now you will cross the Jordan here to go in and take possession of the land the LORD your God is giving you for your own."[4] If it sounds easy, it is anything but.

Joshua, a onetime spy himself, begins his plan of conquest by sending out spies. His major concern is the walled city of Jericho. How will his fighting men ever go up against such an incredible fortress? He would not have heard of Rahab, nor she of him.

Rahab, we can assume, is very familiar with the name Moses. His reputation has preceded him. He is the victorious military leader of a vast assembly of wandering tribes who are now headed directly toward this safe and secure walled town. But is it really so secure? Sure, the walls are thick enough for dwellings to be constructed on them. But the news Rahab has gotten from some of her clients is ominous. They have told her that this massive swarm of people is capable of overrunning everything in its way—not because of its military power per se but rather because of its God.

The story of the battle of Jericho, told in children's Bible storybooks and in spirituals, is very familiar. For seven days Joshua and his men march around the city, the walls crash down, and Joshua's fighting men defeat the security forces there. One might ask, as we glean what the text reveals about Rahab, how necessary is the role she plays in the defeat of her city. It seems as though Jericho is taken, not because of spying or because of a far superior military force, but because God brings down the fortress walls and *gives* victory in what appears to be a foregone conclusion. There is no evidence that the city supports a large standing army.

Rahab does not play a strategic role, as we will later see in the case of Deborah and particularly Jael. Nor is she a key political figure like Esther is. Rather, it appears there is some other reason that this prostitute is highlighted in the text. She does save the spies, but there is no insider

---

The View from Jericho

Rahab studied the distant plain of Jericho from her window in the city wall, her heart stirring with fear and excitement. Out there, just beyond the Jordan River, the Israelites were encamped, only the floodwaters holding them back. Soon they would cross over and come against the king of Jericho with the same ferocity they had shown in battle against Sihon, Og, and the five kings of Midian. And everyone in Jericho would die.

The king had doubled the guard at the gate and posted soldiers on the battlements. But it would do no good. Destruction was on the horizon. . . . Jericho was doomed!

And she was imprisoned inside the city, bound by a life she had carved out for herself years ago. What hope had she, a harlot?

Francine Rivers, *Unashamed*

information that they acquire which in the end would bring down the city. In fact, the only thing the spies accomplish by going to Jericho is to save Rahab and her family. Why, we might ask, would God choose to save a prostitute? Why not decimate the entire city, the kind of military triumph that occurs frequently in the Hebrew Bible? Is there any rhyme or reason for this game plan?

The first verse of Joshua 2 is most noteworthy:

> Then Joshua son of Nun secretly sent two spies from Shittim. "Go, look over the land," he said, "especially Jericho." So they went and entered the house of a prostitute named Rahab and stayed there.

There is no evidence that the spies did what they were told to do—that they scouted out the land, especially Jericho. The text merely says they went and stayed with a prostitute.

On their way to her house, however, they raise suspicions. We know that the people in the town from the king on down have been worried about the approaching Israelites. When strangers walk into town, even when they head straight for a house of prostitution, there would naturally be reason for concern. Normally men would seek out a prostitute only after they had conducted the business that brought them to town in the first place.

We could only wish that the text revealed something about the transactions between the spies and Rahab. We cannot assume that sex was not part of their overnight activities. Indeed, we clearly know by now that the Bible is not squeamish about sex, whether involving prostitutes or family members. The real business, however, has far less to do with sex and spies than with saving Rahab and her family. We easily assume that this account is a story relating to spying. But that does not appear to be the case at all. The spies, it seems, accomplished nothing in Jericho except to warn a prostitute of impending doom and to promise to save her family.

Rahab is truly the leading player in this story. The spies are not even named. It does not require a fertile imagination to realize that information gathering is not what the mission is all about. Though neither Joshua nor the spies would have realized that the reason for this harrowing hike into town had no strategically based purpose, we dare not assume that God was likewise in the dark. But of all the people in Jericho God would choose to save, why a harlot? That she may have been able and willing to provide better cover for the spies might be a reasonable response, but God is typically not constrained by minor difficulties like hiding spies.

It would seem that, out of all the people in Jericho, God has purposely picked a prostitute. Should that shock us? God is often operating on the wrong side of the tracks, and it is no different with Rahab. News now gets around that the men have come to her place of business. The king sends word, ordering her to bring them out. She sends word back that they have, in fact, sought out her services. Further, she hasn't asked personal questions (proper prostitute that she is) and thus does not know where they have come from or where they are going. All she knows is that they have left town at dusk.

In actual fact, she has scurried them up to her rooftop terrace and hidden them under a pile of flax stalks that she had been drying in the sun. Now with their pursuers long gone on the road toward the Jordan River, she sneaks up to have a serious talk. She has their lives in her hands; at any time after she had hidden them, she could have called in authorities. She is the one dealing the cards that determine whether they live or die. What transpires in the dark is not a back-and-forth discussion. Rather, Rahab addresses them for who they are—two hostages under her command. It is a remarkable address that indicates how knowledgeable she is about history and current affairs. And it is one of the the longest orations, apart from a song, ever given by a biblical woman—an oration that clearly acknowledges the power of God. As such, it bears repeating in its entirety.

> I know that the LORD has given you this land and that a great fear of you has fallen on us, so that all who live in this country are melting in fear because of you. We have heard how the LORD dried up the water of the Red Sea for you when you came out of Egypt, and what you did to Sihon and Og, the two kings of the Amorites east of the Jordan, whom you completely destroyed. When we heard of it, our hearts melted in fear and everyone's courage failed because of you, for the LORD your God is God in heaven above and on the earth below.
>
> Now then, please swear to me by the LORD that you will show kindness to my family, because I have shown kindness to you. Give me a sure sign that

you will spare the lives of my father and mother, my brothers and sisters, and all who belong to them—and that you will save us from death.[5]

The spies clearly recognize the power she wields over them, and they readily agree to swear an oath to save her and her family if she does not report them. Only then does she secure a rope to let them crawl out a window and climb down to freedom from her apartment built into the walled fortress surrounding the city. More than that, she gives them the advice they need to safely escape: "Go to the hills so the pursuers will not find you. Hide yourselves there three days until they return, and then go on your way."[6]

Before departing, the spies instruct her to hang a red cord that is visible in the window when Joshua's army arrives to do battle. Further, any family members who wish to be rescued with her must gather at her apartment. As soon as they are gone, she ties a scarlet cord to the window—perhaps the same kind of cord that identifies her establishment from within the city. And then she waits.

She knows that they will not arrive back at their encampment for at least three days, but after that, the hours and days of nail-biting seem endless. She has no doubt heard that the Jordan River is in flood stage, a factor that could delay the assault for weeks. But unbeknown to her, as the Israelite priests (with the ark of the covenant) led the troops to the river's edge, the water had "piled up in a heap," and all the people had crossed over "on dry ground."[7]

Finally, more than ten days after the spies had crawled out her window, she sees in the distance the first signs of troop movement. They slowly come into view. Strange. Seven robed men with trumpets are leading the way, and behind them more robed men. What is it they are lugging with them? Ah, perhaps she remembers her history—those Israelites and the ark of the covenant. And then come the seemingly endless battalions of infantry. We can imagine she's a nervous wreck; the battle could begin any minute.

But that's not what happens. The priests and the entire army begin to march around the city—so many that the last one is marching out of sight as the priests with trumpets come into view again. And then everything is at a standstill. From the inside, the city is on edge. So is she. An oath was made, but in the heat of battle, who's going to remember that? She can never forget after all that she is a mere prostitute living on the wall.

For days she watches the same parade—no clowns, no baton twirlers, not even a marching band, unless you count those guys who haven't as yet even tooted their trumpets. Then after six days of this, things suddenly pick up. On the seventh day, they all march around the city seven times. By this time she knows the battle is close. What on earth is going on? Why hasn't there been a signal for her rescue? She has all but given up when she hears the trumpets blast in unison, followed by a loud bellowing shout from every man in the entire army. Then the walls begin to crumble under her. Now they're all goners for sure.

But somehow everyone in her family is still alive, and then she sees the angels. (Or they might just as well have been.) They are the spies, keeping their word to rescue her. Did she throw her arms around them? Introduce them to her family? All the text says is that they brought out her, her mother, father, brothers, and sisters, and situated them in a safe place outside the military camp.

Rahab's story does not end here. She marries Salmon (speculated by some to be one of the spies, though neither of them is named) and bears a son, Boaz. Boaz will one day marry Ruth, and from that union comes Obed, the father of Jesse, the father of David, through whose line comes Jesus through his adopted father, Joseph. A prostitute is named in the lineage of Jesus. Oh my, what a scandal.

Concluding Observations

The biblical stories of the five daughters of Zelophehad and the prostitute Rahab are arguably the most liberating accounts of women in all ancient history and literature. There are queens and warriors who wield power and demonstrate incredible chutzpah, if not muscular strength, and there are daughters and wives of great men, even marginalized women like Hagar whose honor comes primarily through bearing a son by a great man. But rare is the ordinary woman who can change the course of history—the one who has few if any connections and who is not noticeably gifted with the ability to become a Joan of Arc or a Marie Curie.

Here we have women who are entirely unconnected. Zelophehad seems to be an ordinary schlep, who, like all the other men who began the wanderings in the wilderness with Moses, died in the desert. In his case, however, it is said that he died of his own sin, not the sin of Korah. His orphaned—and seemingly unmarried—daughters are left to find their way, like the rest of us, into complete anonymity, not even qualifying for the dustbin of history. But then they come forward to speak, daring to approach the top dog in the camp. Their well-thought-out plea generates a precedent-setting case that not only gives women in certain situations rights they have not previously enjoyed, but also sets forth the whole concept of women's rights—forever recorded in Scripture.

Rahab's situation is very different. There is no meeting with Moses, perhaps not even Joshua. Her words are spoken privately, but in no less a legal fashion. She demands from the spies an oath—a *word of honor* that cannot for any reason be broken. She is essentially a *nobody*, but she realizes that she has power over their lives. Simply saving herself and her family would be reason enough to include her story in the biblical text—and reason enough to cite hers as a singularly liberating account in ancient history. But that she was singled out by God to be rescued by the Israelite army, per an oath made by nameless spies, is the greatest wonder of all.

Questions to Think About

Imagine yourself wandering in the arid wilderness for forty years. Would you be one of the loyal supporters of Moses? Can you picture yourself complaining and going into the sinkhole with Korah and his crowd?

As a woman wandering in the wilderness, one of hundreds of thousands known as the children of Israel, how would you have felt about giving up cooking and baking for four decades? Is dietary variety important to you, or would you have done okay on manna?

How do you assess the five sisters in their plea for justice? Are there injustices in your own life that you would like to bring before Moses—or the Supreme Court?

What are some of the most obvious practical lessons that we learn from Rahab? Do we too easily look down on individuals because of their immorality or scandalous reputation?

Have you ever known a prostitute personally or become acquainted with one in your ministry? Have you listened to her story? What is your attitude toward prostitutes?

Are we often like Rahab (and the spies—and even Joshua), assuming our actions are accomplishing our ends, while being entirely oblivious to, and unconcerned about, a far greater purpose that God has in mind? Can you think of such situations in your own life?

How would the daughters of Zelophehad and Rahab fit in our circles of friends today, in comparison to patriarchal wives? Are they more modern in their dealings?

9

Deborah and Jael

Military Icons

I never personally knew Carol Irons. I wish I had. She was a friend of an acquaintance, so I was interested when I read a newspaper account of how she had been in divorce proceedings in order to escape an abusive marriage. It was back in 1988, when I also had just recently escaped an abusive marriage to a man who had also made death threats. I recall reading how Carol had been getting her life back together, going out with friends, joining a Bible study, and taking piano lessons. But those details were only embellishments to the story of a life that was viciously snuffed out.

Enter Clarence Ratliff. He was a police officer with a gun and out to kill District Judge Carol Irons, his estranged wife. It was her lunch break. He headed straight for her courthouse chambers. Bam. Bam. Bam. She was dead, Grand Rapids' first female judge.

The shooting and subsequent trial made headlines far beyond Grand Rapids. In the end, Ratliff was convicted of manslaughter for killing his wife. He was also convicted of shooting at fellow police officers who hurried to the scene (and putting shrapnel in one of them). For killing her, he was sentenced to fifteen years; for shooting at them, life in prison. But of course, she was only a woman and a wife, so why should he get life for that? My blood still boils when I think of it. In sentencing him, the judge said: "You struck close to a mortal blow to the peace, dignity, and safety of this community."

In 2011, his son asked that Ratliff, having been diagnosed with terminal cancer, be brought to his home on the Muskegon River to spend his last days. "He deserves," said his son, "a little dignity at the end of his life, a little peace." The judge ruled that life in prison was indeed a *life* sentence. (Otherwise, he could have had his fifteen-year sentence for killing Carol reduced to seven to ten years for good behavior and been out a decade earlier to enjoy life along the Muskegon River.) Ratliff died in prison about a month later.

So, some would say, justice was served. But I'm wondering if justice would have been better served for Ratliff if Jael had gotten him into her tent. She did not take kindly to wicked men and might have driven a spike through his head, nailing him to the ground. Sounds awful, but that's what happened to Sisera, an enemy army general at war against Israel who, like Ratliff, struck close to a mortal blow to the community. In God's sight justice was served.

It is Deborah who is the *Carol Irons*. She is the first female district judge in Israel, also a diplomat and leader of the military. Jael's role is to bring justice through a close encounter with the enemy. She is not, as we might expect, an Israelite. But as we have seen previously, outsiders often serve God more faithfully than do insiders. Both women stand tall in the ancient era of the judges.

Deborah

What is the workday like for Deborah in the generations after the massive Israelite camp crossed over into Canaan? By day she sets up court under a palm tree. It may sound relaxing, almost like sitting in a lounge chair enjoying the breeze beneath a swaying palm on a Florida beach. But life for her is probably the polar opposite, a hectic schedule we can only imagine.

It's past midnight now. She tosses and turns. Why can't she just shut her day job down when she gets home? Lappidoth is understanding. He doesn't complain when she's late. He eats, and when she arrives, she finishes the leftovers the servants have saved and then she goes to bed exhausted. But her brain just won't shut down. The whole day becomes one giant, jumbled ten-hour replay. We can only imagine her train of consciousness.

What was that boy's name again? She can't remember. *Oh my, the viciousness of his father. How could any man want his son stoned, his own flesh and blood, and to say that he'd even throw stones himself? And that poor mother. Well, at least that weeping woman finally convinced him to meet with me under the palm. Sure, the boy did a terrible thing. What was his name? Of course he shouldn't have been sneaking out at night and doing who knows what with that Hittite girl. He must have known his folks would find out. Poor woman.*

How Deborah wishes the woman hadn't told her husband, but that's water over the dam; he would have found out sooner or later. *Why didn't the boy just wait for his father to arrange something with a nice girl? Those Hittite women do have a reputation.*

If she could only relax. The sun will be up soon. Does she see the first touch of dawn through her tent opening? *That boy.* She can't blame him for his impatience. *If his father was so eager for him to marry into the tribe, he should have gone ahead and made the arrangements. Sure money is tight, with all the fighting, and why wasn't he off fighting somewhere anyway?* She can't remember what they said. If she could only get some sleep.

So now he's run off with the girl—bad enough, but to curse his own father. That's just terrible. Kids nowadays. Well, he did strike the boy; that's what the mother said, but to curse his own father. What an awful thing. Sleep, all she wants is some sleep. *At least that poor mother was able to stay the hand of her husband. How could he have even contemplated stoning his own son? What is this world coming to? Imagine a boy cursing his own father.*

And what were they thinking coming after the crowd had been dismissed? After sunset even. Now, if she could only get a few hours' sleep before another day begins.

If deciding tough cases weighs heavily on her and sometimes keeps her awake at night, Deborah is also stressed out by her military responsibilities—

keeping tabs on her fighting men and the continual battles they are waging.

Any attempt to understand Deborah and her work requires a considerable exercise of our imaginations. The text offers few details about her life and virtually nothing about her work as a judge in Israel. But we know human nature, and it is not difficult to believe that she might have encountered many problems that were not easily erased after she had concluded her last session and gone home. And we can imagine the kinds of cases that might have come before her. Family conflict of one sort or another would have been typical. Perhaps a widow is told she is not permitted to glean—hard times, famine in the land. There would have been disputes over grazing boundaries and water rights. Matters of theft, assault, and murder would also have come before her.

The account of Deborah begins in the fourth chapter of the book of Judges, named for the leaders in this era of Israel's history: "Then the LORD raised up judges, who saved them out of the hands of these raiders." One might imagine the people would be grateful. Hardly. "Yet they would not listen to their judges but prostituted themselves to other gods and worshiped them."[1]

Indeed, four times before Deborah's name is mentioned, we hear the scandalous refrain: *The Israelites did evil in the eyes of the Lord.*

A woman judge today, whether sitting on the bench in a hometown courtroom or even on the Supreme Court, is not considered out of the ordinary. Nor are female military commanders. Women in robes and in uniform are a natural part of modern life. Deborah's role as judge and military commander, however, was unique. No other biblical woman took on such *manly* roles. It would be a serious mistake, however, to imagine her filling these positions as we have come to know them. None of these judges served terms in courtrooms as magistrates do today, and warfare in biblical times was far different from modern warfare.

Deborah, however, appears to be as busy as any contemporary career woman who is juggling work and family and a long to-do list. She is married and apparently has children, though they are never mentioned except possibly an allusion in her song. Her hectic schedule involves settling cases as she sets up her courtroom under a palm tree. The text is straightforward:

She held court under the Palm of Deborah between Ramah and Bethel in the hill country of Ephraim, and the Israelites went up to her to have their disputes decided.[2]

As judge, she is Israel's military leader as well. No title of *commander in chief*, but she is expected to see to it that her armed forces prevail in battles against the Canaanites. Another hat that she wears is that of diplomat, a political leader before Israel had a king. She is also a prophet. In that capacity, she hears directly from God and sings a grand song of triumph after the army returns victorious.

Deborah grows up in a time when life in the Promised Land is anything but stable. Acts of terror occur routinely, initiated by both friend and enemy. On one occasion, the fighting men from Judah put the torch to Jerusalem, and from there go to Zephath and on to Gaza, destroying every town in their path. Before that they had captured the Canaanite leader Adoni-Bezek and "cut off his thumbs and big toes." With his missing digits, he laments: "Seventy kings with their thumbs and big toes cut off have picked up scraps under my table. Now God has paid me back for what I did to them."[3] Revenge is the name of the game.

Throughout the era of the judges, there is almost continual warfare. God, working through these judicial and military leaders, gives the people victories. "Yet they would not listen to their judges but prostituted themselves to other gods and worshiped them."[4] The people are virtually unmanageable: "Everyone did what was right in his own eyes."[5] Deborah is fully aware that she has a massive job cut out for her. She depends on God for strength.

Because Deborah is a prophet, God gives her insider information as he had given to Moses and Joshua. One day she calls in Barak, her army commander, and gives him marching orders straight from on high:

The Lord, the God of Israel, commands you: "Go, take with you ten thousand men of Naphtali and Zebulun and lead them up to Mount Tabor. I will lead Sisera, the commander of Jabin's army, with his chariots and his troops to the Kishon River and give him into your hands."[6]

Okay, the orders are the very words of God. Sure, the enemy is fierce. Barak does, however, have ten thousand troops at his disposal. But what if she just *thinks* she's received a message from God? What if she's making that part up so that he'll get out of his tent and go out and fight the enemy? He's nervous. How do you answer a commanding woman like Deborah? So Barak says: "If you go with me, I will go; but if you don't go with me, I won't go."[7]

Deborah knows when she's heard from God, and she doesn't bat an eye. "Certainly I will go with you," she says. "But because of the course you are taking, the honor will not be yours, for the Lord will deliver Sisera into the hands of a woman."[8] It is no surprise to us that the Israelites are victorious, Barak in command, Deborah having accompanied him not just to Kedesh, where the troops are summoned, but also on to the plain below Mount Tabor, where the battle is fought. The ultimate trophy of war for Barak would have been the head of the opposing commander, Sisera. That trophy, however, per Deborah's prophecy, is given to a woman.

But Deborah does not rub it in. Barak joins her in the victory song, though as the lengthy lyrics wind down, he's reminded again that he is not the one who has been granted the honor of killing Sisera. The hymn begins with praise to God:

> When the princes in Israel take the lead,
>   when the people willingly offer themselves—
> praise the Lord!
>
> Hear this, you kings! Listen, you rulers!
>   I, even I, will sing to the Lord;
>   I will praise the Lord, the God of Israel, in song.[9]

The verses pick up on past military victories and then focus on Deborah, and to a much lesser extent on Barak:

> Villagers in Israel would not fight;
>   they held back until I, Deborah, arose,
>   until I arose, a mother in Israel. . . .
>
> Then the people of the Lord
>   went down to the city gates.
> "Wake up, wake up, Deborah!
>   Wake up, wake up, break out in song!

Arise, Barak!
Take captive your captives, son of Abinoam."[10]

Judge Deborah has been absent for some time from *the bench* that is under the palm tree named for her. She's not been in combat herself, but she has been watching over her fighting men, witnessing the battle from close range. Now that's all behind her. What a relief! We can close our eyes and see Deborah singing this song. Deborah, "a mother in Israel," a judge, a prophet, and a revered military leader.

When her judgeship is over or when she dies (whenever either of those landmark events would have occurred), she leaves behind an incredible legacy: "Then the land had peace forty years."[11] How many leaders have such a feather in their cap?

Jael

Deborah's audacity and nerve pale in comparison to Jael's. Though no combat soldier or commando, Jael takes out Sisera in short order. She is the one who slays the fleeing enemy commander. But in fact she's not even on Israel's team. She's a Kenite. The whole story would seem utterly bizarre if we did not already know Rahab and the likes of her. Yet Jael, in Deborah's song, is praised as the "most blessed of women."[12] The *most blessed of women*? Didn't we always think that description would be reserved for someone else?

The prophet Deborah had told Barak straight out that, for his spinelessness, Sisera would be taken down by a woman. God, we presume, had told neither of them who would have the honors and how the deed would be carried out. So, as they go to war, this is a matter of suspense. Indeed, Barak (and perhaps Deborah herself) may have assumed she would be that woman. What other female was around to claim the trophy?

Jael is the wife of Heber and lives in a tent on the plains of Canaan near a mighty tree, so large that it has become a geographical marker. Heber and his extended family had separated from the main tribe of Kenites, who are descendants of Hobab, son of Jethro. That, of course, makes Hobab a brother of the seven sisters watering sheep, whom Moses had defended against the bullies at the well. Hobab's sister Zipporah then had become the wife of Moses. Because he is a brother-in-law to the great Moses himself, one might imagine that his descendants would be allied with the Israelites. But that is not the case. Heber and his family have made an alliance with the enemy king whose commander was Sisera.

After his army has been routed and all his men are dead, Sisera flees for safety to the encampment of Heber. Jael sees him coming and welcomes him warmly: "Come, my lord, come right in. Don't be afraid."[13] He knows his pursuers are hot on his trail and is most grateful for her eagerness to help. She gives him a blanket, and when he requests water, she gives him warm milk from the goatskin. *That will put him to sleep*, she's no doubt thinking.

Before he falls asleep from his exhausting day of battle, Sisera instructs her to stand in the entrance of the tent and deny that he is there, should anyone happen by and ask her. It seems like a reasonable enough request.

But that is not what this wife of Heber has in mind. She bides her time and as soon as he is sound asleep takes a tent peg and drives it "through his temple into the ground."[14] Say what? Jael, we thought, is just an ordinary homemaker. She's not, after all, Shakespeare's Lady Macbeth. So what is she doing, with no apparent provocation, driving a nail through the head of a sleeping man whose army has been allied with her own family? It's a mystery. The text doesn't say. A good guess is that she has realized Sisera is on the losing side and wants the benefits of being on the winning side of history.

> **Jael in Fiction**
>
> In *The Code of the Woosters*, P. G. Wodehouse has Bertie Wooster, the narrator, telling about his awful headache while sleeping off a hangover: "Indeed, just before Jeeves came in, I had been dreaming that some bounder was driving spikes through my head—not just ordinary spikes, as used by Jael the wife of Heber, but red-hot ones."

No sooner has she finished her grisly chore than she sees Barak striding in from the battle carnage, looking for the man he most wants to kill. Jael's a friendly lady. She goes out to meet him and invites him to come right on in. She opens the flap of her tent, and he enters. There is Sisera, dead as a doornail, staked to the ground.

Barak departs to sing a song with Deborah, and Jael is apparently left behind baking flat cakes. Nothing more is heard of her. That is, but for Deborah's ballad, which, like all good lyrics, employs a certain amount of poetic license. The verses featuring Jael are the most lurid and lively of all.

> He asked for water, and she gave him milk;
>> in a bowl fit for nobles she brought him curdled milk.
> Her hand reached for the tent peg,
>> her right hand for the workman's hammer.
> She struck Sisera, she crushed his head,
>> she shattered and pierced his temple.
> At her feet he sank,
>> he fell; there he lay.
> At her feet he sank, he fell;
>> where he sank, there he fell—dead.[15]

Here in the ballad, she strikes Sisera with a hammer, crushing his head and piercing his temple before he's on the ground, and there is nothing about his falling asleep first. Perhaps the actual details were too shocking for a hymn of praise. After all, she is a woman, the lady of the house, Kenite though she be.

The ballad also adds some fascinating details that take place in another setting, the home of another woman—a woman anxiously awaiting her son's return. The first of these verses is sad, a cheerless reminder that even the enemy grieves its lost sons. The second stanza is a remarkable effort to calm the woman's worst fears. The words sound as though they are the dreams of wealth, while in fact they are stalling tactics of her wise servant in a desperate attempt to divert her attention and forestall the inevitable.

> Through the window peered Sisera's mother;
>> behind the lattice she cried out,
> "Why is his chariot so long in coming?
>> Why is the clatter of his chariots delayed?"
>
> The wisest of her ladies answer her;
>> indeed, she keeps saying to herself,

"Are they not finding and dividing the spoils:
    a woman or two for each man,
colorful garments as plunder for Sisera,
    colorful garments embroidered,
highly embroidered garments for my neck—
    all this as plunder?"[16]

Though the text doesn't specifically tell us, we know that Sisera's mother is grief striken when she hears the news of her son's death. But we leave the story of Jael wondering how everything went for her during the forty years of peace in Israel that followed. We might also wonder how Heber felt about his wife's incredible act of daring—dare we say murder? It would not be a stretch to imagine that he was more careful after that not to annoy her, and that on some nights he chose to sleep in a guarded tent.

Concluding Observations

It is easy to sum up Deborah with a list of accolades. She is a superwoman—a contemporary career woman who does it all, one we read about in women's magazines whose accomplishments we ourselves can never attain. How does she do it? Even with all our computer capabilities, our email and texting, we could not imagine accomplishing so much. Her job description boggles the mind: prophet, judge, diplomat, military commander, wife, and perhaps mother. And so successful is she that she paves the way for forty years of peace. We might like to dig up a little dirt on her as we did with Eve, Sarah, Rebekah, Rachel, and others, but the text doesn't allow for it. Absolutely nothing negative is said about Deborah.

And what can we say about Jael? She jumps out of the pages of Judges with no warning, carries out a daring feat, and then just as quickly disappears. Did I say that her name means "mountain goat"? That's a perfect appellation. And not just because my beloved pet as a child was a plucky goat that could practically turn the farm upside down before we knew what was happening. But also because it was a father's nickname for one of my favorite writers, Jeannette Walls, author of *The Glass Castle*. Jael is a fearless woman; nothing is too risky for her, truly a *mountain goat*.

119

Questions to Think About

If you were to take the time to come out and wait in line to see Deborah under her palm, what issue or dispute would you bring before her? Who would you bring along with you?

Does Deborah have enough of a commanding presence to cause unruly teenagers to pay her mind? Abusive husbands? Would you slip her a twenty if you thought her settlement was just?

If Deborah were in your church or your neighborhood association, how would men regard her—especially men who are easily threatened by strong women?

Might some people think Deborah is too forward and cheeky by her seeming put-down of Barak—getting in his face and telling him a woman will claim the prize of killing Sisera?

Does Deborah appear almost conceited when she sings a song of praise, not only to God but also to herself? Do you ever boast of your own accomplishments, though in subtler ways than did she?

What do you make of Jael? Can you put her on your list of heroic women of the Bible? How would you regard her if she had committed her shocking deed from the enemy side and perhaps put a tent peg through the head of Barak or someone like Joshua?

10

Delilah, Samson's Mother,
and Other Nameless Women

Guile and Innocence

Most of the great so-called love stories in history and fiction are characterized by volatility. Whether Samson and Delilah or Anthony and Cleopatra (or the movie stars who played them, Richard Burton and Elizabeth Taylor), their lives are filled with explosive episodes and unpredictable twists and turns.

The most fascinating of these stories, at least for my money, is the medieval real-life drama of Abelard and Heloise—brilliant professor and bright-eyed student. In fact, I wrote a short version of their story some years ago for *Christian History* magazine in three acts, each with two or more scenes. I judged that to be one of the most creative (yet historically based) pieces I had ever done, though I've retold their story in three other publications, each with a different slant. So, here I go again.

The first time I took up their story, I regarded the much older Abelard as a predator in his relationship with his teenage student Heloise. But with each telling, I somehow relaxed a bit and found him less despicable. Perhaps

121

it actually was a story of true love, considering the medieval setting, when girls often married very young.

Cut to the chase. Abelard takes Heloise to bed. Soon Fulbert, her uncle and guardian, learns of her pregnancy. He's in a rage. Why did he hire that scoundrel—famous though he was—as a private tutor? Then when Abelard suggests that she might go to a convent and give birth behind closed doors while he continues his prestigious lecturing, Fulbert is pushed to the limit. He sends thugs in the dead of night to break into the handsome professor's private quarters and castrate him. With a slice of the knife, his sexual exploits are over for good.

Both he and Heloise go on to become well-known monastic leaders. He commits himself wholly to God and ministry, though in later years he is accused of heresy. No such charges mar her reputation, but her devotion to God always seems secondary to her undying love for Abelard.

Samson and Delilah's story is very different. Samson lost only his hair—and with that, his strength and eventually his life. He too was a scoundrel, and, as with Abelard, it's not difficult to think that perhaps he got what he deserved. Delilah was surely no love-struck, naive teenager—though through the years I've come to think that perhaps Heloise was not so innocent as I once thought. All these love stories are private and short on details, but they grab our attention and the names are forever linked in pairs.

The story of Jephthah's unnamed daughter is entirely unrelated to anything analogous to a romance. In fact, she is marked for death—or, if not that, an existence of solitary monastic living, not so unlike that of Heloise.

Delilah's story appears in the text before that of Jephthah's daughter, but before either account there is the story of another unnamed woman who has an unusual visitation from the Lord. Samson's mother stands in for all mothers who wonder if their sons will ever grow up to be responsible men. Samson is set apart for God before he is even born, but what an utterly feckless individual he becomes.

In still another instance in the book of Judges, there is a strange account of a Levite's concubine who is raped and murdered. It is one of four biblical stories identified as a *text of terror* by Phyllis Trible in her classic 1984 study. The other three relate to Hagar (Sarah's slave); Jephthah's daughter; and Tamar, daughter of King David, raped by her brother, featured in chapter 13 (not to be confused with Tamar, daughter-in-law of Judah, in chap. 6). The account of the rape and murder of the Levite's concubine is followed by the story of terror inflicted upon the young women of Shiloh—stories that remind us of the terrible abuse often suffered by women throughout history.

Samson's Mother

Having again done evil in the eyes of the Lord, the Israelites live under the thumb of the Philistines for four long decades. One day from seemingly out of nowhere, the angel of the Lord appears to an unnamed barren woman and tells her that she will give birth to a son who will free Israel from the bondage of the Philistines. She is to rear him as a Nazirite while he is yet in her womb—no alcohol or nonkosher food. The child himself cannot touch alcohol, nor must he ever cut his hair.

The woman tells her husband, Manoah, about this strange man and his message: a baby, *no* alcohol, *no* haircut. He's confused. He cannot understand how he is supposed to raise his son. His wife might have quoted the country lyrics, *What part of no don't you understand*. But she doesn't. Manoah prays to God for the man to return and teach them how to raise their son. God comes again to the woman while she's working out in the field. She runs to tell her husband, who's watching the play-offs or doing something besides working in the field with her.

Manoah, the text tells us, "got up and followed his wife." He asks the man if he's the same one who had showed up before. Satisfied that he is, Manoah asks him to repeat what he has already said. The man does so and says that his wife "must do all that I have told her."[1] Manoah then invites him to stay for a tasty dinner. The man declines the offer of a savory roasted young goat, but he does tell him to prepare a burnt offering to the Lord. When Manoah asks his name, this mysterious man tells him that it is beyond understanding.

Silence follows while the flames begin to consume the offering. Then in an instant, the craziest thing happens right before their eyes. The man ascends to heaven amid the flames. It's a stunning display of pyrotechnics. The woman and her husband fall face down on the ground. Only then do they realize that they have actually seen the angel of the Lord.

123

Manoah panics. "We are doomed to die!" he howls. "We have seen God!"[2] His wife tells him to calm down. *Why would God have accepted our burnt offering if he was simply intending to kill us?*

The months pass, and she gives birth to a boy she names Samson. Time flies. The next we hear of her, Samson is insisting that his parents arrange for him to marry a particular Philistine woman he has seen in the town of Timnah. They protest, arguing that he should marry a nice girl from among his own people—surely not among the uncircumcised Philistines. But he persists, and they give in and arrange for a marriage feast—something like a seven-day bachelor's party, though the women are apparently nearby. We've all heard of *all hell breaking loose* at wedding celebrations. This is exactly what happens. Things get really messy. In the end after Samson's fiancée has betrayed him, he kills thirty innocent men in a fit of rage, and his intended bride marries one of the groomsmen instead.

So angry is Samson about the turn of events that "he went out and caught three hundred foxes and tied them tail to tail in pairs. He then fastened a torch to every pair of tails, lit the torches and let the foxes loose in the standing grain of the Philistines."[3] The Philistines are incensed. They take revenge and kill the woman he was supposed to have married as well as her father. Samson slaughters many of them in return. Now Samson's own people enter the fray. Fearing the Philistines, they tie him up to deliver him to the enemy. He breaks the ropes and kills a thousand of them. After that he rules Israel for twenty years. Where his mother was during this time is not revealed. She simply fades out of the picture.

During this time he displays his incredible strength, as when he travels to Gaza to spend the night with a prostitute. On leaving town, knowing he's been targeted to be killed, he tears down the city gates, posts and all. He hoists the load onto his shoulders and carries it to the top of the hill. Samson reigns supreme.

Enter Delilah.

Delilah

Samson falls in love with her at first sight, this trashy Philistine lady. If she weren't, he wouldn't have spotted her in the first place. She is the very sort of woman country music's Confederate Railroad has sung about. If Samson were the lead singer, he would be crooning in first person about *likin'* his women wild and "just a little on the trashy side" with "their clothes too tight and their hair dyed." They wear "too much lipstick" and "too much rouge"; they get him excited and leave him "feelin' confused." That's exactly what Delilah did to Samson.

She is from the Valley of Sorek, and there is no evidence at all that she returns his love. Rather, she is encouraged by Philistine officials to tempt him into telling her the secret of his incredible strength. They bribe her with cold, hard cash. So she plays along and starts her sweet-talking and more to win his confidence. A straightforward reading of the text gives no evidence that she is subtle. She asks straight out: "Tell me the secret of your great strength and how you can be tied up and subdued."[4] If we were to hear her voice and see her in action, however, the subtlety might be more evident.

Initially Samson hoodwinks her with a bogus story about being tied up with bowstrings. She secretly passes the information on to the officials. They tie Samson up. He snaps the bowstrings as though they were pieces of thread. Delilah is distraught. She's been made a fool. Again she entices him with trash talk and more. Again he tricks her and still again until she's finally had enough. For days on end, she teases him with her most sensuous seductive powers, leading him on only to pull back. No sex without the secret. Her erotic teasing and touching turns into torment. Finally he caves. The secret is his hair.

> "No razor has ever been used on my head," he said, "because I have been a Nazirite dedicated to God from my mother's womb. If my head were shaved, my strength would leave me, and I would become as weak as any other man."[5]

She secretly sends word to the Philistine thugs. When they arrive, he's asleep on her lap. They cut his hair and subdue him. He has lost his strength for "the LORD had left him."[6] The Philistines poke out his eyes, put him in shackles, and force him to grind grain. Here is where the story of Delilah ends, though it is likely that she died with Samson on the day he pulled down the pillars of the temple. He had been unshackled for a Philistine celebration—a celebration of his diminished strength. While he is being made a spectacle, he prays to God for one more moment of superhuman might. God grants his desire. He pulls down the pillars and thousands of celebrants die, Samson with them.

It is difficult to have any sort of favorable opinion of Samson. He's easily caricatured as the ultimate hulk with a brain the size of a small turnip, while Delilah goes on to live forever as everyone's favorite naughty girl.

Jephthah's Daughter

The account of this young woman, daughter of Judge Jephthah, is one of the most curious narratives in the entire Bible. Any attempt to render a straightforward reading of the English text leaves us confused. And, as is true of so many other biblical characters, we wish we had more details to flesh out her story.

Some information, however, is plain as day: she is the granddaughter of a prostitute. Those who are squeamish about God's people consorting with prostitutes should remember that the Bible is very open and honest about such things. Recall Judge Samson going to Gaza and matter-of-factly visiting a prostitute. Previously Judah sought the services of a prostitute who turned out to be his daughter-in-law in disguise. Joshua's spies went to Jericho and visited the prostitute Rahab. The prophet Hosea, as we shall see, marries a prostitute named Gomer. One could almost imagine that from an Old Testament perspective, prostitution is an ordinary aspect of culture.

Nevertheless, the fact that Jephthah's mother was a prostitute is reason enough for his half brothers (sons of his father's wife) to throw him out of the house and deny him any family inheritance. So Jephthah settles in the land of Tob, where sometime later his people seek him out to command an army against the Ammonites. He agrees to do just that. Then in the tense moments just before the battle, he makes a vow to God:

> If you give the Ammonites into my hands, whatever comes out of the door of my house to meet me when I return in triumph from the Ammonites will be the LORD's, and I will sacrifice it as a burnt offering.[7]

Jephthah prevails over the Ammonites and heads home in a victorious mood. But who should joyfully come out his door to meet him? None other than his beloved daughter, his only child. She's thrilled that her father is home safe and sound, so thrilled that she dances to the rhythm of a tambourine. She is no doubt startled when, instead of throwing his arms around her, he breaks down weeping and tearing his clothes. Equally confusing are his words: "Oh no, my daughter! You have brought me down and I am devastated. I have made a vow to the LORD that I cannot break."[8]

Her response to him first makes us cringe and then leaves us completely bewildered:

> "My father," she replied, "you have given your word to the LORD. Do to me just as you promised, now that the LORD has avenged you of your enemies, the Ammonites. But grant me this one request," she said. "Give me two months to roam the hills and weep with my friends, because I will never marry."[9]

Before this response, did he tell her that his vow was not actually to sacrifice her as a burnt offering but rather to offer her in service to God as a perpetual virgin? There must have been some further explanation or else she would have had no idea what his vow entailed. Another way to interpret the passage, as many have done, is to assume that Jephthah actually carried out the vow of sacrificing her as a burnt offering, and therefore until the moment she was consumed she remained a virgin.

Up to this point in the Hebrew Bible, the idea of child sacrifice is at least mentioned (as in Abraham's close encounter with Isaac), unlike the idea of serving God as a perpetual virgin. The text itself is unclear. Her father permits her to go away for two months and weep with her friends "because she would never marry." But then Jephthah carries out his vow "and she was a virgin."[10]

We subsequently learn that it is this very incident that has prompted a tradition: "each year the young women of Israel go out for four days to commemorate the daughter of Jephthah."[11] Would this incident have provoked such a sad annual ritual of roaming the hills if she had merely given herself over to the service of God as a virgin? Perhaps. But for such a tradition to arise, it is not unreasonable to assume that she was actually sacrificed to fulfill a rash vow.

Did Jephthah Really Make A Rash Vow?

[Jephthah vowed:] I will consecrate it to the Lord, or I will offer it for a burnt-offering; that is, "If it be a thing fit for a burnt-offering, it shall be made one; if fit for the service of God, it shall be consecrated to him." That conditions of this kind must have been implied in the vow, is evident enough; to have been made without them, it must have been the vow of a heathen, or a madman. If a dog had met him, this could not have been made a burnt-offering; and if his neighbour or friend's wife, son, or daughter . . . had been returning from a visit to his family, his vow gave him no right over them. Besides human sacrifices were ever an abomination to the Lord; and this was one of the grand reasons why God drove out the Canaanites . . . because they offered their sons and daughters to Molech in the fire. . . . Therefore it must be granted that he never made that rash vow which several suppose he did.

"Judges 11," in *Adam Clarke's Bible Commentary*

An Unnamed Concubine and the Young Women of Shiloh

The era of the judges might appear to be a time of equal rights for women, especially considering the roles played by Deborah and Jael. We will also see (in chap. 11) how Ruth and Naomi are treated with respect and equality, Naomi having land to sell and Ruth taking the initiative in courting Boaz at the threshing floor. While it is true that polygamy is accepted, we will note (in chap. 12) how tenderly Elkanah treats his barren wife, Hannah. But there are many other instances in this era when women endure appalling treatment at the hands of men.

A Levite's concubine is a case in point. She is from Bethlehem, living in that small town some generations before it is identified as Naomi's hometown. The Levite, her husband, as the text refers to him, lives in the hill country, a remote area in Ephraim. She is a runaway wife, having left him to return to her parents in Bethlehem. After four months, he makes the journey there himself in an effort to convince her to come back to his home. She and her parents welcome him and after several days agree that she should return with him, though her father repeatedly seeks to delay their departure.

They leave Bethlehem and spend the night in Gibeah, a town in the tribe of Benjamin. An old man invites them to stay the night at his home. No sooner have they begun to eat the evening meal than they hear a commotion

128

at the door. Men of the town are demanding that the Levite be sent out to have sex with them. The old man is repulsed by their vile demand. He offers instead his virgin daughter and the Levite's concubine and tells them to do whatever they wish with them.

What an awful thing to do, and it is surely not the norm. We will see how protective Boaz is of Ruth, warning his workers not to lay a hand on her when she first arrives and is gleaning in his field. The men of Gibeah pay no heed to the old man, so the Levite pushes his concubine out the door, and he goes back inside to safety. The utterly contemptible men outside then rape and assault the concubine all through the night and then release her at dawn. She returns to the old man's house, where she dies at his doorway.

When the Levite gets up in the morning and opens the door to be on his way, he sees his concubine lying at his feet. He orders her to get up and get going. When she doesn't speak, he loads her onto his donkey and heads for home. There he butchers her corpse into twelve pieces and sends one hunk to each of the tribes of Israel. It is his way of expressing his outrage. But where, might we ask, was his outrage when she was being raped? Why didn't he find her body before he was up and out the door headed for his home?

He does manage to get his point across, however, and all Israel is up in arms, demanding that the men who committed this terrible atrocity be handed over and put to death. But those in the tribe of Benjamin refuse. So the armies of Israel go to war against Benjamin and, after incredible carnage, essentially wipe the tribe off the face of the map, except for six hundred fighting men.

Now they are sorry that Israel has lost one entire tribe. And no one in Israel will allow his daughter to marry a man from this despicable clan. Only then do they recall that the region of Jabesh Gilead had not sent any men to join them in battle, so an army is sent to wipe out the whole region—every man, woman, and child, except for four hundred virgins, who are now offered as wives to the six hundred survivors. But they are still short two hundred virgins. So they come up with a solution. They tell the two hundred men without wives to lurk around in the vineyards in Shiloh during the annual festival. "When the young women of Shiloh come out to join in the dancing, rush from the vineyards and each of you seize one of them to be your wife."[12] They follow orders, and that is how the tribe of Benjamin survives. The story starts with a runaway concubine and ends with kidnapping and rape.

Concluding Observations

As we come to the end of our survey of women in the book of Judges, we are likely to feel utter disgust. And apart from the women who have been singled out, there are tens—if not hundreds—of thousands of women (and men and children) who die in the awful carnage of war and revenge. Judges truly is one of the bloodiest books of the Bible. We readily conclude that women in general are degraded. Samson's mother is certainly honored by God, but there is no evidence that Samson himself shows respect for her. Her husband takes her seriously, but he wants the man with the startling prophesy to confirm to him directly what has already been plainly told to his wife.

Delilah stands above all the others. She is dishonest, but she gives Samson, it seems, his just desserts. Yet above all she is, in the eyes of Samson and in the eyes of the Philistine officials, no more than a sex object. She would be forever remembered as a hero, however, if only she had been on the right side of history. Indeed, the fetching Delilah is to the Philistines what the golden boy David is to the Israelites. We would not expect either one to bring down the strongest man in the land. But each in his or her own way does just that, David with a slingshot and a stone, Delilah with sweet-talk and sex.

As for Jephthah's daughter, the Levite's concubine, and the young women of Shiloh, all we can do is roam the hills for four days each year in commemoration and mourning. What a pity.

Questions to Think About

Do you know of anyone who has had a visitation from God? A visitation concerning the birth of a child? Have you, when pregnant, ever sensed the future of a child or prayed for the future ministry of a child (as was true of the parents of the great missionary Hudson Taylor)?

130

Do you know any mother who has had to contend with a son as out of control as Samson? Does the bad behavior of Samson (a Nazirite by his vow) and the Levite (a member of the priestly tribe)—as well as priests and ministers today—ever cause you to wonder about some men who are ordained to God's service?

Does Delilah demonstrate any redeeming qualities? Do you know of any woman whom you would categorize as a Delilah? How do you feel about such women—and Delilah herself?

Does the prevalence of prostitution in the record of God's people surprise you? Did you know that prostitution was permitted by the Catholic Church in the Middle Ages in order to protect decent young women from being raped? How do you regard prostitution and prostitutes today?

What do you think happened to Jephthah's daughter? Did she live a long life as a virgin, or did she die quickly as a burnt offering? Have you ever had a friend who has suffered in such a tragic way that you still mourned for her years later? How do you assess the annual four-day retreat taken by the young women of Israel to mourn for Jephthah's daughter?

Why do you think the stories of the Levite's concubine and the young women of Shiloh are included in the Bible? Do they have anything to tell us besides *stuff happens*?

11

Naomi and Ruth

Geographical and Spiritual Journeys

I'll never forget that late afternoon. I was sitting alone at my kitchen table weeping and wrenching so hard my whole insides seemed on the verge of coming undone. Then I heard words almost whispered, *I'm so sorry*. I looked up, startled. There stood Melissa, my daughter-in-law, having returned to retrieve one last item after we had parted at the front door. I was totally embarrassed. I pulled myself together, helped her find the item, and said good-bye at the door once more.

I had helped her move out that afternoon with my tiny granddaughter—helped her move, unbeknown to my son. I had purchased a microwave for her new apartment and had wished her well. She had left with an air of confidence. I was good with that, at least that's what I kept telling myself. It had to be. Her short marriage at nineteen to my son, twenty, hastened by a baby on the way, simply wasn't working. Besides, living in my home was anything but ideal. I had hired a carpenter to remodel two adjoining rooms, but they needed a place of their own. Even that, though, would not have mended their broken marriage. And now I knew this clandestine departure signaled the end. I had so looked forward to a long and happy marriage for them. It was simply not to be.

As I now look back, I understand so well the deep mutual love between Naomi and her daughters-in-law, especially the devoted and loyal Ruth. Their love had grown—over how many years we do not know.

I have known Melissa now for almost two decades, first as my son's girlfriend and fiancée, then as his wife and my daughter-in-law, and since then as a very dear friend. At first it wasn't easy, especially when she and my son hurled angry words at each other. Now it is so different. Special occasions, whether our granddaughter's birthday or Mother's Day, are spent together as the happy family almost as I had once envisioned, complete with my husband and me, her own mother and stepfather, my son (her ex-husband), and their daughter. Somehow it works, thanks in large part to Melissa. I love her as Naomi must have loved Ruth. She is my beloved daughter-in-law who is now even dearer to me than she was on that desolate day so many years ago.

Much is made of Naomi and Ruth in a mother-daughter relationship. But it is friendship that most characterizes their bond. Both widowed, they understand grief, but also significant in their enduring kinship is the experience of being an alien in a foreign, and sometimes unfriendly, land. They had each other, and that union proved as strong as marriage or motherhood.

Naomi

So entwined are Naomi and Ruth that it is challenging to analyze them separately, but that is what we seek to do. Naomi lives in the days when the judges ruled. She no doubt had heard about the great judge Deborah and the decisive victory over Sisera's army. And she surely must have heard the heroic story of Jael. In fact, Deborah's song would have been passed along from one generation to the next.

The entire era of the judges—some four hundred years—was marked by violent military strife and, worse than that, the Israelites themselves doing evil in the sight of the Lord. But Naomi's story does not involve any episode that relates to either war or bad behavior. It seems she may very well have lived in one of the periodic times of peace. She faces another problem, however. It is a cyclical crisis that the Israelites endure, dating back to the days of Sarah and Abraham—famine.

Naomi's hometown is Bethlehem, meaning "house of bread." How incongruous that name must have seemed amid a famine. How could a family live without bread? Bethlehem is a small hamlet in Judah. Naomi would have known that on the road to this very town, Rachel had been buried many generations earlier—Rachel the most beloved wife of Jacob and mother of Joseph.

Bethlehem is within easy walking distance from Jerusalem, but we must keep in mind that during this period of the judges, Israel was still only a loose confederation of tribes, with Canaanite kings and their armies possessing vast surrounding areas. Intertribal warfare was only an insult away. In fact, soon after Joshua's death, as judges begin to rule, we read: "The men of Judah attacked Jerusalem also and took it. They put the city to the sword and set it on fire."[1] The burned-down Jerusalem may have been no more than a pile of rubble during Naomi's lifetime.

In times of peace and plenty, Bethlehem would have been a pleasant place to call home. There is a spring close by, and the soil is rich. When the rains come, crops and herds flourish. Naomi is married to Elimelek, both Ephrathites from the tribe of Judah. They are dependent on the land, and when famine comes, they make the critical decision to relocate.

There were many places among other Israelite tribes where they might have taken up residence. Moab was relatively close by as the crow flies, but the road was rocky and steep. It might have taken a week to ten days with small children and baggage to transport. So why Moab? Resettlement among another Israelite tribe certainly would not have assured a warm welcome. And, for whatever reason, Moab beckoned.

Moab after all was populated by descendants of Lot's daughters, kin of Sarah and Abraham. But worship of the true God had gone south. The Moabites were not followers of Yahweh. Rather their national god was Chemosh, who was said to be placated by child sacrifice. It surely wasn't for the worship of Chemosh that Naomi and her husband relocated in Moab, however. With a home in foreclosure and a checking account overdrawn, they were looking to escape the recession.

The next we learn of them, Elimelek is dead, Naomi a widow. Did the neighbors show kindness with covered hot dishes and comfort? All we know is that Naomi in her grief stays on in Moab with her two sons, Mahlon and Kilion, perhaps now adults. Indeed, her rationale for staying put was probably influenced by her sons' enculturation into this foreign land. They may have originally settled in as youngsters, and Moab had become the only real home they've ever known. It's not surprising then that they both marry Moabite women, Orpah and Ruth.

We can imagine the widow Naomi often longing for Bethlehem and deeply regretting the decision to move. But now she has family who will care for her in old age and grandkids to look forward to. Maybe things will be all right. Hardly does she have time to contemplate a better future, however, when both sons die. What an overwhelming sorrow it is to experience the death of a child. Naomi grieves the death of two children, her only ones. Mahlon and Kilion. We pause a moment to remember.

> ### Just for a While in Moab
>
> Elimelech died in Moab. His "just for a while" turned into forever. His sons married foreign wives, a sin against the Law and a disgrace, and then died there too. *They followed in Daddy's footsteps.* The father's compromise led to the sons', and his wife was suddenly left in a foreign, idolatrous land as a childless widow. What good came to Elimelech and his family in Moab? What good *ever* comes from unfaithfulness and compromise?
>
> Cynthia Shomaker, *From Moab to Bethlehem*

Why, a million times over, why, did we ever leave Bethlehem? Anyone who has ever said to herself, *I would sell my very soul* to undo a particular decision knows exactly how Naomi must have felt. Depression is a term that hardly does her state of mind justice. She is weighed down with grief.

That is where we find her when she learns that the economy of Bethlehem is picking up, unemployment down, stock market on the rebound. She informs her daughters-in-law that she will be returning home, and they naturally assume it is their duty to accompany her. They pack up their belongings and head out on the rugged road to Bethlehem. But Naomi has second thoughts. Why should they sacrifice their future for her? There's no one in Bethlehem who would offer them a home—and, as a matter of fact, it would be easier for her alone to simply move in with relatives or friends she had known so long ago.

Go back, she tells them. In fact, she orders them to return—to return each of them to her *mother's* home. We could wish the text explained that little detail. Is it entirely possible that their own mothers were widowed as well? If the order sounds almost harsh, it is not. In fact, it is followed by a compassionate blessing:

> May the LORD show you kindness, as you have shown kindness to your dead husbands and to me. May the LORD grant that each of you will find rest in the home of another husband.[2]

They have come to deeply love Naomi. In fact, only moments later we will hear her referring to them as *daughters*. They are sobbing and crying aloud when she kisses them good-bye. They refuse to go back, insisting rather to go with her and live in Bethlehem. What Naomi says next is tinged with despair and no little sarcasm, though we do recognize that grieving people should not necessarily be held accountable for everything they say.

> Return home, my daughters. Why would you come with me? Am I going to have any more sons, who could become your husbands? Return home, my daughters; I am too old to have another husband. Even if I thought there was still hope for me—even if I had a husband tonight and then gave birth to sons—would you wait until they grew up? Would you remain unmarried for them? No, my daughters. It is more bitter for me than for you, because the LORD's hand has turned against me![3]

She introduces the subject of their remarriages before grass has even grown over the graves of their husbands. And then she suggests a twisted scenario that seems on the surface utterly ludicrous. Her final words indicate her anger toward God.

Naomi returns home bitter, accompanied only by Ruth. And Ruth, as it turns out, is the most loyal and loving daughter-in-law a woman could even imagine. They arrive in Bethlehem during barley harvest, and almost immediately Naomi is being supplied with more grain than she can possibly bake up for bread. This town truly is a *house of bread*.

But besides baking, she's scheming—how to get Ruth and the kindly Boaz together. She plays Cupid most cleverly, and before another barley season has come and gone—at least in a biblical time frame, it seems—she is the proudest grandmother in all Israel. The neighbor ladies rejoice in her happiness: To her, they offer a blessing: "May he become famous throughout Israel! He will renew your life and sustain you in your old age," and to each other they laughingly say, "Naomi has a son!"[4]

Ruth

As a girl and a young adult, Ruth would have known no other culture than that of her people, the Moabites, who were often snarled in a cold war, if not actual warfare, against Israel. Though a narrow strip of land, Moab was rich enough in cattle and land for Israel to fight for. Later, long after Ruth's time, when Joram (son of Ahab) is king of Israel, Moab revolted against its overlord Israel, not wanting to pay exorbitant taxes (one hundred thousand lambs and more). With the help of the king of Judah and the king of Edom, and bolstered by Elisha's prophecy, the "Israelites invaded the land and slaughtered the Moabites" and laid waste to their entire ecosystem.[5]

In Ruth's time, however, the land and the people are productive, and it is a time of peace. Because they have common ancestors, there are many shared religious and cultural traditions. Both the Moabites and the Israelites recognize the law of Moses. But Moab is considered a land of false gods. Chemosh is the main god of Ruth's people. Might she have been aware that sometimes children such as herself were actually sacrificed to him?

Conversion to another religion or god was not considered an option for people in the ancient world. If your tribe worshiped Yahweh, so did you. The same for Chemosh. There were exceptions, of course, particularly in the case of intermarriage. Then the woman would take the religion of her husband.

This would have been the case when Ruth married Mahlon. She would have joined him in the practice of Yahweh worship, though there may have been no real conviction in her conversion. In fact, she and Orpah, who married Kilion, may have never given full allegiance to Yahweh at all while they lived in Moab.

The text reveals nothing about Ruth's marriage to Mahlon. We would be grateful for just one spare verse about how long they had been married and whether Ruth and Orpah were considered barren since no children

---

Moab: A Narrow, Fertile Strip of Land

Moab is rolling plateau (averaging approximately 3,300 feet elevation), bounded on the west by the rugged escarpment which drops down to the Dead Sea (itself almost 1,300 feet below sea level), on the east by the desert, and running through it the steep Wady Mujib canyon (the Arnon River of biblical times). . . . Relatively few springs appear on the Moabite plateau, and the waters of the Mujib/Arnon are virtually inaccessible because of the steepness of the river canyon. Still, the area is well watered by winter rains brought by winds from the Mediterranean. The porous soil holds enough of the moisture for the villagers to grow cereal crops and to find good pasturage for their sheep and goats.

Maxwell Miller, "Moab and the Moabite Stone"

---

are mentioned. Nor are there any details of the demise of their husbands. But according to custom, they are joined to their husbands' family. So it is natural that they would now look to Naomi as the head of the family and accompany her on the road to Judah.

Both Ruth and Orpah protest when Naomi tells them to go back to their mothers' homes, but only Ruth refuses to return. She no doubt sees right through Naomi, knowing all too well that Naomi needs the companionship of at least one of her beloved daughters-in-law. Only now do we see Ruth's conversion for what it genuinely is—one of true conviction.

> Where you go I will go, and where you stay I will stay. Your people will be my people and your God my God. Where you die I will die, and there I will be buried. May the Lord deal with me, be it ever so severely, if even death separates you and me.[6]

Orpah goes back to her people and her god. We easily wonder about this today. Can someone deconvert simply by walking in the other direction down the road? And what of Ruth's conversion? There is no renunciation of her previous religious loyalty, no sorrow for sin. She simply accompanies Naomi to Judah and gets religion in the package—a conversion that could easily be missed by a speed-reader. But we must be cautious about assuming every conversion experience should mirror our own. There is no reason to believe that we are somehow more faithful to God than Ruth was.

138

On arriving in Bethlehem, Ruth and her mother-in-law are immediately the subject of much curiosity. It seems as though Naomi has not kept up over the years with her old neighbors. For all they know, she might have died years earlier. Now she's home again, and who is this young woman who has come with her?

Does Ruth realize how deeply depressed her mother-in-law is? What is she thinking when Naomi, now back home, publicly accuses God of making her life bitter and empty, filled with affliction and misfortune? With Naomi in that condition, Ruth naturally assumes responsibility and offers to go out and glean in the fields during the barley harvest. She knows of Boaz, a landowning relative of her late father-in-law, and it just so happens—by coincidence or by design—that she finds herself gleaning in his field.

Bethlehem is a small town. Ruth is hardworking and, dare we say, an attractive young widow. Naomi is the matchmaker, and Boaz takes the bait with his eyes wide open. It's as simple as that. Boaz notices Ruth and makes sure she is able to glean an ample amount of barley and enjoy a noon meal as well. *So they marry and live happily ever after.* If that were the end of the story, we would sigh and wish more material had been included. As it so happens, in the case of Ruth, we are treated to delicious details that are so often otherwise left out.

A Minimalist Version of the Book of Ruth

When I was growing up in a little country church in the 1950s, I learned Bible stories on flannelgraph. From Creation to the conversion of Paul, biblical truths came alive when my Sunday school teacher rearranged paper figures on the painted flannel backgrounds. The story of Ruth was easy, not nearly as complicated as King Saul and David, or Elisha and Elijah. We started out with four people—Naomi, Elimelech, and their two sons—on the road to Moab to escape famine. It never took them long to get to the other side of the flannel board; and once there, the foursome was suddenly minus one when Elimelech died of unknown causes. Then two female figures were added with the marriage of Naomi's two sons to Orpah and Ruth. . . . Ten years flew by quickly, and the sons died and joined their father in flannelgraph heaven. Now the family was down to three, and they were on the road again, this time in the reverse direction, back to Judah.

Ruth A. Tucker, *Multiple Choices*

In fact, the book of Ruth presents the most developed and detailed courtship in the whole Bible, beginning with a warm interactive conversation, initiated by Boaz:

> My daughter, listen to me. Don't go and glean in another field and don't go away from here. Stay here with the women who work for me. Watch the field where the men are harvesting, and follow along after the women. I have told the men not to lay a hand on you. And whenever you are thirsty, go and get a drink from the water jars the men have filled.[7]

As an older man, he speaks to her in fatherly terms. And she responds as a daughter, giving him the respect due an older gentleman—he, the well-heeled landowner, she, the impoverished widow in need of sustenance. But the motive for Boaz is far more than pity. Ruth, who recognizes this, moves a step forward in her plan:

> At this, she bowed down with her face to the ground. She asked him, "Why have I found such favor in your eyes that you notice me—a foreigner?"[8]

Her question and his reply serve to further their familiarity. He lets her know that he regards her as far more than an indigent foreigner.

> I've been told all about what you have done for your mother-in-law since the death of your husband—how you left your father and mother and your homeland and came to live with a people you did not know before. May the LORD repay you for what you have done. May you be richly rewarded by the LORD, the God of Israel, under whose wings you have come to take refuge.[9]

Now Boaz has clearly moved the conversation into courting territory. He lets her know he's checked her out, knowing full well that she's a young widow. So he blesses her. And what does such a woman need most? It's obvious. She needs a rich reward. She needs a husband. And any prospective Hebrew husband would acknowledge God in her life, which Boaz does so eloquently. She has taken refuge under the very wings of the Lord. Her response continues with a standard courtesy, followed by a self-deprecating assertion that almost begs him to disagree. She says:

May I continue to find favor in your eyes, my lord. . . . You have put me at ease by speaking kindly to your servant—though I do not have the standing of one of your servants.[10]

Come on, Ruth. Does Boaz say such nice things to mere servants? If she is hoping he will take her in his arms and say, "My beloved, you are so much more than a servant to me," he does not. That would have been highly improper. But he does court her. When it's time for the noon meal, he calls to her: "Come over here. Have some bread and dip it in the wine vinegar."[11] How sweet. Almost as good as having a picnic of wine and cheese, lying on a blanket under the shade of a sycamore tree.

After she has eaten all she wants, she overhears him say to his harvesters, "Let her gather among the sheaves and don't reprimand her. Even pull out some stalks for her from the bundles and leave them for her to pick up, and don't rebuke her."[12] In the days that follow, Ruth continues to glean in the field of Boaz, well aware that he is a close relative of her late father-in-law. When the harvest is over, Naomi counsels Ruth to make the all-important next move:

Tonight he will be winnowing barley on the threshing floor. Wash, put on perfume, and get dressed in your best clothes. Then go down to the threshing floor, but don't let him know you are there until he has finished eating and drinking. When he lies down, note the place where he is lying. Then go and uncover his feet and lie down. He will tell you what to do.[13]

It has been said that the reference to feet here is a euphemism for genitals. Perhaps. But her action is certainly salacious as it stands. If this isn't seduction pure and simple, what is? She comes to him alone in the dead of the night while his heart is merry with wine and lies down with him. He asks who she is. She identifies herself and then asks that he spread part of his garment over her. Okay. What happens now? At this point all we need is one *shade of gray* to stir our imaginations.

When he next speaks, he expresses gratitude for her kindness and for her not pursuing younger men. He invites her to stay the night, promising to do what he can to work things out in the morning. This is not what might be termed a routine sleepover. When they awake at dawn, he warns her to sneak away so that no one will learn that she has spent the night with him. She does, lugging a pack of barley that he has put in her shawl—the equivalent perhaps of a promise ring.

With hardly a wink of sleep, Ruth waits. Naomi is optimistic, having heard how Boaz had welcomed Ruth the previous night. She has told Ruth that there is another relative who is more closely related to them than Boaz, one who might claim her as a wife. But she knows Boaz is a clever man. They no doubt quickly learn the details of the negotiations through the social media of the day. Boaz approaches the other relative in the town square, making sure ten reliable witnesses are present. But he does not immediately show his cards. Rather, he brings up the matter of the land that Naomi wishes to sell. The relative immediately agrees to purchase it. It's a deal, then. But there's one minor stipulation in the fine print: Ruth comes with the bargain.

Boaz knows exactly with whom he is negotiating, and he knows this clause in the real estate transaction will cancel the deal. And it does. The relative tells Boaz to go ahead and purchase the land himself and take Ruth as a wife. So Boaz assumes the role of the kindly benefactor, and he marries Ruth. (Or had he already *married* her the night before?) Before the crowd has dispersed, the ten town elders and the people standing around offer a curious marriage blessing, one that brings to mind some familiar women we might not immediately associate with loving marital relationships:

> May the LORD make the woman who is coming into your home like Rachel and Leah, who together built up the family of Israel. May you have standing in Ephrathah and be famous in Bethlehem. Through the offspring the LORD gives you by this young woman, may your family be like that of Perez, whom Tamar bore to Judah.[14]

The next thing we know, Ruth is pregnant. She gives birth to Obed, who will become the father of Jesse, the father of David. So Ruth, the Moabite, like Tamar the Canaanite pretend-prostitute and Rahab the Jericho prostitute, is in the genealogical line of Jesus.

It is hard to imagine a woman who is looked upon in higher esteem than Ruth. Though a foreigner and new to town, she has made an incredible impression on the women of Bethlehem. To Naomi, they praise her as one "who is better to you than seven sons."[15]

Concluding Observations

Naomi's telling her daughters to go back to Moab does not make her an obvious choice as a model for personal evangelism. Here she has a chance to bring them both to Yahweh, and yet she squanders the opportunity—or so it seems. But maybe we have much to learn from Naomi. She is essentially giving them truth in advertising. Too often evangelists—whether professionals or laypeople—make false claims about the faith. Even our songs do that. I remember singing this peppy chorus as a child. The lyrics simply didn't ring true, but we sang them anyway.

> I'm inright, outright, upright, downright happy all the time.
> I'm inright, outright, upright, downright happy all the time.
> Since Jesus Christ came in and took away my sin,
> I'm inright, outright, upright, downright happy all the time.

Naomi has no time for shameless claims about such a faith in God. She's bitter, having gone through economic hard times, adjustments to an unfamiliar culture, the death of her husband, and most recently the death of her only children. Where was God in all of this? Her answer: "The Lord's hand has turned against me."[16]

These are not the words we ought to use in our evangelistic outreach—we assume. But Naomi should never be snubbed as an evangelist. She had two daughters-in-law, and one of them she brings to faith—the one who will be listed in the ancestry of Jesus. Not bad, Naomi!

Ruth's story is entirely different. It is one of the greatest love stories of the ancient world and the best romance in the Bible. If we are uncomfortable with Ruth spending the night with Boaz, perhaps that says more about us than it says about the culture of Israel at the time of the judges.

While it is true that no one will ever know precisely what happened that night on the threshing floor, it would seem that the narrator is telling us that Ruth did more than simply let Boaz know that she was willing to marry him. If Naomi, as head of the household, had set forth a chaste plan (that would satisfy evangelicals today), she could have met with Boaz privately in broad daylight. Instead, she encourages Ruth to bathe and perfume herself and meet him at midnight and sleep with him.

On the other hand, we should not diminish this encounter by imagining it was some sort of hanky-panky. Whatever happened that night, we honor Ruth and Boaz by respecting their privacy.

Questions to Think About

Have you ever given a blessing—written or oral—to someone? There are four blessings offered in the short book of Ruth (Naomi blessing Ruth, Boaz blessing Ruth, town elders and others blessing Boaz, town women blessing Naomi). What can we learn from these blessings that will enrich our spiritual lives today?

Is it a sin to be angry with God? Was Naomi off base in blaming God for her problems? Have you ever expressed anger toward God?

How would you assess Naomi's depression? Is she clinically depressed, or is her sadness the obvious result of seeing a husband and two sons die? Can you relate to her in her sadness and depression?

Is there anything about the budding romance between Ruth and Boaz that you can relate to? Do you enjoy sharing and hearing true stories of romance?

Is there any cause for us to speculate what might or might not have happened between Ruth and Boaz on the threshing floor? Is it important for you to believe that they were chaste according to present-day Christian standards? Do such standards change over the decades and centuries? Have courtship standards changed in your lifetime?

If you were stuck in an elevator for an hour, who would you rather be with, Naomi or Ruth? Which one has the more forceful and interesting personality?

12

Hannah and Peninnah

The Perils of Polygamy

In her book *Letters Never Sent*, Ruth E. Van Reken tells of the nightmare of being sent away as a small child to a boarding school for missionary children in Africa. When the volume was first published in 1988, it was very controversial. Since then, much has changed. Fewer parents are willing to subject themselves and their children to such separations. Homeschooling for missionary kids is an appealing option.

Van Reken's story begins in Nigeria in 1951. She has just departed for her elementary school education. Her first *letter never sent* is dated in September of that year, and letters continue in the following months:

Dear Mom and Dad,

I feel awful. Something inside is squeezing me so bad I can hardly breathe. . . . I couldn't stop crying on the airplane. . . . When I got to school this afternoon, I was still crying and I just couldn't stop. . . . The kids say if the teachers catch you sucking your fingers they'll tie a sock on your hand for a week. You have to keep it on all the time, even in class, and everyone laughs at you. . . . Every night I still cry myself to sleep. If my roommates hear me, they call me a cry baby.[1]

During her second year at school, she is still crying herself to sleep. But then she is assigned a new teacher who becomes very special to her—until the teacher betrays her.

> Dear Mom and Dad,
>
> Today another teacher came up to me on the playground and teased me about how much I love my new teacher. Then she recited the poem I had sent Miss Crown. . . . I tried to pretend I hadn't written it. I wanted to run away and cry. Mom, why did Miss Crown show my notes to anyone else? . . . I have the mumps. . . . I feel extra lonesome when I'm sick away from you. . . . I got your letter today, Mom, saying you hoped I'd act better during Christmas vacation than I did last summer. . . . Each time I come home, it feels harder to let you hug me or hug you back. When I stay mad at everyone, it doesn't hurt so much to think about going back to school.[2]

Writing as an adult, Van Reken was able to express her memories more fully than she could have expressed her actual feelings as a child. And who of us can read these words without feeling this child's awful pain?

Get over it, some mission directors would say, not only to the young child, but also to her mother. It seems cruel, but that is how evangelical missions operated throughout much of the twentieth century. In most cases the kids did just fine, often far better than their mothers did.

It makes us wonder how Hannah could do what she did, leaving a very small boy with a tottering old priest who couldn't even manage his own disreputable sons. It seems almost unthinkable. But that is exactly what she did, and she has been honored for that sacrifice ever since. Peninnah's story is in some ways a foil to Hannah's. But it is important to consider her as an individual who has concerns and needs of her own.

Hannah

The first thing we actually learn about Hannah is that "the Lord had closed her womb."[3] That fact, more than anything else, defines her. True, she is one of two wives, and the one who is most beloved by her husband,

Elkanah. But her barrenness blares out of the biblical text. And it's not merely a matter of a hormonal imbalance or endometriosis or blocked fallopian tubes. In this case, the Lord has intentionally closed her womb. How must she have felt about that? Why was she being targeted?

She is married to Elkanah, an Ephramite with a long pedigree, having descended from Zuph, a Levite, thus putting Elkanah in a priestly line. Although the text is very brief, we might imagine that Hannah is Elkanah's first wife, and when her inability to conceive comes to light, he takes a second wife. In an effort to assuage Hannah's sorrow, he expresses his undying love for her right in front of his other wife and her children. To Hannah he gives a double portion of food each year when they go to the temple in Shiloh to make sacrifice.

It is hardly an overstatement to say that the two women basically hate each other, though Hannah would never admit it. The bitterness between them is palpable. This is especially the case when they all pack up and walk the dusty road to Shiloh about fifteen miles away. Here they see other families making the pilgrimage as well, and Hannah, in comparison, feels intensely the pain of her barrenness. Besides that, this is the very house of the Lord—the Lord who has closed her womb.

On one of these occasions, she is weeping so hard she won't even touch her double portion of food. Elkanah is beside himself. What can he do or say that would make her feel better? One imagines that he would gladly hand over his own portion of food and more—anything to bring her some comfort. He might have just held her in his arms and not said anything. But he thinks he must do something. *Just say anything!* So, nice guy that he is, he puts his foot in his mouth: "Hannah, why are you weeping? Why don't you eat? Why are you downhearted? Don't I mean more to you than ten sons?"[4]

No! she screams, *I want ten sons!* Well, these are not her exact works, but she knows instinctively that this man she is married to cannot fully feel her pain. Elkanah truly appears to be a caring husband, but his words don't seem to matter. His other wife, Peninnah, is giving birth to one baby after another, while Hannah is expected to be satisfied with his kindly words of love and extra food.

Hardly has the meal ended, everyone else apparently still picking at what's left of the roasts and hot dishes, when she gets up and leaves the table. She heads straight for the temple and passes by the aged priest sitting on a stool by the door. Inside, she finds herself alone with God. And perhaps for the first time, she breaks down completely. Amid her sobs, she prays. She wheels and deals with the God who has closed her womb:

> Lord Almighty, if you will only look on your servant's misery and remember me, and not forget your servant but give her a son, then I will give him to the Lord for all the days of his life, and no razor will ever be used on his head.[5]

Although Hannah is exceedingly sorrowful, she is not wailing. And her prayer is not one of calling out to God. In fact, she's almost stifling herself trying not to make a scene. As for the priest Eli, the idea of someone engaging in silent prayer seems unnatural. His corrupt sons, both priests, surely don't darken the temple to pray. So he wonders what is going on. Hannah just keeps on praying as the old geezer squints at her trying to figure out the meaning of her body language. He's confused. "Eli observed her mouth. Hannah was praying in her heart, and her lips were moving but her voice was not heard."[6]

Imagine yourself the spiritual leader at the house of the Lord. Someone who appears to be distraught slips by you and goes inside alone and is silently meditating or praying or thinking. She's not bothering you in any way. How should you respond? Might it occur to you to pray for her, and then as she leaves perhaps ask if there is anything she needs or something you might do for her? Or would you accost her with an utterly unfounded accusation? Would you say to her: "How long are you going to stay drunk? Put away your wine."[7] What's going on? Where did *that* hostility come from? Was he having a really bad day?

Eli's words surely seem to be the worst example ever of pastoral care. How could this man be so unsympathetic? I've always been in awe of Hannah for her calm response to him. I simply do not have the composure she possessed. I would have been tempted to hit him over the head with my handbag and storm out. She has more self-control.

> Not so, my lord. . . . I am a woman who is deeply troubled. I have not been drinking wine or beer; I was pouring out my soul to the Lord. Do not take

your servant for a wicked woman; I have been praying here out of my great anguish and grief.[8]

Here is Hannah, only moments after she has been pouring her heart out to God, having to answer an ugly accusation. We want to jump into the text and demand that the incompetent Eli tell us what his problem is. We will stand up to the old goat. How long has it been since *he* has slipped into the temple and wept before the Lord?

The best thing we can say about Eli is that he doesn't argue and continue his accusation. In fact, he offers a blessing:

Go in peace, and may the God of Israel grant you what you have asked of him.[9]

We might expect her to respond with a *Thank you* or *May God also grant you blessings*. Her response is somewhat baffling. She has been praying to God for a child and knows full well that only God can give her one. But she says to Eli, in reference to herself, "May your servant find favor in your eyes,"[10] as though Eli will be the one to grant the favor.

The good news is that Hannah has come out of her serious depression. With her head held high in front of Elkanah's other wife, she goes to the table and eats. In fact, we imagine that she might have tossed her head a bit. She's convinced that the stigma of barrenness that's been haunting her for so long will soon be history.

Hannah is the greatest woman of faith we have seen thus far (with the possible exception, some might argue, of Hagar). She cries out to God and during these dark moments in the temple becomes convinced that God has heard her and will grant her greatest desire. With that assurance, she's not even bothered by the rude remarks of the priest on duty. Rather, she accepts his blessing as further confirmation of God's favor.

Where does that kind of faith come from? It seems likely that her confidence in God does not necessarily come through the yearly pilgrimages and worship. Too often corruption diminishes any kind of true religion that might have been practiced. The temple at Shiloh was known for wickedness and vice, and not just under the leadership of Eli. In fact, it later became a shrine for false gods.

It is entirely possible that Hannah's faith is inspired less by Shiloh than by stories of old. She surely knows how God opened Sarah's womb in her old age, and later Rebekah's and Rachel's. This same God can give her the baby she has been longing for.

As soon as the extended family returns home, life gets back to the usual routine, which presumably includes lovemaking. "Elkanah made love to his wife Hannah."[11] She waits. Nothing. This is not an instant Cracker Jack prize. Her periods still come like clockwork. It is not until "in the course of time" that she becomes pregnant. Nine months later her baby boy is born, named Samuel "because I asked the LORD for him."[12]

The next year Hannah, with Elkanah's blessing, stays home with her baby during the pilgrimage to Shiloh. She continues to do this until Samuel is weaned, no doubt at least age three, perhaps as old as six. Then the time comes. She and Elkanah take the little boy to Shiloh to spend the rest of his life there. They also bring along a bull to be sacrificed. Eli is still in charge of the place, along with his two utterly ill-disciplined sons. The text is straightforward: "Eli's sons were scoundrels."[13]

What is most stunning is that this time when she encounters Eli, unlike the last time, she is not weeping. For most of us, this would be the time when we are inconsolable. She appears, however, to be entirely in control as we picture her nudging awake the sleeping old man.

> Pardon me, my lord. As surely as you live, I am the woman who stood here beside you praying to the LORD. I prayed for this child, and the LORD has granted me what I asked of him. So now I give him to the LORD. For his whole life he will be given over to the LORD.[14]

She expects him to remember her because she was the woman praying some years earlier. What does that say about the spiritual level of the people at that time? Was it so unusual for a woman to be praying in that sacred place?

Dry-eyed, she gives her little boy over to the Lord, more specifically, to Eli. We shake our heads. We've never known anyone like Hannah. Mary, the mother of Jesus, will get into a real tizzy when Jesus, much older than Samuel, goes missing for only a day or two. We relate to her, not to Hannah. And how, we wonder, did Eli take the news that he now has a young child to raise? The text does not say.

150

To describe Hannah as dry-eyed is missing the point. Before she leaves, she sings a grand song of praise to God, beginning with the words: "My heart rejoices in the Lord; in the Lord my horn is lifted high."[15]

After her song is over, the text tells us that Elkanah returned to Ramah, while the boy stayed and ministered with Eli. It's a strange statement. Did Hannah linger a while to help the little boy get used to his new surroundings? We desperately hope so. But we know she didn't stay on. We soon learn that she is making the pilgrimage to Shiloh every year, taking along for Samuel a little handmade robe.

Each year as they depart for home, Eli blesses Elkanah: "May the Lord give you children by this woman to take the place of the one she prayed for and gave to the Lord." The reader is not left to wait and wonder: "And the Lord was gracious to Hannah; she gave birth to three sons and two daughters."[16]

Samuel will go on to be a great judge and prophet. For the rest of this extended family, including Hannah and Peninnah, their recorded lives are over—almost as surely as the life of Lot's wife is over when she is turned into a pillar of salt.

> **Shiloh**
>
> Shiloh was the center of Israelite worship. The people assembled here for the mandatory feasts and sacrifices, and here lots were cast for the various tribal areas and for the Levitical cities. This was a sacred act, revealing how God would choose to parcel out the land within the tribes.
>
> Generations later, Samuel was raised at the shrine in Shiloh by the high priest Eli. Samuel began prophesying at a young age and continued to serve in the Tabernacle, but not as a priest because he was not from the family of Aaron.
>
> "Shiloh (biblical city)"

Peninnah

Who would name a girl Peninnah? It's actually a beautiful name, but it conjures up only negative attributes from the biblical story. It almost seems to me that you would no more name your daughter Peninnah than you would name her *Potiphar's wife*. It just doesn't seem right. But then I went to Google and came across this lovely Jewish storyteller and university professor Peninnah Schram, the founding director of the Jewish Storytelling Center. She shares her philosophical perspective:

As a storyteller, I never know when a story or an image or words from a story will take hold, like a seed that is planted that may take seven years to root and flower. But I know that with these Jewish stories I have been nourished and nurtured in my understanding of people and the wisdom of Judaism. . . . Several years ago I realized that before I tell stories I needed to have a prayer . . . so that I can become ready to tell the stories, and also to prepare my audience to listen and receive the stories.[17]

Peninnah, the *other woman* in Hannah's life, was very different from Peninnah Schram, though from the latter we gain a refreshing insight on the name, which actually means "pearl." Shram wondered why she had been given that name. "Suddenly, one day I realized that a pearl is created through an irritant, a grain of sand, serving as the catalyst to initiate the process of creating the pearl. Only then are the luminous layers added on one-by-one to form this precious jewel. If Peninnah, the irritant, had not taunted Hannah, Hannah would not have found her strength to pray even harder to God for a child."[18]

Peninnah is the lesser-loved wife, who Schram goes on to suggest is reminiscent of Hagar. But perhaps a better analogy is Leah. Leah has one baby after another, but she is never able to win the love of Jacob. Rachel is loved by him but remains barren. This is essentially the picture of Peninnah and Hannah, though Peninnah seems to carry the mean-spirited aspect of their rivalry further than does Leah. And Jacob, unlike Elkanah, makes no secret of his lack of love for Leah. Moreover, Rachel is no Hannah when we are sizing up quality of character.

But Peninnah takes the prize as a bad apple. The text is unambiguous when it pits her against the flawless Hannah: "Her rival kept provoking her in order to irritate her. This went on year after year. Whenever Hannah went up to the house of the LORD, her rival provoked her till she wept and would not eat."[19] What kind of a woman does that? Does it actually bring her pleasure to inflict pain on Hannah? It is difficult to wrap our minds around Peninnah—except for one huge factor: polygamy.

It is safe to say that the perils of polygamy are enormous. Let Peninnah stand alone with her brood of kids. Take Hannah out of the picture. We might have a very different woman from the one we see in this rivalry. Even apart from her standing as the most beloved who receives the most food,

Hannah is not an easy person for many of us to connect with. She almost seems too good to be true.

So, as we analyze Peninnah, we cannot ignore Hannah's seeming perfection. Let's say these two women are neighbors. One is the kindest woman in town and her husband adores her, but she has no children. The other has a gaggle of kids but gets no love from her husband. Can we imagine the latter sometimes resenting the former? *She's such a goody-goody. Well, if she had a dozen kids, she might scream and holler a little herself!* Now, add polygamy. Let's say that this husband we're speaking of is actually one and the same man. Are we surprised then when Peninnah behaves so shabbily? Maybe not.

Nothing more is said of Peninnah after that first trip to Shiloh. We can assume, however, that she did not throw a baby shower when Samuel was born. Nevertheless, we give her some slack. We certainly wish her well in the raising of all her children, and we hope that she is able to find happiness and goodwill, despite that awful patriarchal practice of polygamy.

Concluding Observations

The Bible is a big book, but brevity is too often the rule. Hannah and Peninnah are cast as opposites in a short narrative of less than two chapters. They are far more, however, than what the Bible tells us. We surely know that Hannah had her bad days before and after this brief account. And Peninnah, we know, must have had good days. She loved her little ones as we all do, and she may, in her old age, have grown to regret her bitter remarks against Hannah.

If Hannah's story were cast today, it would not play well. We want emotion and action. We want characters who are as complex and flawed as we are. There's no room for a sweet, submissive, one-dimensional leading lady. We expect her to stand up for herself and tell off Eli and Peninnah and even Elkanah for thinking a ten-thousand-calorie meal will make things right. Why didn't she storm right past the cranky old priest even as she hissed that he ought to *get a life*? And Peninnah? She was a vicious woman, and Hannah should have stood up to her. We long for action like we got with Sarah and Rebekah and Rachel.

153

Perhaps the most pointed message of this passage, however, is that marriage is to be monogamous. Polygamy, though practiced in biblical times and even today in many cultures, simply does not work. Any benefits that polygamy might have offered to husbands, their wives soon painfully learned were certainly not extended to them.

Questions to Think About

How do you analyze Elkanah as a husband? Is he a decent man but essentially clueless? How do you suppose his giving Hannah more food serves to lessen the pain and hostility that permeates his polygamous marriage? Does his effort at comforting Hannah fall flat?

Imagine yourself in a polygamous situation with your husband having taken one or more additional wives. How would you survive? Do you have any coping mechanisms that would help you make it through each day?

If you were Mr. Rogers, would you tell Hannah that you like her just the way she is? Peninnah? If you were to spend a day in a park with Hannah, would you want her to present herself any differently than she does in the scriptural account?

Do you prefer getting the silent treatment, for example, having someone get up and leave the table without saying a word, or would you rather have the person say right out exactly what is bothering her?

Is there anything positive you can say about Peninnah? Have you ever felt as though you yourself were behaving just like her?

Have you ever known anyone who has given up a young child? Could you ever do what Hannah did? Have you ever bargained with God? How would you know for sure whether it is God who is asking you to make a great sacrifice?

13

⌘⌘⌘⌘⌘⌘⌘⌘⌘⌘⌘

Abigail and Michal

Unfortunate Wives of David

I often wonder if women, perhaps more than men, are predisposed to heartbreak when the heart leads the mind astray. How many times have I laid out a cogent course of action, only to have my heart take me into a quagmire? I make lists; I arrange priorities in ascending and descending orders; I stay awake nights logically setting out a formula that I think will serve me well. Then, in a heartbeat, rational thinking is hijacked by an utterly undisciplined and unruly heart.

It sometimes feels like my brain has been sucked right out through the top of my head. And I'm not alone. Many of us fall into a category identified by two male clinical psychologists, Connell Cowan and Melvyn Kinder. The title of their 1985 best-selling book says it all: *Smart Women, Foolish Choices*. My testimony: *been there, done that*.

After enduring seventeen years of singleness (my son having flown the coop), I met a widower, accurately summed up as a charming gentleman. Highly educated and having been very successful as a physician, he was now active in retirement. Our interests coincided on many levels, and there was a spark that soon led to romance. I was head-over-heels in love. I had finally found *Mr. Right*, and we became engaged.

Over the next year and a half (our marriage plans having been postponed), I realized that the relationship simply would not work. I had made lists of reasons, had written detailed journal entries, and had spent long hours talking with him. As much as we enjoyed each other's company, I knew rationally that I should never make a *till-death-do-us-part* commitment with him. It was a no-brainer. My head was screaming *no*, while my heart was melting—*yes*.

We like to quote philosopher Blaise Pascal's great line: "The heart has its reasons that reason knows nothing of." But it should come with a warning label for our love life.

Fortunately for me, after an off-again, on-again love affair, we ended up going our separate ways. Last I heard, he was happily married. I am happy for him—and for myself. For me, both head and heart were joined together in complete harmony when two years later I married John. I will never forget that misery, however, of enduring the warfare of head and heart. When the heart prevailed, foolish choices littered the battlefield. But when my heart held up the white flag of surrender, my head and common sense triumphed, though not without tears and a sense of loss.

Abigail was a smart woman who, I will argue, made a very foolish choice. Not necessarily in marrying Nabal. True, he was a fool and worse. The Bible says so. But that first marriage might have been arranged when she was young. No, her foolish choice was when her heart overruled sanity in a rash decision to marry David. He was a heartthrob and by any standard a trophy husband. And we could make a strong case that he was a good man, though surely not a good husband for Abigail. Rational thinking would have told her to listen to her head and not become entangled with him.

There were many women who found themselves in orbit around David, that great biblical figure who posed so perfectly for Michelangelo. A few years ago when we visited Florence, we gazed at him up close and personal, and not just once. As we strolled through the piazza, I found myself being pulled back again and again to this most alluring hunk of humanity. But David does not get high marks for his treatment of women.

A case in point. When David's son Absalom makes war against his father with superior military force, David flees the palace, leaving behind

156

his ten concubines to keep house. Upon arriving at the palace, Absalom, prodded by his chief adviser, rapes (or "sleeps with") all ten concubines. This he does to humiliate and make himself "obnoxious to" his father in an attempt to make his own followers even more loyal.[1]

When David returns to the palace, having heard about Absalom's wicked deeds, he places his ten concubines under house arrest, with armed guards preventing their escape. He feeds them but never again has sexual relations with any of them. "They were kept in confinement till the day of their death, living as widows."[2] In the eyes of David, it appears that these women were no more than sex objects. They had served him in that capacity, and now that they had been sullied by his son Absalom, they were sentenced to life in virtual prison.

Besides these ten concubines and Abigail, there were other women who might have rightly resented David's treatment of them, not the least of whom are his first wife, Michal (daughter of Saul), and his daughter Tamar. Did Abigail ever commiserate with them? We'll never know.

The world of the Bible is a small one, and it is fun to speculate how closely connected various individuals might have been. Hannah and Abigail, for example, were separated by only two generations.

There is a theory, first set forth by Frigyes Karinthy, that everyone in the world is connected to everyone else by only six degrees of separation. For example, I know Mayor Heartwell of Grand Rapids, who knows President Obama, who knows Vladimir Putin, and so on for three more steps to cover everyone in Russia. Since the president knows leaders from all over the world, I'm within six steps of connecting, so the theory goes, with all seven billion people in the world. True, *knowing* may be very superficial, as in my knowing the mayor and the mayor knowing the president. But this worldwide grid does show us how closely each one of us is connected to everyone else, and even more so in the biblical world.

Abigail

Hannah and Abigail were much closer than six degrees. Abigail's story begins with a solemn announcement: "Now Samuel died, and all Israel assembled and mourned for him."[3] Hannah's son Samuel was the last judge of

Israel. God had harkened to the pleas of the Israelites, who wanted a king like the surrounding enemy tribes had. So Samuel anoints Saul to become the first king of Israel. Due to Saul's serious deficiencies, however, Samuel later anoints David to succeed him (while Saul is still on the throne). That is a huge mess we pass over in this study. But Hannah, we discover, is then only three degrees of separation from Abigail: Hannah's son Samuel has anointed David, Abigail's husband.

When David meets Abigail, Saul is still the reigning monarch. That factor is more than a footnote; it frames the remainder of her life.

Abigail is a wealthy woman, by marriage if not by inheritance and dowry. She lives with her husband, Nabal, near the settlement of Carmel in the highlands of Judah, south of Jerusalem. Theirs is a big operation, with house servants, herdsmen, and thousands of sheep and goats. Abigail, as the text clearly emphasizes, is the captivating charismatic half of this duo. "She was an intelligent and beautiful woman." *Well-heeled* is all that can be said for Nabal, who is "surly and mean in his dealings."[4] He is identified as a descendant of Caleb, one of the spies sent by Moses to scout out the Promised Land.

The reason we learn about this affluent married couple is that David and his guerrilla army are in the region. Abigail may have heard about the upstart David, who was celebrated in the popular little song crediting him with killing ten thousands of the enemy while King Saul had only killed thousands. Now he and his fighting men are close by, and unlike other rag-tag militias they have not raided or even threatened their plantation.

One day Abigail is at home with her servants, while Nabal is with the herdsmen. It is sheep-shearing time, and there is a general atmosphere of celebration, though she and her house servants would not have been involved in those festivities. One of the servants who has been out with the herdsmen suddenly appears with an alarming report. He informs her that David has sent messengers to make a request of Nabal.

The servant tells the whole story, emphasizing that the messenger has come with warm greetings and a reminder that David and his men have never attacked Nabal's men or stolen from their flocks. Now David would like Nabal to share his bounty and provide some much-needed victuals. The servant, in fact, is clearly taking the side of David, not Nabal, who, according to the servant, has insulted the messengers. Abigail, her heart pounding, listens as the servant (who knows firsthand how David has protected them) continues:

> Yet these men were very good to us. They did not mistreat us, and the whole time we were out in the fields near them nothing was missing. Night and day they were a wall around us the whole time we were herding our sheep near them. Now think it over and see what you can do, because disaster is hanging over our master and his whole household. He is such a wicked man that no one can talk to him.[5]

Imagine that. A servant is telling you this about your own husband. But she doesn't waste a second trying to defend him. She is decisive. She instantly takes charge, ordering servants to take foodstuffs from storage and load everything onto donkeys: "two hundred loaves of bread, two skins of wine, five dressed sheep, five seahs [some eight gallons] of roasted grain, a hundred cakes of raisins and two hundred cakes of pressed figs."[6]

Without informing Nabal of what's going on, she orders her servants to head for David's encampment, as she follows on her own donkey. Just as this entourage is heading down into a ravine, she sees armed men coming toward them from the other side. She immediately spots the commander of the militia, this man named David, who could easily put an end to them all. She alights from her donkey, walks over to him, and bows prostrate before him, her face to the ground. (She truly is as smart as the text says.) Her words confirm her absolute helplessness before him:

> Pardon your servant, my lord. . . . Please pay no attention, my lord, to that wicked man Nabal. He is just like his name—his name means Fool, and folly goes with him. . . . And now, my lord, as surely as the LORD your God lives and as you live, since the LORD has kept you from bloodshed and from avenging yourself with your own hands, may your enemies and all who are intent on harming my lord be like Nabal. And let this gift, which your servant has brought to my lord, be given to the men who follow you.[7]

Abigail goes on to add more lines to this blessing suggesting she knows that David is more than a small-time militia commander. "The LORD your God will certainly make a lasting dynasty for my lord," she prophesies.[8]

She ends this long blessing with continued prophecy and one last plea for herself and her servants:

> When the LORD has fulfilled for my lord every good thing he promised concerning him and has appointed him ruler over Israel, my lord will not have on his conscience the staggering burden of needless bloodshed or of having avenged himself. And when the LORD your God has brought my lord success, remember your servant.[9]

Dare we say that Abigail, besides being intelligent and beautiful, is a prophet? On hearing these words, David responds with, "Praise be to the LORD, the God of Israel, who has sent you today to meet me."[10] After accepting her load of provisions, he concludes with the very words she wanted to hear: "Go home in peace. I have heard your words and granted your request."[11]

Abigail returns home only to find Nabal presiding over "a banquet like that of a king." Not surprisingly, "he was in high spirits and very drunk."[12] She says nothing to him of her little foray to David's encampment, but by morning, when he has slept off his hangover, she tells him straight out exactly what she has done. It is such shocking news that "his heart failed him and he became like a stone."[13] He lingers in a coma for ten days and then dies.

Abigail is not a grieving widow. In fact, she is now free. She has loyal servants, and the herdsmen realize she doesn't suffer fools gladly. If Nabal's family were to rush in and attempt to divvy up the property, they would have had to face her head on. She has before her the opportunity of a lifetime. But then she receives a message. David, having heard of Nabal's death, is once again praising the Lord. But he also sends servants to Carmel with what almost appears to be a threatening message: "David has sent us to you to take you to become his wife."[14] She's a strong woman. Why didn't she send a return message: *Not on your life!*

She doesn't. Rather she bows and says . . . (Oh please, Abigail, we beg you, don't say it. Don't. Don't. Don't say it!) She says: "I am your servant and am ready to serve you and wash the feet of my lord's servants."[15] With her head having been overruled by her heart, she does not hesitate a minute. She gets on her donkey and, with five female servants, joins David's camp and becomes his wife. Does she know that he already has two wives, Ahinoam and Michal?

We could only wish her story would have ended with Nabal's death, but it doesn't. To comprehend the remainder of her life, we depend largely on conjecture. Unlike Hannah, her marriage to a polygamous husband involves far greater peril than merely a malicious other wife. No sooner is the honeymoon over than David and his men (along with Abigail, Ahinoam, servants, and children) move for safety into Philistine territory, where they live for one year and four months in the little village of Ziklag.

From there, his militia makes raids on various towns. Whenever David went on the attack, "he did not leave a man or woman alive, but took sheep and cattle, donkeys and camels, and clothes."[16] How does Abigail feel about this, or doesn't she know the details? Does she ever think, *Well, maybe Nabal wasn't so bad after all?*

Sometime later Abigail, Ahinoam, children, and servants are taken hostage by the enemy Amalekite army. Exactly how long they are held in captivity before David and his men rescue them is not recorded. But we cannot assume that these wives were treated with respect. If they were not raped and assaulted, they were most fortunate. In fact, as David and his militia approach the enemy camp, he finds the Amalekite army "eating, drinking and reveling because of the great amount of plunder they had taken," including Abigail.[17]

Having been rescued from the Amalekite revelers, Abigail is back in the camp with her husband's six-hundred-man army. Then comes the news of King Saul's death (as well as the death of his son Jonathan, David's good friend). David is heartbroken and mourns for days on end. Then, with his extended family, he moves to Hebron, where he is anointed king of Judah. If we imagine Abigail as a queen sitting on a throne in palace splendor, we are quite mistaken. Warfare continues. "The war between the house of Saul and the house of David lasted a long time."[18] But in the midst of the fighting, David does manage to get under the covers with his Abigail and Ahinoam, and other women:

> Sons were born to David in Hebron: His firstborn was Amnon the son of Ahinoam of Jezreel; his second, Kileab the son of Abigail the widow of Nabal

of Carmel; the third, Absalom the son of Maakah daughter of Talmai king of Geshur; the fourth, Adonijah the son of Haggith; the fifth, Shephatiah the son of Abital; and the sixth, Ithream the son of David's wife Eglah.[19]

After living in Hebron for more than seven years, David relocates to Jerusalem where he resides for thirty-three more years and fathers many more children, four by Bathsheba, nine by other wives, "besides his sons by his concubines."[20] How long Abigail survived is not recorded, but she is never mentioned after her move to Hebron. Did Abigail ever reminisce about what might have been had she not gotten involved with David and his warfare and wives? David gave her at least one son, and we want to believe that this child brought some measure of joy into her life.

Tamar

In the enumeration of all of David's sons by his various wives in 1 Chronicles 3, there is added a five-word sentence: "And Tamar was their sister."[21] We might wish that the biblical text simply left it there. But no one can ever accuse the writers of the Bible of leaving out shameful episodes. What if all the writers of family Christmas letters were as honest and open as the writers of the Bible? Instead, we get a litany of promotions, honors, awards, and exciting travel. Never a brother raping a sister.

Tamar is living at the palace in Jerusalem when she receives a message from her father: "Go to the house of your brother Amnon and prepare some food for him."[22] Amnon is her half brother living nearby, and she may have heard that he was haggard and not feeling well. His request, made to his father and presumably passed on to her, may have seemed unusual. He expects her to "make some special bread in my sight, so I may eat from her hand."[23]

If he's really sick, why would she need to make bread for him while he's watching? And why not a servant? Something's up, we immediately suspect. But this order has come from her father the king, so she makes haste to do his bidding. She goes to Amnon's house dressed as usual in her lavish royal gown. There, as expected, she finds him lying down apparently sick in bed. She kneads the dough and bakes it. Bread, fresh out of the oven.

What could be better? In fact, a recent study shows that the smell of freshly baked bread lightens the spirt and supposedly makes a person kinder.[24]

This was certainly not the case with Amnon. When she brings the bread over to him and tries to serve him, he refuses to eat. Then he demands that all the servants leave immediately and insists that she bring the bread right into his bedroom. By this time she is getting nervous, but he's a lot stronger than she (and is obviously not sick), so she follows orders. No sooner has she stepped inside the door than he grabs her and pulls her to his bed.

She screams for him to stop. She's a virgin. "Don't do this wicked thing," she pleads. She would be terribly disgraced. And him? Why isn't he concerned about his own reputation? If he forces her to have sex, he would be no better than just another "one of the wicked fools in Israel." She's begging him to stop and saying anything to try to stall him. In fact, she tells him to "speak to the king." She's desperate, insisting that their father "will not keep me from being married to you."[25]

But Amnon, in his violent rage, spurns her pleas and rapes her. The unspeakable brutality is over as soon as it has begun. Is it any surprise that he now despises her? He screams at her to get out of his house, no doubt calling her every crude expletive in the book. As violated as she has been, she stands up to him and argues that he simply cannot do that. Now that he's committed this vile act and she's lost her virginity, he can't simply order her out of his home. But he calls for his servant and demands: "Get this woman out of my sight and bolt the door after her."[26]

We shudder to imagine this awful ordeal for Tamar and we wonder why she didn't run screaming out of the house. After she is ordered out of Amnon's house, she returns home and tears up her beautiful gown that had signified she was not only the daughter of the king but also a virgin. She puts ashes on her head and a garment that corresponds with her grief, and weeps aloud as she leaves the palace.

The first person she meets is her dear brother Absalom. He knows immediately what has happened. To say he's irate is an understatement. He would kill Amnon in a heartbeat, but he is determined to bide his time. In the meanwhile, Tamar lives with him in utter desolation. When David gets word of what has happened, he is furious. But he refuses to take action.

Two years later, Tamar hears that Absalom is having a big party to celebrate the end of sheep shearing, though not at his house, where she is living. He invites all his brothers. It is a night of merrymaking and murder. The morning after, Tamar learns that Amnon is dead, struck down when he was drunk with wine. After that, Absalom flees for his life, and Tamar, we presume, now lives alone, abandoned in her brother's house, forever damaged goods.

Michal

"Michal was in love with David."[27] She is the only woman in the Bible who is said to have loved a man. The daughter of King Saul, she would become the wife of David. Her story begins before Abigail enters the picture and ends after Abigail has faded from the scene.

There is no evidence that David loved Michal. In fact, he weds her, if not for the prestige of marrying a princess, then for the daring challenge of earning her bride-price. King Saul, by any account, is insane. He sends word to David that the only payment he requires for his daughter's hand in marriage is one hundred Philistine foreskins. In Saul's mind, this is certain death for his young rival. But for David, this is a dare he cannot resist. So he goes out with his men and brings back not one hundred but two hundred Philistine foreskins.

So Michal marries the man she loves, while her father, with two hundred Philistine foreskins, recognizes David's military might and is now more determined than ever to fight him until the day he dies. What kind of a bind does this pose for Michal? Imagine your father conspiring to kill your husband, who is actually an officer in your father's army. In fact, on one occasion she overhears alarming news of a vicious plot and warns David: "If you don't run for your life tonight, tomorrow you'll be killed."[28] The threat is dead serious, so Michal helps him escape out the window, letting him down with a rope. Then she concocts a disguise, taking an idol, laying "it on the bed, covering it with a garment and putting some goats' hair at the head."[29]

When her father sends men to arrest David, Michal tells them he is ill. They leave but later return on Saul's orders to bring David to him in his bed. It is only then that they discover the idol and the goats' hair. Saul is furious with his daughter and demands to know why she has deceived him. She responds by quoting David, her husband: "He said to me, 'Let me get away. Why should I kill you?'"[30] Apparently he meant that if he were killed she would be also, and that by escaping he was saving her life.

The next we learn of Michal, David is out of the picture. Her father has given her in marriage to Paltiel. Now she is married to two men. Indeed, she is the only woman in the Bible for whom the word *polyandry* fits. Later, after Saul's death (before the war between the opposing sides is over), word comes to David from Abner of the house of Saul that he is ready to deal. David is willing, under one condition: "Do not come into my presence unless you bring Michal daughter of Saul when you come to see me."[31]

So the order goes out that she must be forcibly "taken away from her husband Paltiel." What follows is one of the saddest little passages in the Hebrew Bible: "Her husband, however, went with her, weeping behind her all the way to Bahurim. Then Abner said to him, 'Go back home!' So he went back."[32]

Here is Michal, once more a pawn, taken from the only man who has ever really loved her, being brought back into David's polygamous household. She should be happy. She's now a queen living in the City of David. Or is Abigail queen? Or Ahinoam? Or another wife? How many queens are there? Are some of them now deceased?

To celebrate David's reign, the ark of the covenant is brought back to Jerusalem. As it enters the city, David, clad only in a scanty linen ephod, begins to wildly dance in the street. When Michal looks out the window and sees him "leaping and dancing before the LORD,"[33] she is thoroughly disgusted. She is perhaps still grieving over Paltiel (as well as her father, King Saul), and here is her *other* husband making a fool of himself. Later when he comes back into the house, her words are dripping with sarcasm: "How the king of Israel has distinguished himself today, going around half-naked in full view of the slave girls of his servants as any vulgar fellow would!"[34]

David is furious and comes right back at her, pointing out that he was dancing before the Lord—the Lord who picked him over her father to be king. And further, he will become even more disgraceful. So there!

It was not a happy marriage. Poor Michal. What a grim life, daughter and wife of kings. The remainder of her life is summed up in one verse: "And Michal daughter of Saul had no children to the day of her death."[35]

Concluding Observations

Abigail's story is an excursus in the narrative of David's exploits against King Saul. In fact, it falls between two episodes in which David could have killed the king but did not. He likewise could have killed the wealthy Nabal but did not, having been warded off by the beautiful Abigail. Some scholars have speculated that Abigail funded David's military expeditions with the wealth from Nabal's estate, but the text gives no indication of that. Rather, except for her personal servants, she seems to have left it all behind in exchange for camp life with David, another wife, and his fighting men.

Many students of Scripture contend that Abigail, having been suddenly widowed, was awarded *God's gift to women*, namely, David. Who more ideal could a Hebrew woman ever dream of marrying? But that assessment typically comes from men. A woman being led by her head rather than her heart—perhaps even Michal—might consider herself fortunate to be married to Paltiel rather than to King David.

We know Paltiel only because he is the devoted husband of Michal, Saul's daughter and David's first wife. She initially loves David and protects him. But it is not a love that lasts. Did David's dancing cause her to despise him, or was it something else? All we know for sure is that this princess became a pawn in the hands of powerful men. She has been faulted for having an idol (used as a disguise for David in bed), but surely David was aware of that idol.

Tamar's story is also very sad. She is the daughter of David and Maakah, one of his many wives. A young virgin dressed in royal apparel, she is raped by her brother. The joy in her life is gone—almost a reminder of Jephthah's daughter.

The biblical text suggests that all three of these women were as capable and intelligent as their male counterparts, if not more so. But because of their gender, opportunities were severely limited, and their risks for abuse were many times greater.

Questions to Think About

Have you ever known of a husband as difficult as Nabal? How do you rate David as a husband? If you were living in Old Testament times, would you consider it a privilege to be married to him?

How are these accounts of women and the men in their lives parallel to Hollywood's frequent portrayal of love? Does the Bible show us the rarity of true love and how love and hate are sometimes difficult to differentiate?

Considering Michal and Tamar, what do Saul and David have in common in their role as fathers with daughters? Can it be true that we have seen no good fathers of daughters so far in our study of biblical women? What does that say about the ancient world? About our own fathers? About how things have changed?

Have you ever, like Michal, been torn between a husband and a parent? Have you known of such situations? Have you ever been embarrassed, as she was, by the behavior of a husband or someone very close to you?

Which one of these three women do you most resonate with? Have you ever let your heart rule your head in matters of love? Have you ever loved someone, as Michal did David, only to have that love disintegrate?

Have you ever dealt with a situation involving rape or incest in a family? How are such situations far more complicated than similar cases in which the individuals are not related to each other? Do you often wish this were not such a messy world that we live in, or that the Bible were not so explicit in its exposure of sexual misconduct?

14

Bathsheba

Seducer, Widow, Wife, and Mother

Rembrandt painted Bathsheba, a naked bathing beauty as he imagined she would have looked in the eyes of King David. "From the roof he saw a woman bathing. The woman was very beautiful."[1] Looking at the painting from our perspective, nearly five hundred years after Rembrandt van Rijn painted her in 1654, she's not necessarily beautiful at all. His ideal would never make the February swimsuit issue of *Sports Illustrated*. Standards change significantly over the centuries. As a matter of fact, her actual appearance some two thousand years earlier might not have impressed Rembrandt at all.

Today we're looking for something very different in female beauty: a woman with toned arms who might be running in a marathon or kayaking the rapids. If she can dance like Beyoncé, all the better. We expect that this beautiful woman will have just the right measurements, and that she'll have a face fit for a princess—as Diana or Kate Middleton.

Rembrandt's Bathsheba would never be mistaken for Diana or Kate. In fact, if we didn't know that he was depicting her bathing soon after King David looked down from his balcony in lust, we might imagine her already six months pregnant with his child.

Her shoulders are narrow and her breasts small considering her wide hips and protruding belly. Her head is small in comparison to the rest of her body, her thighs heavy, ankles thick, and feet perhaps a size 10. Her pale white skin and thin lips give no hint of Jewish or Palestinian heritage.

What is beauty? Is it the perfect specimen of a woman in the twenty-first century? The truism begins with Eve: *Beauty is in the eye of the beholder*. In the eyes of Adam, she was beautiful. Sarah, Rebekah, and Rachel were deemed beautiful apparently by any ancient standard. Delilah was a beauty in a trashy sort of way. Abigail was not only beautiful but also intelligent. Vashti and Esther, we will see, were both beautiful, though Esther is the first person we meet with her own personal beauty consultant. But after her story, the beautiful Bible woman disappears, except for the idealized woman in the Song of Songs.

> **Beauty and the Bible**
>
> It is interesting to note that the word "beauty" is not found in the New Testament and that "beautiful" is found only 4 times in it. "Beautiful" is found 19 times and "beauty" is found 49 times in the Old Testament. "Beauties" is found once and "beautify" is found 3 times in the Old Testament.
>
> Howard E. Wright, "What Does the Bible Say About Beauty?"

In the New Testament women are regarded more for their inner beauty and ministry than for their appearance. Proverbs 31:30 (perhaps Bathsheba's own Proverbs 31?) is apparently taken to heart: "Charm is deceptive, and beauty is fleeting; but a woman who fears the LORD is to be praised." In fact, not one of the many named women in the Gospels, Acts, or the Epistles of Paul is described as beautiful.

Bathsheba

As a name for baby girls, *Bathsheba* ranks low, number 14,856 in 2012. Only three in a million, some nameless statistician tells us, were given the same name as this biblical woman. The name Abigail ranked number 12. Ahinoam didn't rank at all.[2] But imagine naming your baby Bathsheba. It's more than a name; it's a label she would carry the rest of her life.

They say it's a wonderful time of the year: springtime in Jerusalem. It could almost be a song title. But in the biblical world it is "the time when kings go off to war."[3] Bathsheba is personally well aware of that. She has said good-bye to her soldier husband, Uriah, only days (or maybe weeks) earlier. And she has probably heard through the grapevine that King David has remained back in Jerusalem for this springtime season of carnage. In fact, his palace is close by, and she may have seen him in the early evening taking a walk on the elevated roof of the palace.

It's a warm evening, and we imagine her going outside to bathe, perhaps in her backyard or maybe on the roof of her own home. She stretches and washes and luxuriates in the fragrant bath oils. If Uriah were home, he would be panting by now, putty in her hands. But he's not. She yearns for a man's strong arms, especially when her own muscles are tight with imaginings of war—of corpses and limbless bodies and bloody battles that never seem to serve any real purpose. Her mind goes to David, how he paces the roof and gazes out over his city and off beyond the horizon where his men are fighting. He's probably as tense as she is. She turns her breasts toward the palace, slowly stroking her underarms and thighs. She's in no hurry.

Is she seductively displaying herself in full view of King David? Or is he a voyeur? The text does not say. All it tells us is that he sees a *very* beautiful woman bathing and sends someone to ask who she might be. It turns out she is Bathsheba, wife of Uriah the Hittite, who is off fighting in the springtime war. David sends a message to her, requesting that she meet him at the palace. She does.

An Interesting Profile of Bathsheba

Almost every painter who ever painted the story of Bathsheba chose the moment when David spied on her while she was bathing. But not Rembrandt in this case. His choice fell on the moment of Bathsheba's dilemma: should she obey the king's command—and that weighed heavily in those days—or should she stay faithful to her husband? From her troubled expression it looks as if she already senses the suffering that will result from her decision: the death of her husband, God's reproaches which the Prophet Nathan would pour forth upon David, the death of the first child she was to bear David. X-rays have revealed that at first Bathsheba held her head up more confidently. Only later did Rembrandt choose to make her bow her head in troubled contemplation.

"Bathsheba at Her Bath, 1654 by Rembrandt"

Bathsheba is well connected. She's the daughter of Eliam, no mere schlep. He is one of David's "Thirty,"[4] an elite force—the Navy Seals of ancient Israel. Eliam's own father is, in fact, one of David's top military advisers. Why would David ever become involved with a woman with such important connections? Has he begun to believe his own press releases?

She spends a night, maybe more. She may not have been ovulating on the first night they jumped into bed together. The text tells us, albeit in parentheses, that on that momentous evening she had been "purifying herself from her monthly uncleanness";[5] thus ovulation may have occurred some days later. ("When a woman has her regular flow of blood, the impurity of her monthly period will last seven days.")[6] When she does recognize the seriousness of the situation, perhaps after missing only one period, she sends a terse message to David: "I am pregnant."[7]

No. It can't be true. David's heart pounds. Bathsheba is a married woman, and not to just anyone. Her husband is one of his most faithful soldiers—a mighty man of war. Bathsheba pregnant? This can't be happening. David is stunned beyond words. Only rage and terror. But whatever shocking expletive that erupts from his mind will soon slither as a serpent into a strategy for murder.

All Bathsheba can do is wait. David is the one who initiated this tryst, and now he needs to come up with a solution. Barely a week goes by, and she hears that Uriah has unexpectedly returned to Jerusalem. Strange. It's springtime, the season of war. He should be fighting. *Okay*, she thinks, *so this is David's solution.* Uriah will be coming through the door any minute eager to make love, and the baby will be his.

We imagine her taking long baths, perfuming herself, baking bread in an apron only. She waits. Thinking he'll slip in at night; she sleeps naked with a candle and a jar of Bordeaux on the lamp stand. The hours drag. Then word comes that he's refusing to darken her door. Has he heard something? Why would he not even stop by to check in on her? The next thing she hears is that he's been sent back to the front lines.

But why did he purposely avoid her? Turns out that her husband is simply a decent man behaving as a faithful soldier should. In fact, she learns later that David had tried every trick to lure her husband to his own house, but he had refused to go. How could he possibly enjoy a furlough

---

Military Letters

From David to Joab: "Put Uriah out in front where the fighting is fiercest. Then withdraw from him so he will be struck down and die."

From Joab to David: "The men overpowered us and came out against us in the open, but we drove them back to the entrance of the city gate. Then the archers shot arrows at your servants from the wall, and some of the king's men died. Moreover, your servant Uriah the Hittite is dead."

2 Samuel 11:15, 23–24

---

of eating, drinking, and lovemaking while his comrades are risking their lives on the battlefield?

Bathsheba broods. Uriah's a good man. She's really gotten herself in a fix. No word from David. She despairs. He'll deny everything, and she'll be great with child for the whole world to see. What a disgrace to her family and her faithful husband.

Each day finds her in knots. The nights are long with worry. She dusts and sweeps and mends, tends the fire and paces the floor. Then there's a knock. She cautiously opens the door. Two men in military garb. She listens, but she can't take it in. They're sorry. They're deeply sorry. The king has been notified. They take their leave. She's numb.

The hours and days that follow are a blur. She properly mourns in public and inwardly weeps dry tears of guilt and loss. Uriah is dead. Neighbors still come with casseroles, but she can't eat. She hasn't bathed in weeks. Her hair is matted, her gown soiled. The smell of regret makes her nauseous—worse than morning sickness. She's got to pull herself out of this at least for the sake of the baby.

She would have had no way of knowing what sort of underworld crime the king had concocted. But in the back of her mind suspicions linger. They will all say her little one looks just like Uriah, but she will know otherwise. There's no one to talk to. Perhaps she will seek out the prophet Nathan. He's a man of God with a sympathetic ear.

Her period of mourning is coming to a close. Her waistline is expanding. A message comes from David. He has remembered. This isn't a one-night stand after all. She no doubt has mixed emotions, but she packs up her bags and moves to the palace.

Palace living is not all it's cracked up to be. How many wives? How many queens? Where is she in the pecking order? She may be high on David's list, but among the other wives and concubines and servants, there is seething resentment. Who is she to just show up with a big belly and assume she has David's ear—and bed? She'll find out soon enough that the role of queen is surely no picnic.

But Bathsheba, we can imagine, is struggling with more than petty squabbles in the palace. Alone in her bed at night, does she ever cry herself to sleep thinking about Uriah? He was an honorable man, one of the very few she had ever known. He loved her and was faithful. Why did she ever get entangled with David? Why?

Her due date is now approaching. David is attentive, desperately hoping for a son. Doesn't he have enough sons already? But she too wants a son, a badge of honor for any woman in the ancient world. It's not an easy labor, but David is ecstatic. A healthy bouncing baby boy? No, he seems sickly. Bathsheba nurses her little one, and the bond of maternal love that had begun months earlier is now becoming so fierce it's almost scary. She has never known such love.

Then, with no warning from her nurse, she realizes something's seriously wrong. Her little one is not responding to her nipple. For seven days the baby hovers between life and death. David is weeping and crying out to God, throwing himself on the ground, refusing to eat. Bathsheba is worried sick, rocking the baby in her arms. And then he's gone, just like that.

She has known her little one for such a very short while, and she'll have more children in due time. She's still young. God gives and God takes away. That's life. It's sad, but she'll get over it. How easy it is sometimes for people to make stupid judgments. Everyone grieves in her own way, but for most mothers there's never a *getting over* the loss of a child. She will grieve until the day she dies.

For David it is different; his lament in sackcloth and ashes ends the moment news comes that the baby is dead. He had sought to change God's mind, but to no avail. Now it is over, and he can go right on with his life.

To his credit, "David comforted his wife Bathsheba" in her deep sorrow. Sometime later, "he went to her and made love to her. She gave birth to a son, and they named him Solomon."[8] But no sooner have they named him than

173

word comes from the prophet Nathan that the baby should be named Jedidiah, meaning "friend of God," a name never used elsewhere in the entire Bible.

That Nathan would interfere with the naming of the baby boy is most curious. David had only recently been called on the carpet by this bold prophet. Had Bathsheba known about that? Had she learned from either one of them how Nathan had accosted David about his sin? Nathan was sly. He had begun the conversation with a parable: A rich man who has all the sheep and cattle anyone could want seizes the one and only beloved little lamb belonging to a poor man and roasts it for dinner to feed his guest.

David had been irate. The rich man "must die," either that or "pay for that lamb four times over." Nathan had shot back: "You are the man!" David had been startled, but Nathan didn't blink an eye. He had reminded David of all that God had given him as king over Israel—all his wealth and wives. And what had he done in return? He had stolen a little lamb from his faithful soldier. "You struck down Uriah the Hittite with the sword," Nathan had railed, "and took his wife to be your own. You killed him with the sword of the Ammonites."[9]

Does Bathsheba know that Nathan took David to the woodshed? Does she know that David killed her faithful husband? Does she know that the death of her beloved baby is punishment for David's sin? For Bathsheba, it would have been a heavy burden to carry. She is married to this man—a murderer. Another baby boy brings her joy, but beneath the surface there surely is sadness.

David is good with words, and he pleads for God's forgiveness:

> Have mercy on me, O God,
>   according to your unfailing love;
> according to your great compassion
>   blot out my transgressions.
> Wash away all my iniquity
>   and cleanse me from my sin. . . .
> Create in me a pure heart, O God,
>   and renew a steadfast spirit within me.[10]

David is a man after God's own heart. Bathsheba is merely one of his many wives. Actually, she is a lot more than just another wife. She is the mother of Solomon as well as three other sons, the second of whom is named—should we be surprised—Nathan. But her role as mother of Solomon (a.k.a. Jedidiah) is one that allows our imaginations to soar.

It is fair to assume that she was a significant power behind David's throne even before he became gravely ill in old age. In fact, the text offers a fascinating glimpse of this old man who needs more than Bathsheba, now getting on in years herself. Was a beautiful maiden needed to rouse him sexually and improve his circulation?

> When King David was very old, he could not keep warm even when they put covers over him. So his attendants said to him, "Let us look for a young virgin to serve the king and take care of him. She can lie beside him so that our lord the king may keep warm."
> Then they searched throughout Israel for a beautiful young woman and found Abishag, a Shunammite, and brought her to the king. The woman was very beautiful; she took care of the king and waited on him, but the king had no sexual relations with her.[11]

Bathsheba has too many court duties to be lying abed with her husband keeping him warm. She knows David is very near death, and she knows he has other sons who will be vying for the throne, most notably Adonijah, Solomon's half brother. In fact, even while King David is on his deathbed, Adonijah has pronounced himself his father's successor. He "put himself forward and said, 'I will be king.' So he got chariots and horses ready, with fifty men to run ahead of him."[12] With Joab and other big names falling in behind him, he can hardly wait to hear the news that the old man is dead.

Bathsheba is not taking this lying down. She consults with the prophet Nathan, who encourages her to go straight to the king. Had she simply gone to him, without Nathan's support, she might have been regarded as an intruder, just another one of David's wives. Having a star prophet in her camp is critical. Here we have the words of Bathsheba herself:

> My lord, you yourself swore to me your servant by the LORD your God: "Solomon your son shall be king after me, and he will sit on my throne." But now Adonijah has become king, and you, my lord the king, do not know about it. He has sacrificed great numbers of cattle, fattened calves,

175

and sheep, and has invited all the king's sons, Abiathar the priest and Joab the commander of the army, but he has not invited Solomon your servant. My lord the king, the eyes of all Israel are on you, to learn from you who will sit on the throne of my lord the king after him. Otherwise, as soon as my lord the king is laid to rest with his ancestors, I and my son Solomon will be treated as criminals.[13]

Right on cue, Nathan arrives at the door. As Bathsheba exits, he enters. Nathan repeats Bathsheba's talking points—same little speech almost word for word. So David sends for Bathsheba, who we suppose is eavesdropping from behind the door. David makes an oath to her that Solomon indeed is the designated prince to ascend the throne. "Then Bathsheba bowed down with her face to the ground, prostrating herself before the king, and said, 'May my lord King David live forever!'"[14]

Bathsheba's power behind the throne is evident when Solomon, riding a mule (no horse and chariots), makes his way to Gihon accompanied by Nathan and Zadok the priest and other important dignitaries. Why not anoint him king in the palace? The text does not say, but Gihon Spring was the major water source for Jerusalem. As such, it was close to the palace and was a setting with great symbolic significance.

After Solomon is anointed with oil, the trumpeter sounds the announcement of a new king, and the people shout, *Long live King Solomon!* In fact, a flash crowd assembles and makes so much noise with their pipes and voices that the ground actually shakes beneath them. We can imagine Bathsheba looking out her window with mixed emotions. Her husband is dying in the room next door, while her son is crowned king in the distance.

Solomon's reign is remembered for ostentatious luxury, and his mother would live on to enjoy the perks. That he would acquire a thousand wives and concubines must have upset her. But his reputation for wisdom and encyclopedic knowledge in many fields is what truly set him apart, and it is likely that she played an important role in his education.

While it is true that Solomon's wisdom was granted as a special favor from God, his many interests may have been encouraged by his mother from a young age. There was nothing, according to the biblical text, that escaped his interests: botany, zoology, ornithology, herpetology, ichthyology, astrology, musicology, and a wide variety of other specialties. He wrote more than a thousand songs and some three thousand proverbs.

In fact, Bathsheba may have been the voice behind the words of Proverbs 31, under the name of King Lemuel. This passage describing the ideal woman is identified as "an inspired utterance his mother taught him."[15] But before describing the "wife of noble character," the mother warns her son about spending his "strength on women" (advice he obviously didn't heed) or alcohol.[16] Then she goes on with the best advice a ruler could ever receive:

> Speak up for those who cannot speak for themselves,
>   for the rights of all who are destitute.
> Speak up and judge fairly;
>   defend the rights of the poor and needy.[17]

What an incredible testimony this is to a mother's effort to influence her own influential son. More than all the book learning she could have passed on to him, this plea for him to care for the poor will centuries later parallel the words of Jesus.

Concluding Observations

Perhaps it should not surprise us that what are apparently Bathsheba's words in Proverbs 31 sound so similar to the words of Jesus. Her concern for the poor could almost make us think that she was a follower of Jesus himself. She was not, but she was a great-great-grandmother many times removed. We find her in the genealogy of Jesus, though sadly not by name. Her son is there: "Solomon, whose mother had been Uriah's wife."[18]

It is difficult to assess Bathsheba as we are initially introduced to her. Is she aware that David will see her while she is bathing? It's hard to imagine that she is completely innocent. Furthermore, when he calls for her, she could have sent word back that she is a married woman and thus cannot spend the night with him. David's guilt is clearly evident. Hers is not. But we cannot let her entirely off the hook.

After her faithful husband, Uriah, is ordered killed by David, his own commander in chief, Bathsheba becomes another one of David's wives.

She might have gotten lost in the polygamous crowd, but she does not. She works behind the scenes preparing her oldest son to succeed his father. With a vow from David and loyal support from the prophet Nathan, she carries out one of the biggest coups in history.

She stands alone as David's most prominent and influential wife, as King Solomon's fiercest and most loyal defender, and as the unnamed wife of Uriah in the genealogy of Jesus. Yet her reputation is forever marred. She is more often associated with the trashy Delilah than Queen Esther. David becomes the daring and darling hero of the Bible, while Bathsheba is easily pushed out of polite company. Such a dismissal of her is wrong, and we dare not let it stand.

Questions to Think About

How do you assess Bathsheba? Would she be welcome to participate with other mothers in local school functions? Do you think that women are judged more harshly for sexual sins than men in biblical times? Today?

Are we too easily attracted to men with flair? Are we enamored with the Davids while ignoring the Uriahs? Uriah the Hittite may have been a descendant of Esau and one of his Hittite wives whom Rebekah so disliked. Again, do we easily overlook the good, solid men like Esau while idolizing the wily Jacobs?

Put yourself in Bathsheba's shoes. Could you have willingly become the wife of a charismatic ruler like David, knowing he is a murderer? Do you assume Bathsheba did not suspect David of murdering her husband?

How would you rank Bathsheba as a woman, wife, and mother alongside Sarah and Rebekah? Does the Bible reveal her story as openly as it does theirs? Which one of the three would you most want to spend time with?

Does a wife ever fully get over the death of a husband? Does a mother ever get over the death of a child, even a small child or a baby miscarried before birth? Does the story of David and Bathsheba speak to us on gender differences and this kind of grief?

How much should a mother become involved in paving the way for the success of a child? Should a mother work behind the scenes like Bathsheba did? Rather, should a mother avoid interfering and playing the role of stage mother?

15

Jezebel, Athaliah, and Huldah

Strong Voices for Baal and for God

Who, more than any other person, personifies pure wickedness? Hitler? Stalin? Pol Pot? For me, on a more personal level, Ed Gein stands alone. I was in middle school when he made headlines. Though he lived on the edge of a small town in Wisconsin some two hundred miles south of our farm west of Spooner, and though he was in custody when I first heard his name, he scared me witless. He was a serial killer, specializing in women. That in itself is not so rare. His madness, however, had a unique twist. He hung the bodies up on meat hooks, their torsos "dressed out" like a deer. With their skin he upholstered his furniture, and he boiled the heart and other organs for eating.

It was late autumn of 1957, and my older brother had recently left home for college. I had taken his job of milking our twenty dairy cows each evening, now dark with the hours of daylight growing shorter. The barn was dimly lit, shadows everywhere. There were a thousand places where Ed Gein might be hiding—and that was inside the barn alone. He could be lurking outside in the nearby woods or behind the chicken coop or in a corncrib.

I'd like to say my fears subsided in the months that followed, but there is a sense in which Ed Gein, now dead for more than thirty years, still haunts me. Imagine how I would feel if my own mother or aunt had been one of his victims.

Women do not factor significantly as serial killers or as evil dictators, except perhaps Marie Antoinette. But unless we are historians or read historical fiction, most of us know little about her. And some argue that her reputation as an evil queen is more myth than fact. Jezebel more easily comes to mind. A *Jezebel* is a synonym for an evil woman.

To understand Jezebel, however, we must go back to Bathsheba and her son Solomon. Wise man that he was, he was unfaithful to Yahweh in his worship of other gods. His acquisition of so many wives and concubines was certainly not for sex alone. The wives were first and foremost political trophies from neighboring kingdoms, and they brought with them their gods—gods who in time were acknowledged by Solomon himself.

It was Solomon's intention for his son Rehoboam to be his successor, and he would be, but only over Judah, the southern half of what would become the divided kingdom. One of Solomon's trusted officials, Jeroboam, had rebelled and became king of Israel, the ten northern tribes of the divided kingdom. He is forever remembered as *the son of Nebat who made Israel to sin*. God allowed this division because of Solomon's unfaithfulness. The prophet Ahijah made this clear in his prophecy to Jeroboam.

> See, I am going to tear the kingdom out of Solomon's hand and give you ten tribes. But for the sake of my servant David and the city of Jerusalem, which I have chosen out of all the tribes of Israel, he [Rehoboam] will have one tribe. I will do this because they have forsaken me and worshiped Ashtoreth the goddess of the Sidonians, Chemosh the god of the Moabites, and Molek the god of the Ammonites, and have not walked in obedience to me, nor done what is right in my eyes, nor kept my decrees and laws as David, Solomon's father, did.[1]

Solomon died after ruling forty years over a united kingdom. Fast-forward more than fifty years and we find Ahab reigning as the seventh king in the northern kingdom of Israel. During the more than half century since Jeroboam, Israel's kings had not seen a straight line of succession from father to son. Ahab, however, was the son of King Omri (who had succeeded King Zimri, whose seven-day reign ended with his suicide).

Ahab and Jezebel's son Ahaziah would succeed Ahab, and after Ahaziah died of accidental injuries, Joram (another son of Ahab and Jezebel) would ascend the throne. He would reign until he was overthrown by Jehu, thus ending the *house of Omri* and Jezebel's influence over Israel. No biblical queen has ever reached a higher rank of notoriety than she. Her daughter Athaliah, also a Baal worshiper, would reign as a wicked queen over Judah, but would never rise to the name recognition of Jezebel.

During the reign of Ahab and Jezebel, the prophet Elijah railed against their worship of Baal. In fact, prophets came and went during the reigns of the kings of Israel and Judah. Only one stands out for her gender: Huldah, who spoke for God in King Josiah's reign during the renovation of Solomon's temple. The Bible makes reference to other women during this era, including three nameless mothers who interacted with Elijah and Elisha.

Jezebel

She is a princess, daughter of King Ethbaal, who reigns over Sidonia (including the coastal cities of Tyre and Sidon), another name for Phoenicia. It is an advanced and very important kingdom, known for its great sailing vessels, shrewd merchants, and lucrative trade throughout the Mediterranean world. In fact, more than three hundred years before Jezebel was born, the proficient Phoenician sailors were the first to use the North Star for navigation and the first to sail around Africa, bringing along with them their functional twenty-two-letter alphabet, a precursor of the Latin alphabet.

According to Josephus, Ethbaal had been a priest of the goddess Asherah (consort to Baal), but he switched careers by usurping the throne of the Phoenician ruler and went on to reign for more than three decades. Jezebel then is anything but an untamed wild woman or an ugly old hag. We can imagine her as a highly educated, cultured, classy, rich girl—spoiled rotten. She gets everything she wants—except that she is handed over in a politically arranged marriage to a Jewish king in a backwater realm.

Back in the day, several decades earlier, Solomon's kingdom had been the glory of the known world. Now it is divided, and Ahab could hardly be considered a dream-come-true for a sophisticated Phoenician princess. And why would Ahab want to marry her? Could it be that he wants easy access to some of the world's busiest ports?

No sooner are they married than Jezebel insists that Ahab build a temple with an altar to Baal, and that he join her in worship. To us it's utterly blasphemous, but for Jezebel that would have been a standard provision in the prenup. She would have found Asherah and Baal far more appealing than the stern Yahweh. She had grown up with the explicit sex and fertility rituals associated with Asherah. And Baal was primarily a weather deity called upon for sunshine and rain. With a husband who is less than faithful to Yahweh, why should she convert? It would not have been expected. Besides, the leading preacher of the day, the prophet Elijah, is hardly reaching out to her in friendship evangelism.

It is only natural for her to bring prophets and priestesses with her to her new kingdom of Israel. To please her, Ahab also provides her with an Asherah pole and does more to "arouse the anger of the LORD, the God of Israel, than did all the kings of Israel before him."[2] As for Jezebel, as soon as she is securely in power, she begins killing the prophets of Yahweh. As such, we regard her an evil woman, though killing prophets of opposing religions was not a practice she invented.

It is true, however, that Jezebel is unusually loyal to her religion. When Elijah orders Ahab to summon 450 prophets of Baal to meet him at Mount Carmel for a showdown, he stipulates, in addition, "the four hundred prophets of Asherah, who eat at Jezebel's table."[3] This may have been a sarcastic remark since it is doubtful that Jezebel was hosting that many dinner guests. But his remark is telling.

The face-off at Mount Carmel ends in a triumph for God and Elijah. Jezebel doesn't attend, but she quickly hears about the loss and the aftermath: "Now Ahab told Jezebel everything Elijah had done and how he had killed all the prophets [of Baal] with the sword." Jezebel's fury has no bounds. To Elijah she shoots off a message: "May the gods deal with me, be it ever so severely, if by this time tomorrow I do not make your life like that of one of them."[4]

She is not playing games. Elijah knows it, and he runs for his life. In fact, he is so well hidden that not even Jezebel and her scouts can find him.

Jezebel in Jerusalem Today

"Jezebel, Jezebel, fornicating under the walls of God's holy city!" The words intruded into what had been, until that moment, a beautiful Jerusalem spring morning. I'd been walking peaceably along when I was suddenly confronted by this irate, shabbily dressed stranger who seemed to have appeared out of nowhere. . . . To judge by his grandiose phrasing, I was being denounced to both heaven and earth—or at least as far as the walls of the Old City, where he trailed me, ranting and raving all the way. . . . Never mind that the real Jezebel had never set foot in Jerusalem. . . . This true believer had seen a secular woman whose long-sleeved shirt and jeans hid nothing from his righteous vision. I was flaunting myself in public, a shameless hussy inflaming his basest desires by my mere presence. In his mind, I could only be another Jezebel out to pollute holiness.

Lesley Hazleton, *Jezebel*

In the meantime, Ahab is doing battle with King Ben-Hadad of Aram. Twice he is victorious, but in the end, instead of killing Ben-Hadad, he agrees to a treaty. God is not pleased. He sends a prophet to Ahab with an ominous message: "This is what the LORD says: 'You have set free a man I had determined should die. Therefore it is your life for his life, your people for his people.'"[5] It would be an understatement to say that Ahab is upset when he returns to his palace. Unlike Jezebel, he fully understands the power of Yahweh.

Ahab will soon come to a bitter end but not before the *vineyard incident*. Here the very different upbringings of Ahab and Jezebel are most clearly observed. Ahab wants Naboth's vineyard in the worst way. It's close by the palace, and he wants to grow some vegetables. But Naboth doesn't want to trade or sell even at a good price; it happens to be the land of his ancestors, and that means more to him than money. So Ahab goes home despondent and won't eat. What is noteworthy is that, though he is upset, he accepts the verdict.

Not so Jezebel. She's going to get what she wants, come hell or high water. When she learns what is bothering her husband, she promises to take care of it, and she does. She forges letters in Ahab's name with his seal and sends them to the leading citizens:

Proclaim a day of fasting and seat Naboth in a prominent place among the people. But seat two scoundrels opposite him and have them bring charges that he has cursed both God and the king. Then take him out and stone him to death.[6]

Jezebel's scheme works, and Ahab gets his garden plot. Sounds reminiscent of David, who, rather than for a vineyard, killed a man for a woman. As with David, who is dressed down by Nathan, Ahab is denounced by Elijah, who shows up at the vineyard with a dire message from God: "'Have you not murdered a man and seized his property? . . . In the place where dogs licked up Naboth's blood, dogs will lick up your blood—yes, yours!' . . . And also concerning Jezebel the LORD says: 'Dogs will devour Jezebel by the wall of Jezreel.'"[7] Death comes to everyone, but in ancient times having one's body treated in such an ignominious manner is virtually equivalent to a double death.

> **Israel, Apostasy, and Prophets**
>
> The northern kingdom of Israel became a symbol in the Hebrew Bible of apostasy and faithlessness, as her kings and people abandoned faith in the Hebrew God and turned to idols and the worship of the forces of nature. It was often to the northern kings that the great prophets, the so-called "conscience of Israel" were dispatched to recall them to the faith of their ancestors. Men such as Amos and Hosea were among the witnesses to the Hebrew God whose words are preserved in the Bible.
>
> Gregory Elder, "Ahab and Jezebel, One of the Bible's Most 'Colorful' Couples"

But that is not all Elijah has to say. God, he thunders, will bring down all of Ahab's descendants. This is a serious penalty, especially if Ahab had known nothing about his wife's plot. Whatever the case, he tears his clothes, wears sackcloth, and humbles himself before God. For that show of sorrow, God temporarily delays the disasters. But Ahab soon thereafter does die a violent death in battle and dogs do lick up his blood.

Though the text does not specifically say, we assume that Jezebel mourns his death. She now becomes queen mother as her son Ahaziah ascends the throne and worships Baal during his two-year reign, cut short due to a fall through the lattice of an upper palace room. Jezebel grieves once again. Now her other son, Joram, becomes king. His reign extends for twelve years, during which time he turns against the religion of his mother and rids the land of its shrines to Baal.

But in other ways, Joram is essentially as wicked as the kings before him. His reign ends quickly, after the prophet Elisha pegs Jehu as the next

185

king. Jehu ends up killing the king with an arrow—in the very vineyard for which his mother had conspired to kill Naboth.

And now Jezebel is the only one of the family who is left, but not for long. The new king Jehu heads for the palace, Jezebel having already heard he was on the way. Proud to the very end, she is getting herself gussied up with makeup and hair combs when he rides into town. She yells down to him, calling him a murderer and wondering if he has come in peace. He looks up and demands to know whether her eunuchs are on his side. They apparently nod because he then orders them to hurl her down into the street. They do just that. Her blood spatters, and she is trampled underfoot by horses.

> Jehu went in and ate and drank. "Take care of that cursed woman," he said, "and bury her, for she was a king's daughter." But when they went out to bury her, they found nothing except her skull, her feet and her hands. They went back and told Jehu, who said, "This is the word of the Lord that he spoke through his servant Elijah the Tishbite: On the plot of ground at Jezreel dogs will devour Jezebel's flesh. Jezebel's body will be like dung on the ground in the plot at Jezreel, so that no one will be able to say, 'This is Jezebel.'"[8]

It is not until after her death that we even learn that Jezebel has a daughter, Athaliah. During her reign as queen of Judah, the names of the kings easily become mixed up in our minds. Jehoram is also called Joram, and there is another Joram who is king of Judah, and there are two kings named Ahiziah, one a son of Ahab and Jezebel and another a son of Athaliah, grandson of Ahab and Jezebel. So we plod on with caution.

Athaliah

Jezebel's story is straightforward and easily understood in comparison to that of Athaliah, her daughter. Or was she her sister-in-law? Biblical scholars continue to argue over dates and the meaning of the Hebrew term for *daughter*. Was she Ahab's sister or daughter—or daughter by a wife other than Jezebel? (Jezebel's flamboyant claim to the stage easily obscures the presence of other wives.)

For our purposes, Athaliah is the daughter of Jezebel, with Ahab perhaps a distracted and distant father. Yes, we picture her *all* Jezebel, though perhaps not enjoying cultural and educational opportunities so easily accessible as to her mother growing up in Phoenicia. Jezreel, where the palace is located, is a fortress city with little influence from Egypt and other ancient cultural centers.

Following in the footsteps of her mother, she is an ardent worshiper of Baal. We know nothing of her childhood, though she may have been little more than a child when she is married to Jehoram, king of Judah, for political purposes. Her father, Ahab, remember, is king of the northern kingdom; her new husband, king of the southern kingdom. This alliance should not surprise us. Although Israel and Judah have been enemies, they have periodically also been allies. But this is the first significant instance of intermarriage between the opposing dynasties.

The biblical text offers no details on how this marriage was arranged. Jehoram's father, Jehoshaphat, had allied with Ahab in his battles with Ben-Hadad, and the marriage of their children seemed to follow naturally. Jehoshaphat is rated by many biblical scholars as a good king, except for his arranging the marriage of his son with Ahab and Jezebel's daughter, Athaliah.

Jehoram descends to the depths of evil that might even have caused Jezebel to wince, though apparently not Athaliah. Once he has established himself securely on the throne, he orders the murder of all his brothers. But his reign, not surprisingly, is filled with turmoil. After eight years, he dies of a serious abdominal affliction: "his bowels came out."[9]

His older sons having also been killed off, he is succeeded by their young-est brother, Ahaziah, twenty-two, son of Athaliah. "He too followed the ways of the house of Ahab, for his mother encouraged him to act wick-edly."[10] He reigns only one year before he is killed, and that sets the stage for his mother to take over the throne of the southern kingdom. The murder of her son had taken place during his state visit to the palace of the late King Ahab (her father). The murderer? Jehu, usurper of the throne who had killed Jezebel and his rival Joram.

Back in Judah, Athaliah thus becomes its first female monarch. What is her first line of action as ruler? Does she expand welfare for widows? Does she open educational opportunities for girls? Not Athaliah. She "proceeded to destroy the whole royal family of the house of Judah."[11] It is a bloody reaction to what has just happened up north, and it is the only way she has of securing the throne of Judah.

Very little is known about her reign except that after six years her own life ends in bloodshed. It is a story of intrigue. Unbeknown to her, Jehosheba, the daughter of her husband (by another wife), had hidden the infant son of her brother Ahaziah (the murdered son of Athaliah). For six years he grows up secretly in the temple. But then in the seventh year of her reign, the priest Jehoiada, nephew of Jehosheba, stages a coup, kills Queen Athaliah, and establishes the seven-year-old Joash on the throne.

That she had managed to reign for more than six years suggests that Athaliah was a shrewd and perhaps even popular monarch. By today's standards, she would be considered open-minded for her religious tolerance—worship of both Baal and Yahweh. But in the minds of many students of Scripture, she was worse than the other bad kings; in fact one list of *bad* and *good* kings describes her uniquely as *devilish*.[12]

Huldah

A prophet by profession, Huldah makes her home in the New Quarter of Jerusalem, a development not far from the Fish Gate, northwest of the old town. She is married to Shallum, whose grandfather had the distinction of being "keeper of the wardrobe."[13] Josiah is now sitting on the throne.

King Josiah began his reign as king over Judah some two centuries after the reign of Athaliah and is considered by some to be the best king of Judah since David. He was preceded by his father and grandfather, who were among the worst. In fact, his grandfather King Manasseh "shed so much innocent blood that he filled Jerusalem from end to end."[14]

Josiah begins his reign at eight years old and carries on for more than thirty years, during which time he orders the repair of the temple. In the process, the high priest finds the Book of the Law. It has apparently been collecting dust for centuries, and its discovery is big news. He passes it on to the king's secretary, who delivers it to the king and reads from it. Josiah is beside himself and tears his clothes. He then sends out an important delegation, including his secretary and the high priest, to discern what all this means.

> ### Huldah Consulted over Jeremiah
>
> Josiah does not seem to have told his messengers where to go; but they knew, and went straight to a very unlikely person, the wife of an obscure man, only known as his father's son. Where was Jeremiah of Anathoth? Perhaps not in the city at the time. There had been prophetesses in Israel before. Miriam, Deborah, the wife of Isaiah, are instances of "your daughters" prophesying; and this embassy to Huldah is in full accord with the high position which women held in that state, of which the framework was shaped by God Himself. In Christ Jesus "there is neither male nor female," and Judaism approximated much more closely to that ideal than other lands did.
>
> Alexander Maclaren, "Josiah and the Newly Found Law"

So all five of them head straight to the New Quarter to find the prophet Huldah.

We can just imagine her in the middle of her afternoon nap being roused by the *fabulous five* standing on her doorstep. After they explain their mission, she doesn't hesitate a minute before breaking out in prophecy. After the standard first line, "this is what the LORD says," she gets down to business:

> I am going to bring disaster on this place and its people, according to everything written in the book the king of Judah has read. Because they have forsaken me and burned incense to other gods and aroused my anger by all the idols their hands have made, my anger will burn against this place and will not be quenched. . . . This is what the LORD, the God of Israel, says concerning the words you heard: Because your heart was responsive and you humbled yourself before the LORD when you heard what I have spoken against this place and its people—that they would become a curse and be laid waste—and because you tore your robes and wept in my presence, I also have heard you, declares the LORD. Therefore I will gather you to your ancestors, and you will be buried in peace. Your eyes will not see all the disaster I am going to bring on this place.[15]

So, despite the scary introduction to Huldah's prophecy, the news the five bring back to the king turns out to be good. He cleans house and gets rid of all the false gods, and Huldah is never heard from again—at least in the pages of Scripture.

The Widow at Zarephath

She is just another unnamed woman in the Bible. She lives near the gate in the town of Zarephath, a place far to the north along the shore of the Mediterranean Sea. A widow with a young son, together they have endured a prolonged famine. She's out picking up sticks one day when she hears a stranger call out to her asking for a drink of water. She might have said, *Excuse me? Who are you talking to?* But, hospitable as she is, she turns around to get him water only to hear him call after her for a slice of bread as well. Now he has her attention. "As surely as the LORD your God lives," she retorts, "I don't have any bread." She's from outside the land of Israel, but she can spot an Israelite in a second. *Your God* is the one she swears by. She goes on to explain—perhaps bitterly—that she has "only a handful of flour in a jar and a little olive oil in a jug," which she has saved to make a final meal for herself and her son "that we may eat it—and die."[16]

The stranger, who turns out to be Elijah, tells her to make him a small loaf of bread and bring it to him, and then do the same for herself and her son. God, he continues, will give her enough flour and oil for all three of them until the rains return.

Later on when her son becomes very ill and dies, the woman berates Elijah: "What do you have against me, man of God? Did you come to remind me of my sin and kill my son?"[17]

The prophet takes the boy up to his bedroom. She waits, nerves on edge. He's her only child. *What's going on up there?* The minutes seem like hours. She paces the floor. And then he appears, the boy in his arms. He's alive. He's breathing again. His breath is to her the breath of God: "Now I know that you are a man of God and that the word of the LORD from your mouth is the truth."[18]

The Shunammite Woman

Unlike the widow of Zarephath, she is a wealthy married woman who admires Elisha, Elijah's successor, as a man of God, and whenever he is in town she invites him for a meal. But she wants to do more. She consults her husband: "I know that this man who often comes our way is a holy

190

man of God. Let's make a small room on the roof and put in it a bed and a table, a chair and a lamp for him. Then he can stay there whenever he comes to us."[19] Now Elisha has his own prophet's chamber, apparently large enough for his servant, Gehazi, as well.

So appreciative is Elisha that he sends Gehazi to ask what he can do for her. She has all the flour and oil she needs. She sends word back that the one thing she most wants is a son. She's still in her prime; the biological clock has not run down. But she's married to an old geezer, and she's simply lost hope. Now, Elisha himself wants to talk with her. She stands in his doorway as he informs her, "About this time next year, . . . you will hold a son in your arms." She's not buying it. "No, my lord!" she protests.[20] *Don't toy with me.*

But wouldn't you know it, she starts missing her periods, and before the year has ended she's nursing a baby boy. What a joy he must be to his parents. But then one day the little tyke goes to the field to be with his father and the hired hands at harvest time. Without warning, he cries out to his father, "My head! My head!" The father tells a servant to carry the boy to his mother. She holds him tight all morning and then his breathing stops.

Imagine her terror—her sense of helplessness. She rushes upstairs, puts the little boy on the bed in the prophet's chamber, then races out calling to her husband for a servant and a donkey so that she can fetch Elisha. Her husband's reaction is inexplicable: "Why go to him today?" he asked. "It's not the New Moon or the Sabbath."[21]

She takes matters into her own hands. She saddles the donkey and orders the servant: "Lead on; don't slow down for me unless I tell you." She comes upon Elisha at Mount Carmel. When he sees her in the distance, he tells Gehazi to run out and inquire if something is wrong. She responds: "Everything is all right."[22] Huh?

She hurries right past the servant on to Elisha and grabs hold of his feet. The servant pushes her away, but Elisha orders him to leave her alone— that she's obviously distraught. Then, knowing she's got his attention, she speaks: "Did I ask you for a son, my lord?" she said. "Didn't I tell you, 'Don't raise my hopes'?"[23]

Elisha hands Gehazi his staff and orders him to run with all his might to her house and lay the staff on the boy's face and bring him back to life.

But she will have none of it. *Don't even try it!* She demands that Elisha come himself. Still hanging on to his feet, she cries out: "As surely as the LORD lives and as you live, I will not leave you."[24]

So Elisha has no choice but to get up and hurry after her. Gehazi arrives first and lays the staff on the boy's face. Nothing. He races back to Elisha to tell him that the boy is still dead. When Elisha arrives, he goes up to his room, where the boy is, and after a time calls down for Gehazi, who reports back to the woman to come fetch her son. "She came in, fell at his feet and bowed to the ground. Then she took her son and went out."[25] And she lives happily ever after. Well, not quite.

Some years later, Elisha tells the woman to move away because God has decreed a seven-year famine. She does and then returns after seven years to find her house and land in foreclosure. She goes to the king for redress, and it just so happens that when she arrives she finds Gehazi there. Indeed, "just as Gehazi was telling the king how Elisha had restored the dead to life, the woman whose son Elisha had brought back to life came to appeal to the king for her house and land."[26]

She confirms Gehazi's testimony and gets her house and land back, plus the income from her land for the past seven years. And there ends the account of the Shunammite woman.

Concluding Observations

When we study women of the Hebrew Bible, we encounter many queens, including Ahinoam (wife of Saul), Michal, Abigail, Ahinoam (of Jezreel), Bathsheba (and other wives of David), Jezebel, Athaliah, Vashti, Esther. Indeed, if the Bible were more politically correct, there would be not just two books of Kings but also 1 and 2 Queens. We want their lives detailed even as their husband's lives are. But alas, we must be satisfied with what we get.

Both Jezebel and Athaliah are regarded as wicked queens, but from our perspective their actual crimes were no worse than those of their male counterparts. Killing those who challenge royal authority is par for the course. Their offense was against God in their worship of Baal. Today, in the name of religious freedom, we are less judgmental.

192

Huldah stands alone. Here she is, receiving a delegation of top officials. And she makes no attempt to demean herself, as we often see with holy women in the historical record. She's no worthless woman. She's a prophet with an attitude. She tells it like it is.

The nameless women are sometimes seen as props for Elijah and Elisha. They are not. They are struggling with real issues, ordinary women—women like us.

Questions to Think About

If you were assigned a partner for a bus tour of Holy Land sites, who would you rather be paired with, Jezebel or Athaliah? What question would you ask first? Which one seems most devoid of redeeming qualities?

Have these two queens been unfairly demonized, or does the Bible give us no other alternative in our assessment of them?

How do you compare the carnage we read about in the Old Testament with that of today? Have you ever known war firsthand or through a loved one? Have you ever known real danger from enemies?

Have you ever been so poor that you needed a prophet's miraculous help? Have you ever been in an area of the world experiencing famine or utter poverty? How do we best respond to such situations?

How does Huldah differ from other female prophets we have previously met? Have any other such prophets been sought out by a delegation of leading men? Does this have anything to say about women in ministry today?

If you were asked to play a role in your local theater for charity and could choose to play either the widow of Zarephath or the Shunammite woman, which one would you pick? Do you see yourself more passive or active as you interact with others?

16

Vashti and Esther

Queens of Persia

Many years ago, soon after I had begun my first teaching position at Grand Rapids School of the Bible and Music, I stopped by the office of student services to pick up the newly minted basketball schedules. One side was emblazoned with the title *Men's Basketball*, the other side *Girls' Basketball*.

What! I did a double take. Something is wrong with this picture—or these titles. The players were the same age, mainly upperclassmen—or should I say, *upperclasspersons*. Why then men and girls? Well, of course, it was no real mystery. This is how most people talked in those days. In fact, when I questioned the *woman* who had formatted the schedules and sent them to the print shop, she was confused by what appeared to be my initial stage of a snit. *That's the way we've always done it*, she responded.

Now the snit was taking form. I had argued such cases before. Okay, if you don't consider these players to be adults, make the titles *Boys'* and *Girls'*. But if one gender gets a manly title, the other should get a womanly one. I'm sure she rolled her eyes after I left, but to get rid of me she assured me that from now on there would be gender equality in the titles. And there was.

If I could have changed a common phrase in marriage ceremonies that easily, I would have done it then and there. In those days (the late seventies), it was common for a minister to say, "I now pronounce you *man and wife*." Now, unless a woman is marrying a boy, who, by virtue of the wedding ceremony, becomes a man, the minister should pronounce them *husband and wife*. There are other aspects of wedding ceremonies I might mention at this point, but I won't.

Having been raised in a family that assumed girls had full equality with boys, I found unacceptable anything that smacked of gender inequality. And it never occurred to me that my mother had anything other than straightforward equality with my father. They were full partners on the family farm.

So, when I read the book of Esther, I easily find myself siding with the Bible's first (and perhaps only) protofeminist. Queen Vashti is the one who stood up against her husband when he sought to demean her. She is a dignified queen, and she deserves honor. Because she will not do the bidding of her drunken husband, he sends her packing and issues a decree against not only her but all the women in the realm.

Esther, by virtue of her beauty, comes along and takes Vashti's place. I surely know that this is all part of God's plan, but nevertheless, my allegiance naturally favors Vashti. She had the self-respect to stand up against a bully, and she suffered for it. Unfortunately, this Persian queen often gets lost in the story of the great Jewish heroine Esther. Indeed, the feast of Purim is celebrated in her honor, forever giving tribute to this woman who saved her people from certain death.

As we are now moving into the era of the exile, we once again need a brief history lesson. Under Saul, David, and Solomon, God's people were united as one nation. Then the nation split into the northern kingdom of Israel and the southern kingdom of Judah, with its capital at Jerusalem.

> **Jewish Tradition of Purim**
>
> Traditionally people would dress up as characters from the Purim story, for example, as Esther or Mordechai. However, nowadays people enjoy dressing up as all manner of different characters: Harry Potter, Batman, wizards, you name it! The tradition of dressing up is based upon the way Esther concealed her Jewish identity. . . . Many synagogues will put on plays (shpiels) that reenact the Purim Story and poke fun at the villain. Most synagogues also host Purim Carnivals.
>
> Ariela Pelaia, "The Jewish Holiday of Purim"

The northern ten tribes of Israel, with the capital in Samaria, carried on under mainly wicked kings for some two centuries until the kingdom was gradually taken over by the Assyrians and eventually assimilated into Assyrian society. These peoples are sometimes referred to as the *Ten Lost Tribes of Israel*.

More than a century after this dispersion of Israel's population, Babylon conquered the southern kingdom of Judah. Many of the Jews were taken into captivity, among them ancestors of Esther. After Babylon fell to the Persian armies, large numbers of Jews returned to rebuild Jerusalem and later the temple. In succeeding generations Jerusalem and the surrounding region would be conquered by Alexander the Great, only to fall under Egyptian control, and then come under Roman domination only decades before the time of Christ. The era of Persian dominance forms the backdrop to the lives of Vashti and Esther.

Queen Vashti

She is married to the most powerful man in the world. Her husband, King Xerxes (son of Darius the Great), rules over a vast Persian empire that stretches from Egypt to India. She lives in the grand palace at Susa and has every luxury money can buy. Is she happy? The text does not say. Studies show, however, that wealthy people, including ones who have suddenly acquired great wealth, are not necessarily happier than those of moderate means. In the 1970s, UCLA economics professor Richard Easterlin identified the "hedonic treadmill" as a psychological condition of always desiring more and more wealth even after great wealth is amassed. Likewise, individuals who acquire lavish assets, whether mansions or cars or jewelry, are rarely satisfied and are as prone to depression as the rest of us. Did great wealth bring happiness to Elvis or Princess Diana or Michael Jackson?

Do great riches bring happiness to Vashti? To Esther? So far we have not detected happiness among the wealthy women of the Bible, including such women as Sarah, Rebekah, Abigail, and Bathsheba. Contrasted with them are downhearted women like Naomi and the widow of Zarephath who are struggling to barely eke out a living. We can imagine, however, that Ruth might have been a happy and cheerful woman. Though widowed and poor,

196

she put her relationship with Naomi above material well-being. She married a good man and, we want to believe, found deep contentment with him.

But palace splendor, without strong family ties, is not likely to lead to happiness and fulfillment. Vashti's husband is now three years into his reign. Things are settling down; the borders are relatively secure. Now he is seeking the goodwill of the people. So he announces a grand celebration, inviting "the military leaders of Persia and Media, the princes, and the nobles of the provinces."[1]

For months on end, he opens the gardens and courtyards for all to marvel at his ostentatious lifestyle. This show of wealth culminates in a weeklong feast in an enclosed palace garden. From the detailed description, we quickly understand how one might easily be impressed with a king who possesses so many luxuries and has such fine taste:

> The garden had hangings of white and blue linen, fastened with cords of white linen and purple material to silver rings on marble pillars. There were couches of gold and silver on a mosaic pavement of porphyry, marble, mother-of-pearl and other costly stones. Wine was served in goblets of gold, each one different from the other, and the royal wine was abundant, in keeping with the king's liberality.[2]

At the king's command, the wine flows freely. He spreads a sumptuous smorgasbord—all you can eat and drink. But men only. The wives and fair maidens, however, are not forgotten. Queen Vashti hosts a banquet for them, though unfortunately there is no recorded description of this feminine feast. What do women do for seven days? Are they exchanging recipes? Are they reveling like the men? Not likely. With Vashti in charge, we can assume there was proper decorum.

On the last day of this celebration, Vashti is confronted with a delegation of seven eunuchs. And not just any eunuchs. They, unlike many women in the biblical text, are all named: Mehuman, Biztha, Harbona, Bigtha, Abagtha, Zethar, and Karkas. They have come at the king's bidding to bring her over to the men's feast so that she can flaunt her beauty. Is she surprised by this unusual request? She no doubt assumes that there would be pole dancers and strippers or whatever else the men would want for lewd entertainment. But a queen wearing her crown? What on earth is the king

> **The Heroic Vashti**
>
> To Vashti, the command of the king—her husband, who alone had the right to gaze upon her beautiful form—was most revolting to her sense of propriety, and knowing what the consequences of her refusal to appear before the half-drunken company would entail, refused in no uncertain terms to comply with the king's demand. She stood strong in womanly self-respect. . . . What the king sought would have infringed upon her noble, feminine modesty, therefore she had every right to disobey her wine-soaked husband. A wife need not and may not obey her husband in what opposes God's laws and the laws of feminine honor and decency. All praise to the heroic Vashti for her decent disobedience.
>
> Herbert Lockyer, *All the Women of the Bible*

thinking? It would be very inappropriate—demeaning to her as an individual and to the position she holds.

We can almost see this lovely and strong-willed woman looking at the seven eunuchs with a mixture of contempt and pity. She's obviously not going to strut her stuff in front of a courtyard of drunken men. Perhaps all she does is shake her head, roll her eyes, and give a toss of the hand indicating that they would do well to take their leave. Or maybe she simply says, *No thanks*, and sends her regrets. She doesn't seem like the sort of woman who would retort with: *Tell his royal highness that hell will freeze over before I show up at his boorish Hooters bash.*

She is very proper and is not about to sully her reputation and lower herself to his standards. But the king, no doubt tanked-up himself, is irate. How dare she blow him off in front of his underlings! She's making a mockery of him.

Unbeknown to her, he is handling her *regrets* as an audacious affront to his sovereign rule. He ratchets up what should have been a marital spat to a *war against men* so serious that it requires a public response. He calls together his advisers, seven named men: Karshena, Shethar, Admatha, Tarshish, Meres, Marsena, and, last but not least, Memukan, who offers a resolution:

> Queen Vashti has done wrong, not only against the king but also against all the nobles and the peoples of all the provinces of King Xerxes. For the queen's conduct will become known to all the women, and so they will despise their husbands and say, "King Xerxes commanded Queen Vashti to be brought before him, but she would not come." This very day the Persian and

Median women of the nobility who have heard about the queen's conduct will respond to all the king's nobles in the same way. There will be no end of disrespect and discord.

Therefore, if it pleases the king, let him issue a royal decree and let it be written in the laws of Persia and Media, which cannot be repealed, that Vashti is never again to enter the presence of King Xerxes. Also let the king give her royal position to someone else who is better than she. Then when the king's edict is proclaimed throughout all his vast realm, all the women will respect their husbands, from the least to the greatest.[3]

King Xerxes immediately goes into action, texting the bureaucrats in each of the 127 provinces of his kingdom, "proclaiming that every man should be ruler over his own household."[4]

Now what? The next piece of information that comes to Vashti is that she is being deposed. Does she also hear how her successor will be chosen? That it will not be on the basis of a political alliance? Perhaps that would not be so hard to take. But instead, the king jumps at the first proposal his personal attendants put forward, one in which beauty is the only criterion.

Let a search be made for beautiful young virgins for the king. Let the king appoint commissioners in every province of his realm to bring all these beautiful young women into the harem at the citadel of Susa. Let them be placed under the care of Hegai, the king's eunuch, who is in charge of the women; and let beauty treatments be given to them. Then let the young woman who pleases the king be queen instead of Vashti.[5]

What happens now? The Bible doesn't say whether Vashti was locked up or exiled or executed. We are left hanging. After all, this book of the Bible is not about her. It's about her replacement, Esther.

Esther

Esther, whose Hebrew name is Hadassah, is an orphaned daughter of Abihail. What a lovely name, Hadassah, meaning "myrtle tree" and the fragrance thereof. It has a wonderful, smooth, romantic sound. Can't we just imagine a tender masculine voice whispering the name *Hadassah*, accompanied by sweet nothings into the ear of his beloved? Yes, *Hadassah* more so than the harder sounding *Esther*. But we have come to know her by her Persian name, meaning "star."

She is reared in the house of Mordecai, her cousin. We know nothing more about this household, apart from the fact that he is her guardian and she is raised as a daughter. Were there other siblings in the household? Did Mordecai have a wife who became a mother to her? It is noteworthy that she is not the only young Jew whose name would become a household word in Persia. Daniel lived only a generation before her. In fact, the old man Daniel may still have been alive in Susa while she was growing up. Both would come to know the palace in that city very well.

It is often the case that a gorgeous little girl does not necessarily mature into a stunning woman. But we know that Esther as she approached maturity "had a lovely figure and was beautiful."[6] After the king's proclamation to search out the most beautiful young women of the realm, many are brought to the palace harem, among them Esther escorted by Mordecai.

Are some of the girls turned down at the gate? It's hard to imagine that every girl who enters this contest will go all the way to the finals. Hegai is the king's right-hand man in charge of the harem. He quickly takes to Esther and provides her a salon with seven beauty specialists. In fact, she and her seven attendants are moved "into the best place in the harem."[7] Is Esther ever asked about her background or nationality? If so, does she lie or evade the truth? All we know is that Mordecai forbids her to tell anyone that she is a Jew.

Before she can even be judged by the king, each girl must undergo a full year of beautification—"six months with oil of myrrh and six with perfumes and cosmetics."[8] Was this twelve-month process stressful—or boring—for Esther? Imagine Miss America contestants required to spend a year of preparation before they even have a chance of wearing the crown. Of course, winning the crown of Persia is more significant than wearing a tiara at a pageant.

What happens when she finally goes in to spend a night with Vashti's ex-husband? We can assume the king is not interviewing her for typing and shorthand skills. She enters the royal bed chamber in the evening and takes her leave in the morning. On exiting, she is moved into a different wing of the harem—those on one side awaiting their turn, those on the other awaiting a callback from the king.

The pageant rules specify that all young women must have a minimum of a year of preparation. But Esther might have waited longer if there were a lot of young virgins ahead of her in line. We do know that Xerxes deposed Vashti in the third or fourth year of his reign but did not see Esther until the tenth month of the seventh year of his reign. Three years is a long time to wait.

What happens next is devoid of details—details we would eagerly devour if they were in the text. She spends a night with the king. Voilà! She wins the contest. "Now the king was attracted to Esther more than to any of the other women, and she won his favor and approval more than any of the other virgins."[9] So he puts the crown on her head, and she takes Vashti's place—just like that. Then he throws another grand banquet, proclaims a holiday throughout his entire realm, and lavishes gifts on important people.

Queen Esther reigns. But there will be bumps along the way. The next information the text offers, without explanation, is that "the virgins were assembled a second time."[10] And we thought they'd all gone home. Did Xerxes want a second go-round, or was he simply looking for some more virgins to fill slots in his harem?

If we are kept in the dark about the second set of virgins, the king is kept in the dark about not only Esther's nationality but also her continuing relationship with Mordecai. In fact, the king doesn't have a clue that his new queen is Jewish. Nor is he aware that she continues "to follow Mordecai's instructions as she had done when he was bringing her up."[11] This seems like a serious security breach, but Xerxes doesn't appear to have a crack intelligence team, and Esther clearly wasn't vetted as we would have expected her to be.

Sometime after her coronation, Queen Esther reports to the king that there is an assassination plot under way. He's the target. She tells him that Mordecai, who apparently enjoys some prestige as one who sits at the king's gate, can name the culprits. (Again, where is the king's security detail?) Soon after this Esther learns that the conspirators have been put to death.

Time passes, and Esther, we imagine, carries out her queenly duties, hosting the wives of provincial governors and foreign dignitaries. It is now past the twelfth year of Xerxes' reign. She learns one day that Mordecai is out in the street "wailing loudly and bitterly,"[12] having torn up his clothes and wearing only sackcloth and ashes. She's mortified. In an attempt to shush him up, she sends him new clothes, but to no avail. He just keeps wailing. So she dispatches her most trusted eunuch to find out what's going on.

The eunuch returns, informing her that Haman, one of the king's chief officers, has hatched a plan to exterminate all the Jews in the realm, and that the king himself has issued the edict (a copy of which the eunuch brings to Esther). Esther also hears from the eunuch that Mordecai is instructing her "to go into the king's presence to beg for mercy and plead with him for her people."[13]

Esther's response to Mordecai (through her eunuch) gives us pause. She's the official queen. Mordecai's instructions seem perfectly in line. But she is not moved. Her relationship with the king, we learn, is most unusual, as indicated by the message she sends back.

> All the king's officials and the people of the royal provinces know that for any man or woman who approaches the king in the inner court without being summoned the king has but one law: that they be put to death unless the king extends the gold scepter to them and spares their lives. But thirty days have passed since I was called to go to the king.[14]

What is she thinking? She has gotten alarming news of the plan to kill all Jews in the realm, including Mordecai, who has been a father to her. But she is most concerned about her own life. If she thinks this is the end of it and that she'll simply stand by as her fellow Jews are slaughtered, she's wrong. Mordecai sends a caustic retort, essentially saying: *Who do you think you are? Just because you're the queen doesn't mean you'll escape. One day the Jews will find relief, and you will perish with all the rest of those who would not lift a finger to help.* The remainder of his short message is not so harsh: "And who knows but that you have come to your royal position for such a time as this?"[15]

Esther sends word back to Mordecai that she will go to the king if he and all the Jews in Susa will fast for three days. Then she adds the words he's been waiting to hear: "And if I perish, I perish."[16]

Imagine being married to a guy, whether a king or a carpenter, who is likely to kill you if you come into his presence failing to follow precise protocol. It's safe to say this couple is not real close. But after waiting two days, Esther dons her royal gown and goes to the king's hall, where she takes a position just outside the entrance. She sees him and is relieved; he's holding out his scepter, signaling her to approach. She must be astonished by his greeting: "What is it, Queen Esther? What is your request? Even up to half the kingdom, it will be given you."[17]

If we are hoping she will cry out, *Save the Jews*, we will be disappointed. Instead she invites him, along with Haman, to come to a feast that her servants have already prepared. They come, and again the king asks Esther what she wants—anything, but not more than half his kingdom. She's biding her time. So she invites them to another feast, this one the following day. Only then will she tell him what she wants.

At the big banquet the following day, the king again asks Esther what her request is. This time she asks him straight up to spare her people. The king acts as though he doesn't know anything about the edict and asks who is behind it. (Apparently Xerxes is spending too much time with his harem.) As a matter of fact, he had supported Haman's petition to eradicate the Jews by giving him his signet ring and saying, "Do with the people as you please."[18]

Esther responds to the king's inquiry. "An adversary and enemy! This vile Haman!" she blurts out. *He's sitting right there at the table.* Is the king shocked? The text says he's furious and stalks out into the garden. Haman, alone with Esther, pleads for mercy, "falling on the couch" where she is reclining. At this point the drama turns into pure comedy. Here is Haman desperately pleading with Esther, even grabbing her wrists and falling on top of her as he begs for his life. The king returns to the stage and angrily exclaims: "Will he even molest the queen while she is with me in the house?"[19] (And to think that every year this scene—as well as the whole story—is reenacted by Jews to celebrate Purim!)

From this point on things move quickly. Haman is impaled on the very stake he had prepared for Mordecai, Esther is given Haman's estate, and

A Hang-Up regarding Haman

Was Haman hanged or impaled? . . . In the work of the Greek historian Herodotus, impalement is regularly presented as a Persian punishment. . . . Given the setting of Esther, it thus seems likely that the manner of punishment for Haman was in fact impalement. In other words, the fifty-cubit "tree" built by Haman was intended to display Mordecai's body impaled in such a way that no one could avoid seeing it.

Benjamin Shaw, "Was Haman Hanged or Impaled?"

the Jews are saved. But now Esther's on a roll. She asks not for more land but for more public executions: "If it pleases the king . . . let Haman's ten sons be impaled on poles."[20] Who would have thought this of Esther? She is making sure he has no sons left to exact revenge. But it's no less than brutal—*cruel and unusual* punishment. Wasn't hemlock or some other poison available?

No other biblical queen outshines Esther. But unlike the other great monarchs of the Bible, her rule is not over Israel or Judah. She reigns as queen over a pagan realm. She serves *for such a time as this* to save God's people.

Concluding Observations

Vashti disappears from the scene by the end of the first chapter of Esther. What happened to her? Neither the Bible nor history tells us. Was she also impaled on a pole? We hope not. There are so many things we would like to know about her. Did she have children by Xerxes? If so, how did they fare in their father's realm after their mother was deposed?

Esther is considerably less assertive than is Vashti. In fact, in her plea for her husband to save the Jews, she qualifies her request: "If we had merely been sold as male and female slaves, I would have kept quiet, because no such distress would justify disturbing the king."[21] That's not how Vashti would have responded.

Although Esther serves as queen and is honored with her name on a book of the Bible, she is in the end trumped, dare we say, by her cousin and guardian, Mordecai. After Haman has been done in, Mordecai is elevated by the king, and we learn that when he leaves the king's presence, he is "wearing royal garments of blue and white, a large crown of gold and a purple robe of fine linen."[22]

Not once in the book is Esther described as *great*. Mordecai is heralded, however, for his greatness. The final chapter, short as it is, focuses entirely on him:

> King Xerxes imposed tribute throughout the empire, to its distant shores. And all his acts of power and might, together with a full account of the greatness of Mordecai, whom the king had promoted, are they not written in the book of the annals of the kings of Media and Persia? Mordecai the Jew was second in rank to King Xerxes, preeminent among the Jews, and held in high esteem by his many fellow Jews, because he worked for the good of his people and spoke up for the welfare of all the Jews.[23]

Questions to Think About

Are we missing the point of the book of Esther when we give a place of respect to Queen Vashti? Was she justified in defying her husband the king?

Have you ever encountered behavior (by men or women) that could be considered demeaning to you as a woman or to women in general? Does it bother you? Do women ever show sexist bias against their own gender? Is a woman overreacting to insist that basketball schedules titled *men* and *girls* must be changed to represent equality?

Describe the different personalities of Vashti and Esther. If you were in a Purim drama production, which queen would you want to play?

How do you think you would have responded if Mordecai had contacted you, the queen, asking you to go straight to the king to save your people? Do you think Esther's timidity was justifiable?

Does Esther seem fainthearted, on the one hand, and almost bloodthirsty, on the other? Was her request to impale all ten of Haman's sons overkill?

How do you rate Esther alongside other prominent women of the Bible? Do you like her? Would you want to have her as one of your three intimate female Bible friends?

17

Job's Wife, Proverbs 31 Woman, Song of Songs Lover, and Gomer

Symbolism and More

Curse God, and die. These are the infamous words of Job's wife. *Curse God.* I have never heard anyone curse God. But if anyone ever might have felt justified in doing so, Job would be a likely candidate. Rather than cursing in the name of God, as people often do, it would be a reversal of the words. But Job did not take the bait. He suffered and eventually was rewarded.

Today the phrase *Curse God and die* might be shrugged off as easily as cursing in God's name. It wasn't always that way. I was reminded of that recently when my husband was reading to me (as he always does at bedtime) *Caleb's Crossing* by Geraldine Brooks. Bethia is the main character growing up on Martha's Vineyard in the seventeenth century. After her mother dies and after her father is lost at sea, her grandfather arranges for her to become an indentured servant in Cambridge, Massachusetts, in order to pay for her brother's schooling.

Painful as it is to leave the home and island she loves so much, she willingly carries out her indenture. But when her brother fails to make the grade and is forced to drop out of his schooling, he schemes to pay off her term of servitude by arranging for her to marry a young man she does not love. It is a done deal, as he tells her matter-of-factly. She is flabbergasted and outraged. She damns him in God's name. Where has she learned a curse like that in Puritan New England? Her brother is shocked. He reports her to the schoolmaster, who sentences her to be whipped by her brother. The next Sunday she is ordered to stand up in church and confess her grave sin.

Though the book is fiction, it rings true. Decades ago my master's thesis required that I spend time doing research in Boston, poring over seventeenth-century selectmen's minutes. There I found shocking stories of youth and adults being imprisoned, having their tongues bored through with a hot spike, and even executed. And sometimes for crimes that seemed far less serious than cursing a brother. Indeed, Bethia got off easy.

Job's wife is almost entirely symbolical. She bears Job ten children and serves as mistress of the household. But her only role in the story is to act as a onetime adversary to a suffering man. His arguments and emotions are laid bare chapter after chapter. Hers are stifled but for one offensive outburst. What was her state of mind—her sentiments—behind those words? We ask the same questions regarding the Proverbs 31 woman and Gomer. One is working her fingers to the bone; the other is a prostitute married to a prophet. There must be some pent-up anger or sadness or doubt that would fill out their stories. And even the woman in the Song of Songs, apart from her romantic expressions, seems distant, her character flat and undeveloped. Where is the passion, and where are the honest outbursts that we saw in Sarah and Hagar, Rebekah, Rachel, Leah, Naomi, and Hannah?

To understand Job's wife or the other three women found in Proverbs 31, the Song of Songs, and the book of Hosea, we must recognize their immense significance as symbols. As such, we would not expect the text to reveal their personalities and private thoughts. Beyond their symbolism, however, we seek to know them through our own intuition and imagination.

There are similarities among these women as well as differences. An amusing way to exercise our imaginations is to switch the roles of these women. How, for example, would the Proverbs 31 woman have reacted to the terrible misfortunes that befell Job—and herself, were she his wife? And could the Song of Songs lady ever have kept up with the Proverbs 31 woman, not in lovemaking but in a hectic daily schedule? What if the woman Hosea acquires as a wife becomes for him the Song of Songs lover? Would he have even been able to carry on with his prophesying? We ponder such lighthearted hypotheticals as we seek to better comprehend what the Bible is telling us about these women.

Job's Wife

She's gotten a bad rap. How could anyone criticize this woman? Just imagine. She's going about her household duties and still active in the lives of her ten children, all of whom have turned out well. Then suddenly all is gone. Since a book of the Bible is named after him, most of us know Job. He is a healthy, wealthy, and righteous man who has a wife and ten kids. Within the space of a day, he loses everything except his wife. That Job gets top billing in this drama is an understatement. His wife is barely a shadow.

When Job first hears of his terrible losses, his response is truly amazing:

Job got up and tore his robe and shaved his head. Then he fell to the ground in worship and said:

"Naked I came from my mother's womb,
    and naked I will depart.
The Lord gave and the Lord has taken away;
    may the name of the Lord be praised."

In all this, Job did not sin by charging God with wrongdoing.[1]

Hardly has Job processed his incredible losses when he's struck down with *boils from hell*. There's no other way to describe them—oozing, itching, burning, ugly red sores from the top of his head to all ten toes. It is at this point that his wife makes her one speaking appearance. She's heard him practically sing the words *The Lord giveth and the Lord taketh away; blessed be the name of the Lord*. For her the words ring hollow—and worse. Now he's suffering beyond description, and her protest is one of desperation. "Are you still maintaining your integrity?" *What's wrong with you? How can you bless the Lord at a time like this?* She's beside herself. "Curse God and die!"[2] We can see right through her. She's bitter. Her sarcastic rhetorical question belies her anger. The curse is aimed directly at God, though she is demanding her husband carry it out. All hope is gone. Things can't get any worse. He might as well—at least, as a manner of speaking—die and curse God on the way to hell. Could hell be any worse than this?

For most of us, losing our house and all our possessions would be enough to put us in an awful funk of bitterness or depression. Job's wife loses all ten children as well. When I contemplate her, I think of Scott Willis, a Baptist minister, and his wife, Janet.

The accident was horrific. I will never forget it as long as I live. Local reporters were at the scene. It was midmorning, November 8, 1994. I was teaching at the time at Trinity Evangelical Divinity School in Deerfield, Illinois. From the seminary you can see Interstate 94, which connects Chicago with Milwaukee. Janet and Scott Willis, from the south side of Chicago, were on that very highway headed for Milwaukee. It was to be a fun getaway—a visit to one of their nine children. With them in the van were their six youngest children.

Normal traffic, good road conditions, temperature in the forties. A truck passes. Then without a moment's warning, a huge steel rod flies off the truck and strikes their vehicle. It explodes in a fireball. Burned to death are Ben, thirteen; Joe, eleven; Sam, nine; Hank, seven; Elizabeth, three; and Peter, six weeks.

Neither Job's wife nor Job himself, for that matter, knows anything of God's dealings with Satan behind the scenes that have allowed such a terrible tragedy. But would it have made any difference? She's lost her children, and that blinding grief is all-consuming.

For Janet and Scott Willis, the *Satan* behind the scenes was Governor George Ryan, who was deeply involved in a Mafia-style bribery scheme that sold drivers' licenses to unqualified drivers (such as the one driving the truck). At the time they knew nothing of the governor's corrupt dealings. They would find out later when the case was brought to court, and he would be sentenced to prison. But would it have made any difference then if they had known? They were crushed with the unspeakable loss of Ben, Joe, Sam, Hank, Elizabeth, and Peter.

Scott and Janet, both burned badly themselves, were numb with shock. Early on they spoke of their profound trust in God. They almost had to. He was a pastor, she a pastor's wife. They had comforted others with God's goodness in times of tragedy. As the weeks and months passed, they healed physically, but beneath the surface were deep emotional scars. In fact, they encountered many of the same spiritual struggles that Job did—and more, not only anger but severe depression, thoughts of suicide, and fear of insanity.

In the years since that terrible day, Janet and Scott have been healing emotionally and spiritually. With a monetary settlement, they established a nonprofit ministry and Janet wrote a children's book, *A Dad's Delight*, with her own lovely illustrations. At the time of the writing, they had nine grandchildren—almost a Job-like story ending.

Job's wife. When I try to comprehend her incomprehensible grief, I ask: Would we have faulted Janet Willis if she had uttered to Scott (had he been writhing in pain himself), *Curse God, and die*? Such an angry outcry, a grief therapist would tell us, is hardly abnormal. Yet we easily beat up on Job's wife, a woman who seems so utterly alone in the Bible. How did she manage to paddle her way through that painful river of grief? Did she receive

---

The Devil's Accomplice?

Her name was never revealed and yet she may be the most infamous woman in the Bible. Augustine labeled her "the devil's accomplice." Calvin called her "a diabolical fury." And the contemporary understanding of Job's wife hasn't improved on Calvin or Augustine. It's difficult to find a book or sermon treatment of the life of Job that doesn't include the usual condemnations toward his wife. It has become a standard joke to pity Job, as if his wife was yet another cross God called this man to bear. If the Proverbs 31 woman represents a model of Christian virtue, the wife of Job occupies the role of least desirable, sharing space in the Hall of Shame with the likes of Jezebel, Delilah, and Michal. But is this image an honest assessment of her character? Or is there a possibility that in our rush to empathize and identify with Job, we've rushed to cast judgment on his wife?

Daniel Darling, "The Most Misunderstood Woman in the Bible"

cards and other expressions of sympathy? Did she pour out her anguish to a counselor? Or was she censured, even as we in the generations since have censured her? Job's wife. A sorrowful woman without a name. Will we forever shun her as a symbol of spiritual rebellion?

Proverbs 31 Woman

No name, just the *Proverbs 31 woman*. She's the polar opposite of Job's wife. Mother's Day sermons come alive and sing her praises. She is exactly what every woman ought to be. You know her. Not personally, but you've seen her from a distance, especially if you've ever been to a large church in Birmingham. She's a prim and proper Southern Baptist preacher's wife, Alabama accent, high heels, and a delicate way of holding her legs together and slightly to the side when seated. Wife, mother, hostess, home decorator, garden club president, symphony cellist, Women's Missionary Union secretary, ladies' day emcee, and chauffeur with honor-student sticker on her SUV. She does it all—in a pleasing southern drawl. And we hate her.

This, however, is how some picture the Proverbs 31 *Christian* woman. The actual passage was penned before the Christian era and offers a different slant. And it is critical to note that it is introduced with a qualifier: Who can find a wife of such noble character? No one. If someone actually did come upon this rare find, she'd be worth her weight in rubies.

Okay, so what are the qualities of this nonexistent woman? She shops till she drops with a particularly good eye for fabric—sometimes spinning and weaving her own—which she makes into draperies, duvets, and dresses: purple and scarlet with embroidered borders and hems. She's out early every morning (after having set out breakfast on the patio for husband and kids) and is the first one in line at the farmers' market dickering for produce, meat, and spices. On her way home she texts her realtor, buys forty acres, sells thirty, and with the profit plants a vineyard on the remaining ten.

But her day is far from over. She's anything but a pale, fragile Victorian lady. Her muscular arms and legs outstrip most men in her determined pace. She heads through downtown, where she volunteers at a food pantry and soup kitchen. Then she returns home to oversee household management and burns the midnight oil in her sewing room where she fashions stylish

211

clothes with *Made in Palestine* labels that are sold in bazaars throughout the Mediterranean world. In the morning, with no plan to purchase more real estate, she gets back into the routine of homeschooling, always days ahead on her lessons—wisest woman on the block. And, just for good measure, this woman fears the Lord.

"Her children arise and call her blessed; her husband also, and he praises her."[3] Well, at least we sure hope they do. Too often such superwomen are handed only higher expectations, but little thanks.

What about her looks and personality? Is she beautiful and charming? Don't count on it. "Charm is deceptive, and beauty is fleeting."[4]

The Song of Songs Lover

The Proverbs 31 woman, albeit symbolic, is anything but a sex symbol. She works twenty hours a day. Should we be surprised that in the enumeration of all her assets, there's not one word about her being really *good in bed*? We imagine her waiting on her husband hand and foot, but there's nothing about her being the lover of his fantasies. Not so with the lady lover in Solomon's Song. She opens the book with a tease of erotic sensuality: "Let him kiss me with the kisses of his mouth—for your love is more delightful than wine."[5] She knows how to lay it on, and men find her utterly irresistible.

She continues with what we might expect to see in a dating-site personal ad, though without the usual *size 6* and *easy on the eyes*:

> Dark am I, yet lovely,
> daughters of Jerusalem,
> dark like the tents of Kedar,
> like the tent curtains of Solomon.[6]

He reads her words as he's cruising the personals and responds. But she wants to get a little background on him. She questions him about where he grazes his flocks and where he rests them when the sun is high in the sky. Or rather does she want to know where he's grazing so she can meet him there? Unidentified friends assume the latter and tell her to "follow the tracks of the sheep and graze your young goats by the tents of the shepherds."[7] So, now we know that he's a shepherd and she's a goatherd. They meet not at Starbucks but out in the field in broad daylight. From there things progress quickly.

She readily introduces lusty language that is sure to excite him: "My beloved is to me a sachet of myrrh resting between my breasts. . . . And our bed is verdant."[8] No erotic desire goes unspoken by either of them:

> I slept but my heart was awake.
> Listen! My beloved is knocking:
> "Open to me, my sister, my darling,
> my dove, my flawless one."[9]

We should not view this as a one-night stand. Early on he speaks of her as his bride, but then they lose each other, perhaps as lovers often do. One searches for the other, and they are back in each other's arms. Then the other is lost, and so it goes.

Many of the figures of speech are familiar today: *rose of Sharon, lily of the valley,* and *lily among thorns.* Others seem odd to our modern ears, one such describing a handsome man as *a gazelle or a young stag* and another, a beautiful woman's hair *like a flock of goats.* (Actually that metaphor does have current usage—at least with my husband's occasional description of *my* hair!) The words we so enjoy hearing as descriptive phrases from a lover today are clearly not the same as they were thousands of years ago:

> Your teeth are like a flock of sheep just shorn,
> coming up from the washing.
> Each has its twin;
> not one of them is alone.
> Your lips are like a scarlet ribbon;
> your mouth is lovely.
> Your temples behind your veil
> are like the halves of a pomegranate.
> Your neck is like the tower of David,
> built with courses of stone;
> on it hang a thousand shields,
> all of them shields of warriors.

Your breasts are like two fawns,
    like twin fawns of a gazelle
that browse among the lilies.[10]

One of the most romantic passages of this poem consists of her words to her lover. They are filled with images that we can easily visualize in our mind's eye:

I belong to my beloved,
    and his desire is for me.
Come, my beloved, let us go to the countryside,
    let us spend the night in the villages.
Let us go early to the vineyards
    to see if the vines have budded,
if their blossoms have opened,
    and if the pomegranates are in bloom—
there I will give you my love.[11]

I read those words and my mind goes back to a moonlit night in the small village of San Lorenzo, Italy. My husband and I were teaching a course at an American-based Bible institute there. After a long day of classes and after excusing ourselves from the evening meal, we walked out into the countryside. Vineyards bordered the one-lane roads, and budding blossoms filled the air with fresh fragrance. *Come, my beloved,* I surely must have whispered, *I will give you my love.*

Some scholars believe that this book of the Bible was actually written by a woman. The main character is certainly female, though her lover also has a significant speaking role. Whether she is the female author or only an imagined lover, she possesses a profound understanding of love that has never been surpassed:

For love is as strong as death,
    its jealousy unyielding as the grave.
It burns like blazing fire,
    like a mighty flame.

Many waters cannot quench love;
    rivers cannot sweep it away.

> If one were to give all the wealth of one's house for love,
> it would be utterly scorned.[12]

The Song of Songs truly is just that—the most lovely of all songs, of all lyrical poems. Is it too good to be true? For all of us romantics in the ages since, we would surely hope not. But it does not ring true for the couples we have seen thus far in the Hebrew Bible. Imagine our pleasure if we had come upon Eve and Adam or Sarah and Abraham repeating these sensual words throughout their long marriages. Or perhaps Rebekah and Isaac. Delilah whispered sweet nothings, but they were the conniving words of conspiracy. Gomer, we will discover, surely must know how to use words to enhance her profession, but any such sentiment is not even an echo of true love.

Gomer

She's a prostitute, the daughter of Diblaim. And she has a name: Gomer. It is safe to say it is not high on the list for girl babies today. Unlike Rahab, the most popular prostitute of the Hebrew Bible, she offers no service other than bearing babies for Hosea and symbolically representing Israel's unfaithfulness. Why she agreed to marry him, we can only wonder. He was ordered by God to marry her, but in her eyes, he could hardly have been the most eligible bachelor in town.

The book of Hosea opens with a familiar phrase that we would expect in a prophetic writing: "The word of the LORD that came to Hosea." What follows, however, is startling. It must have shocked the sensibilities of Hosea's contemporaries as much as it shocks us: "Go, marry a promiscuous woman and have children with her, for like an adulterous wife this land is guilty of unfaithfulness to the LORD."[13]

God has certainly told prophets to do strange things before in order to grab people's attention and pull them out of their stupor. But to actually marry a promiscuous woman (or a prostitute, as she is elsewhere identified) is hard to understand. We hold the bond of marriage so very high, a union that should never be used merely as an object lesson. But this seems to be God's very point. When God's people are unfaithful spiritually, it's comparable to being unfaithful in marriage.

Gomer bears Hosea children whose names recall God's wrath. The first: "Call him Jezreel, because I will soon punish the house of Jehu for the massacre at Jezreel."[14] The second child is a girl whose name means "not loved." Then a son with a name meaning "not my people."

Hosea is a prophet, not a poet per se. But his words are in poetic form, though hardly the tender love lyrics of the Song of Songs. His lyrics are cruel, expressing God's wrath toward unfaithful Israel. He begins as though he is speaking to his own children:

> Rebuke your mother, rebuke her,
>   for she is not my wife,
>   and I am not her husband.
> Let her remove the adulterous look from her face
>   and the unfaithfulness from between her breasts.
> Otherwise I will strip her naked
>   and make her as bare as on the day she was born;
>   I will make her like a desert,
>   turn her into a parched land,
>   and slay her with thirst.[15]

Hosea goes on to say that he will not show love to his children. Why? *They are children of adultery.* Apparently he thinks one or more are not his biological offspring—that she, while married to him, has been having affairs with others who trade sex for food and clothing, "my wool and my linen, my olive oil and my drink."[16]

> "She decked herself with rings and jewelry,
>   and went after her lovers,
>   but me she forgot,"
>   declares the LORD.[17]

Now God instructs Hosea, who is utterly disgusted with his adulterous wife, who has run away with another lover, to seek her out and bring her back home and show her how much he loves her. She's not simply going to return without some remuneration, however, so he pays in silver and barley what might total somewhat less than one hundred dollars in today's currency. Most working prostitutes would insist on at least that much for an hour of service. But she is to come and live with him. So they renew their vows, or at least he does: "You are to live with me many days; you must not be a prostitute or be intimate with any man, and I will behave the same way toward you."[18]

She returns home and is never mentioned again. Hosea carries on with his prophecies, threatening downfall and pleading with Israel to return to the Lord. Indeed, if the people of Israel will return and repent, God will "love them freely" and "will be like the dew" in a parched land.[19] Israel will then flourish and blossom. All will be well.

Concluding Observations

We would like to hear *the rest of the story* of each of these four women. Did Gomer and Hosea settle down in a bungalow with a garden and a white picket fence? When did the lovers in the Song have their first marital fight, and what was it about? Sex? Did the Proverbs 31 woman finally burn out?

The last time we heard from Job's wife, she had hurled a curse. Later on Job laments that his sewer breath disgusts his wife (and, we can assume, is not conducive for kissing). In the days and weeks that had followed her curse, he sat on a heap of ashes and was joined by three friends who insisted that his misfortune was a result of his sin. Although Job reacts with indignation not only toward his friends but also toward God, he is amazingly long-suffering. Indeed, *the patience of Job* is a common axiom that comes from his story. And for him, there is a *happily ever after* ending.

> The LORD blessed the latter part of Job's life more than the former part. He had fourteen thousand sheep, six thousand camels, a thousand yoke of oxen and a thousand donkeys. And he also had seven sons and three daughters.[20]

Job's wife is not mentioned. We would like to think, however, that she also had a fulfilling life, and perhaps we catch a glimpse of her through her second set of daughters: Jemimah, Keziah, and Keren-Happuch. "Nowhere in all the land were there found women as beautiful as Job's daughters, and their father granted them an inheritance along with their brothers."[21]

Whether penned by the hand of Solomon, Bathsheba, or palace court-iers, Proverbs 31 and the Song of Songs are wonderful writings filled with engaging figures of speech. Both present very different symbolic profiles of the perfect woman, one who does it all in the community and in her own household, the other who does it all in lovemaking. Love is clearly the theme of the Song, but it is also the theme in a very real sense of the book of Hosea—perfect love versus distorted love, or rather absence of love. But both the Song of Songs and the story of Gomer in Hosea stand as powerful symbols. The love lyrics in the Song have long been seen by many Jewish rabbis (as well as Christian scholars) as a metaphor for God's love for his people. As such they are a stark contrast to the unfaithfulness symbolized by Gomer.

But there is even greater significance in the marriage between Hosea and Gomer. How many times are men in the Bible told by God (or an angel of God) to marry a particular woman? Only two incidents come to mind. Hosea is ordered to marry Gomer, and Joseph is told to marry Mary. It is difficult to contemplate two more opposite women. But, in a sense, the message is similar. The prophet Hosea's marriage to a prostitute is an object lesson that shows God's people their sinfulness—an object lesson so brazen that it will jolt people to abandon their wicked ways and turn to God.

In a startlingly similar way, an angel of the Lord speaks to Joseph in a dream telling him to marry a pregnant woman:

> Joseph son of David, do not be afraid to take Mary home as your wife, because what is conceived in her is from the Holy Spirit. She will give birth to a son, and you are to give him the name Jesus, because he will save his people from their sins.[22]

In both instances God's love so profoundly symbolized in the Song of Songs reaches out to humankind—to save his people from their sins.

Questions to Think About

Is it possible to even imagine the depth of sorrow Job's wife endured? Have you ever experienced or known anyone who has experienced the pain of losing multiple children? Does such anguish serve to bring the individual closer to God, or does it do the opposite?

Why do you think Job's wife has so often been treated so badly by preachers, Bible teachers, and writers of commentaries? Is she easily lost amid the pain and arguments Job himself is encountering? How would you respond to a friend bowed down in grief who used such words?

How do you assess the Proverbs 31 woman? Have you ever heard a sermon on her that made you feel that you simply couldn't rise to the standard? Do you wish there were a comparable Proverbs 32 man?

How do you regard the Song of Songs? Does it have uses today in the context of romance and marriage? Does it offer far more than the usual erotica of the twenty-first century (or do you know nothing about that genre of literature)? Does it serve us well by leaving much to the glorious imagination?

If you were to mix and match these symbolic women, how would you do it? Would you have Job's wife stand in for the lover in the Song of Songs? Gomer transformed into the Proverbs 31 woman?

Which one of the four women do you find the most intriguing? If you were assigned to write a murder mystery featuring one of them, which one would you choose?

18

Anna and Elizabeth

Preparing the Way with Prophecy and Song

Family relationships today are often very complex, and there is sometimes no simple way of explaining to people where the precise connection lies. For example, how am I related to my husband's mother-in-law? She's not *my* mother, though she reminds me in many ways of my late mother—an outspoken, hardworking farmer's wife. Sue Kraker is the mother of my husband's second, dearly departed wife—thus no in-law of mine. So to make it simple, I just call her *Mom*, and that's fine with her.

What an incredibly dear and delightful woman she is. She's past ninety-five and still has a very good mind—and a mind of her own. She's not about to let anyone push her around (though in her frail condition, it would not be difficult to physically do that). Dad, whose mind is as sharp as hers, is more mild-mannered and easygoing. She, however, is not about to let age get in the way of making her own decisions and having her own opinions.

When I think of the eighty-four-year-old prophet Anna, who witnessed the temple dedication of baby Jesus, I think of Mom. Anna was an alert, quick-witted, old-age anomaly in her day even as Mom is today, and I can imagine Anna also having a mind of her own. She didn't stand by mute during this momentous occasion, though at the time it would have appeared to be anything but momentous. She spoke up for all to hear.

Mom is hardly one who grabs the center of attention, and I doubt very much that Anna was either. But recognizing the Messiah would be enough for either of them to let go of proper decorum and make a scene—enough of a scene to let others know exactly who this baby is.

Anna lived in the temple. Mom doesn't live in the church, but sometimes we almost accuse her of that. Despite their age and frequent ailments, she and Dad go to church every Sunday, and not just once. If they are not there for the Sunday-night service, people wonder what's wrong.

One of these years, Mom will join Anna, and they will be singing together with a grand choir, *Worthy is the Lamb*. Jesus was the little lamb whom Anna recognized as the Messiah. Another very old lady who will join in this heavenly songfest is Elizabeth. Unlike Anna, she gets some traction in the text as both cousin and friend of Mary and also as mother of John the Baptist. Perhaps she knew of Anna, that faithful old prophet who for decades never set foot out of God's house.

Anna

What would it have been like for Anna, the daughter of Penuel, living in Jerusalem in the generation before Jesus? Though she is one of the earliest figures in the New Testament, she is really much more of an Old Testament character. She makes her home in the temple, the center of Jewish worship and would have known a lot about life in that ancient city.

It is primarily because of Jesus that Jerusalem and its environs in that first-century time frame have so captured our interest. Take away Jesus, and the Jerusalem of this era would appear to many to be drab and uninviting. There would be far fewer archaeological digs and tourist sites. Most of the popular books that have spawned a publishing industry would not exist. Of course, there would be scholars interested in the history, archaeology, geography, anthropology, and sociology of the time. But there would be no Christian *Holy Land*.

Anna, perhaps as much as any other individual, walked right out of the Old Testament into the New—except that there were four hundred so-called *silent* years between the two testaments. How can four centuries possibly be silent? Well, of course they were not, but as the Hebrew Bible was later combined with what became known as the New Testament, a full four hundred years (or thereabouts) went missing. It is important to refer to the Hebrew Bible (or *Tanakh*) as just that. More than two hundred years before Christ, this Hebrew text was translated into Greek, and at about the same time additional writings were incorporated.

This Greek Septuagint was necessary because so many of the Jews living in exile had long forgotten their Hebrew tongue, and those who returned to Jerusalem brought back with them the prevailing language of the day, Greek. Thus, the need for the translation. But the Septuagint included more than just the Hebrew Bible (the first five books of Moses, or the Torah; the books of the Prophets; and the books of the Writings, all which are equivalent to the Old Testament in Protestant Bibles today). It also included what has become known as the Apocrypha.

> ### Between the Two Testaments
>
> The period between the two testaments was a turbulent one for the Jews. They were under the authority of Egypt, then Syria, and finally Rome. Much of their literature that was written during this period reflected their struggle. With evil all around them there were hopes for better days when the Messiah would come and bring them into a new golden age of peace. The writings of the Apocrypha reflect this hope. . . . Jesus and his disciples basically used the Septuagint as their Old Testament. They quoted from it extensively. However they never cited the Old Testament Apocrypha as Scripture.
>
> Don Stewart, "What Is the History of the Old Testament Apocrypha?"

These apocryphal books were thus part of the only Bible that would have been available to literate Jews in the first century. In the centuries that followed, additional writings were collected that would become known as the New Testament. All these writings were combined for a Latin translation by Jerome in the fourth century, now referred to as the Vulgate. Jerome himself did not regard the Apocrypha as part of the scriptural canon, but others like Augustine did. The Apocrypha has thus remained in the Catholic Bible ever since, while it was deleted by the sixteenth-century Reformers in the Protestant Bible.

Anna no doubt would have been familiar with the Apocrypha, and she might have been especially intrigued by the book of Judith, which tells the story of a courageous, beautiful, widowed woman almost reminiscent of Jael. Judith, however, also serves as a prophet. She calls upon the Israelites to come back to God and to trust him to deliver them from their conquerors. When they take no heed, she goes into action. In disguise and accompanied by her maid, she sneaks into the enemy camp and sallies up to the general. Then one night when he's drunk, she simply does what any nice Jewish widow would do; she cuts off his head. Now she has an object lesson to bring back home—the head of a great general. The enemy soldiers, without their leader, scatter in panic, and Israel is saved.

These centuries were bloody beheading times that flowed right into the New Testament era. John the Baptist, Elizabeth's son, would also give up his head as an object lesson. Though Anna blesses Jesus, she probably dies long before John the Baptist and Jesus would begin their ministries. The Bible says very little about Anna, relegating her story to only three verses in the book of Luke. She is paired with Simeon, and one might imagine them to be husband and wife but for the fact that she is identified as a widow.

Simeon is simply a very devout Jew who, moved by the Holy Spirit, walks into the temple courtyard, and takes Jesus into his arms and blesses him. Anna, on the other hand, is a prophet who actually lives in the temple, apparently not even going out and treating herself to an occasional latte at Starbucks. "She never left the temple but worshiped night and day, fasting and praying."[1] How long had she done that? The text doesn't say, but she had been widowed after only seven years of marriage, thus perhaps ever since she was thirty or maybe even younger. Imagine living in the temple for a half century. We picture her almost like a cloistered nun.

Very few things happen in the temple, we can assume, that escape Anna's attention, including Simeon's blessing. Indeed, his prayer must have caused her to tremble:

> For my eyes have seen your salvation,
>   which you have prepared in the sight of all nations:
> a light for revelation to the Gentiles,
>   and the glory of your people Israel.[2]

Simeon praises God for allowing him to see the Messiah before he dies. Anna also thanks God, but she goes a step further. She does exactly what any prophet would have done upon recognizing the Messiah; she "spoke about the child to all who were looking forward to the redemption of Jerusalem."[3] Her audience would have included devout Jews milling around the temple and the courtyard. Who knows, news like that might have taken her out of the temple into the city for the first time in more than fifty years. At least we would like to think so.

Elizabeth

Like Anna, Elizabeth is in many ways an Old Testament character. A descendant of the priestly line of Aaron, she is thus also distantly related to Miriam and Moses. Such a lineage was a matter of pride and surely would have been noted on a business card and a résumé. For Americans, ancestry can also be a point of pride. When I married John, the game of Dutch bingo came with him. He plays well, though surely not with me. The game pops up everywhere, most recently when we were purchasing new kayaks. The store manager overheard the name *Worst*. He moved closer: *Any relation to* . . . And so it went. I examined the cigarette lighters on the counter, while they named an assortment of Worsts going back through the generations.

There are no known priests in the Worst lineage, but that doesn't mean my husband has no bragging rights. Harold Worst, his second cousin once removed, was the 1965 world champion three-cushion billiard player—beat the pants off Boston Shorty. Elizabeth's ancestral connection with Aaron was no doubt a critical factor in her marriage to Zechariah. (A billiard champion wouldn't have cut it.) Zechariah himself "belonged to the priestly division of Abijah."[4] Though without the name recognition of Aaron, Abijah is actually a descendant of Aaron himself and plays an important role in the books of Ezra and Nehemiah.

Elizabeth and Zechariah live in the hill country of Judea and are both known in the community as good, upstanding Jews; *righteous* is the term for them. That we learn they are elderly when we are introduced to them is balanced against the stark reality of their being childless. Being old is a biblical mark of pride, but when *barren* is added to such vintage wine, it tastes as bitter as vinegar. Her longing for children reminds us of barren women we've come to know in the Hebrew Bible.

Periodically Zechariah travels to Jerusalem for priestly duty at the Temple. It is part of his profession, and Elizabeth no doubt takes his absences in stride. On one occasion, unbeknown to her, he had been chosen to go inside and burn incense. We would imagine that he would have come home and told her of this honor, but he's been struck mute. So he comes home and is unable to say a word. Imagine her confusion when all he can do is play charades, and she's trying to figure it all out. (He could have written it down for her, since he knows how to write, but we must assume that she, like most women of her day, is illiterate.) Here's what he would have wanted to communicate to her:

So I'm there at the temple, and would you believe it, I get picked by lot to go inside and burn incense. What a privilege. Now I'm all alone, carrying out this ritual exactly like I'm supposed to, and out of the blue an angel appears, standing right there beside me, claiming to be Gabriel. I was so scared I almost peed in my pants. [How do you say all that in charades?] I'm shaking and hyperventilating and dizzy. I'm thinking I've lost my mind. Gabriel tells me to calm down and listen to his message. Then he tells me you will get pregnant! I'm not kidding. And more than that, this baby we will have won't be any ordinary child.

If she were initially into his game of charades, by now she's given up and stepped outside to try to comprehend what is going on. Has he had a serious stroke? But if he's had a stroke and can't speak, why is he otherwise physically normal? Why is he completely mute—not the usual slurred speech of a stroke victim?

If he could have responded, he would have told her that he lost his voice because he had irked the angel. All he had done was to ask Gabriel how he could be sure all this would happen since he and his wife are so old. But not liking the question, Gabriel struck him mute. So here he is with this incredible information and not able to tell her.

Had he not been mute, he surely would also have quoted Gabriel word for word on the most startling fact of all about this baby: "And he will go on before the Lord, in the spirit and power of Elijah, to turn the hearts of the parents to their children and the disobedient to the wisdom of the righteous—to make ready a people prepared for the Lord."⁵ Here we see the close connection between the Old and the New Testaments. Malachi prophesies (in the last chapter of the last book of the Old Testament): "See, I will send the prophet Elijah to you before that great and dreadful day of the LORD comes."⁶ And now the angel has informed Zechariah that his son will come in the power of this very Elijah.

Elizabeth, who no doubt has long ago gone through menopause, now finds herself pregnant. She would have been in complete denial had she not been so familiar with the story of the laughing old Sarah, who had a baby at age ninety. Her own reflections are, in fact, similar to those of Sarah: "The Lord has done this for me," she says to no one apparently other than herself. "In these days he has shown his favor and taken away my disgrace among the people."⁷

Elizabeth lives in a time when visitors suddenly appear without warning—no text, no phone call, not even a postcard. She's in her sixth month of pregnancy, and her young cousin Mary shows up at the door. Mary exuberantly greets her, and at that moment Elizabeth, "filled with the Holy Spirit,"⁸ feels the baby leap in her womb. What appears most startling about this encounter is Elizabeth's recognition that Mary, without having had time to break the news, is also pregnant:

> Blessed are you among women, and blessed is the child you will bear! But why am I so favored, that the mother of my Lord should come to me? As soon as the sound of your greeting reached my ears, the baby in my womb leaped for joy. Blessed is she who has believed that the Lord would fulfill his promises to her!⁹

After Mary sings a song, she settles in for three months with Elizabeth. What did they do during this time besides fashioning little quilts and crocheting baby booties and bonnets? Elizabeth surely would have shared household tips and offered spiritual counsel. And we want to think that before Elizabeth bade Mary good-bye, they enjoyed many moments of reminiscence and laughter.

Soon after she leaves, Elizabeth gives birth, much to the joy and surprise of her neighbors. She has been in seclusion inside her house, and it's possible that until the moment she called in the midwife, none of them had known. As is the custom, she and Zechariah take the baby when he is eight days old to be circumcised. Those about them have assumed he would be named for his father, but Elizabeth insists otherwise—that he is to be named John. They argue that there is no one in the family by that name and look to the mute Zechariah for support. He asks for a tablet and confirms in writing that John is the name. In an instant, he is filled with the Holy Spirit, and his silence is transformed into speech and a song of praise to God.

After this, Elizabeth fades quickly from the scene. We learn only that her son grows up strong in spirit and heads out to live in the wilderness until the time when he will reappear as a prophet known as John the Baptist—the very one who will baptize his cousin Jesus, proclaiming him the Messiah. Elizabeth is most likely deceased by this time. Had she been alive, she might have been as confused as Mary would later be about the complex identity of her own son.

Concluding Observations

What fun it would be to find an inspired manuscript that would fill in many of the missing links in the Bible. Anna is a prophet. But who really is this mystery woman? What brought her to the temple as a young widow, or was she widowed at age sixty? How long did she live after she prophesied to her fellow Jews about Jesus? Is it possible that she was still at the temple when the twelve-year-old Jesus stayed behind to talk with the learned men? Imagine her peeking around the tapestry, eyes gleaming in recognition of this supernaturally brilliant boy taking on those men. She knew; they didn't have a clue.

Like her, Elizabeth is an old woman, assuming that she is about to wind down and wait for death. She couldn't have even imagined that she'd be nursing an infant, changing diapers, and hobbling after a toddler, knowing full well that it's only a matter of months till he'll be able to escape her grasp every time. We're glad there are neighbors around to pitch in, and who knows, maybe old Zechariah steps up to the plate sometimes.

The account of Elizabeth's barrenness is interesting. She is the only woman who will be identified with that awful b-word in the entire New Testament. And it is also noteworthy, that among the many miracles that Jesus performs, there would be no miracle of a barren woman conceiving and having a baby. Why not? Were there no women who longed for *barren* to be transformed into *baby*? Perhaps the stunning mystery of his own conception and birth is fully miraculous enough for one testament of the Bible.

Questions to Think About

Could you ever imagine yourself involved in long-term ministry primarily involving prayer, similar to that of the prophet Anna? Have you ever contemplated becoming a cloistered nun? Do you admire that lifestyle? Have you ever spent even a weekend at a silent retreat? Do you consider yourself deeply spiritual?

How does Elizabeth's story of barrenness differ from those of women we've come to know in the Hebrew Bible? Who are these women, and how does the matter of polygamy factor into their stories in comparison to Elizabeth's?

If you were Zechariah and wanted to communicate the angel's message to Elizabeth through charades, how would you do it? Could you demonstrate your communication skills to other people?

How has the condition of being childless changed since biblical times? For Elizabeth it was a disgrace. Does that stigma ever attend women without children today?

Elizabeth may have been fully old enough to be Mary's grandmother. Do you have friends who are significantly older or younger than yourself? How does that friendship differ from same-age friendships? What is there to be gained by such relationships?

How would you feel if someone (a good friend or close relative) without warning showed up at your door and stayed for three months? Are you and your household today prepared for such a gift of company?

What makes a person a Christian? Righteous living? Confession of creeds? Faith in Christ, his shed blood on the cross and resurrection from the dead? Ability to defend and spread the gospel message? Do you think that Anna and Elizabeth were "Christians"?

19

Mary

Mother and Disciple of Jesus

*C*ounterfactuals, the *what ifs* of life, have always interested me. *What if*, for example, my mother had married someone other than my father? I certainly wouldn't be around to wonder about it. Going back a generation earlier to the last decade of the nineteenth century, *what if* my paternal grandparents had not emigrated from Germany? Even before that to 1836, *what if* the pregnant, unmarried forty-two-year-old Maria Anna Schicklgruber had gotten an abortion and not given birth to Alois, the father of Adolf Hitler?

If we go back to the very beginning, *what if* Eve had not bitten when Satan tempted her? And if we go back to the beginning of the Christian era, *what if* Mary had not given birth to Jesus? More than two decades ago, I wrote a counterfactual fictionalized story about Mary, an unmarried, pregnant teenager. Here I offer an abbreviated version of that narrative:

> Mary is greatly troubled. She has never had sexual relations with anyone. How could she possibly be pregnant? And how will Joseph react? She can't bear the thought of losing him. What was it the angel had said? It just seems

so utterly preposterous. She buries her face in her hands and weeps. "What have I done to deserve this?"

It is an impossible situation, and there is no one she can turn to. Her parents would be devastated. In her despair, she thinks of the woman who lives at the edge of town. Mary's girlfriends have whispered that women pay her money so that they won't have babies.

It is dark and everyone is asleep when Mary slips out of the house. Occasionally a dog barks, but otherwise the streets of Nazareth are silent. She sees a lamp flickering in the window as she nears the house. What if the woman gets angry and wakes the neighbors? Mary's heart is pounding. She knocks and is invited into a tiny room lit only by the flickering lamp in the window. Mary is silent, her eyes fastened to the floor. Then she begins sobbing. The woman waits. "I'm going to have a baby," Mary whispers. The woman understands. Mary agrees to come back the following night.

It is pouring rain the next night as Mary hurries through the dark streets. Her head is throbbing. If only a bolt of lightning would strike her dead, how much easier it would be. The coins weigh heavily in her pocket as she knocks at the door. She enters and follows the woman into the back room.

Mary's mother is distressed the next morning to find her daughter feverish and ill. For three days Mary slips in and out of consciousness as the fever rages. Then it subsides, and she slowly regains her strength. But she is not the same. She doesn't smile and laugh as she used to; her cheery disposition is gone. Joseph is relieved that they can carry on with their wedding plans.

Settling into married life, they are summoned to Bethlehem to pay taxes. They journey, as do many of their neighbors, by foot and by donkey over the dusty roads to the south. It is late when they arrive. Joseph locates a stable where they can spend the night. They find a spot in a corner on some dry hay and lie down, exhausted from the journey.

But Mary cannot sleep. Finally she gets up and walks over to the open door. There are stars in the night sky—ordinary stars, nothing unusual. And there are shepherds out in the field some distance away, barely visible in the moonlight. They are watching their sheep as they normally do.

Mary reflects on the months that have passed. This is just about the time that her little one would have been born. She thinks of what might have been. She looks back at Joseph sleeping in the hay. He is a good man. She weeps softly, pondering in her heart what she has done. Her muffled sobs break the stillness. Otherwise, it is a silent night in Bethlehem.[1]

Mary, Mother of Jesus

What if . . . These are thought-provoking words to ponder. Of course, we know that this fictional story is simply a counterfactual. Mary did give birth to her baby in Bethlehem.

But who was Mary, and why was she chosen to bear the Messiah? This is not a foolish question. Unlike Anna and Elizabeth and most of the women we've come to know in the Hebrew Bible, she is an unknown. She has no lineage, no ancestry, no *pedigree*, is not even daughter of someone as unfamiliar as Penuel (as was Anna). Sarah, daughter of Abraham; Rebekah, daughter of Bethuel; Rachel, daughter of Laban; Zipporah, daughter of Jethro; Bathsheba, daughter of Eliam. Even Gomer has a named father, Diblaim.

Mary, daughter of someone. We know that for sure, but he is unnamed in the text. Tradition has it that her parents were Joachim and Anna, but you'll never find that in the Bible. Why not? Is it possible that trying to track down her parents and Jesus's grandparents would create some sort of a saintly lineage that would simply distract us from who Mary really is? She's essentially an unknown young woman from Nazareth. Don't even try to trace her family tree.

Yet it is tempting to try to track her down and fill in all the blanks with tradition and legend and papal decrees, which not only names her parents but in some cases tells us that she was sinless and forever a virgin. Really? Was Mary sinless? Or did she struggle with a sinful human nature as we all do? And the biblical text clearly implies that she bore more children, several of whom survived to adulthood.

The most important detail we immediately learn about Mary is that she is betrothed to Joseph, whose lineage winds its way back to King David. Their engagement is far more than a diamond ring and a notice in the local newspaper. Betrothal is a binding commitment that can be broken only with a divorce. Are they in love? The text gives no hint of a love story—not even the kind of love Isaac had for Rebekah, surely not the head-over-heels passion of Jacob for Rachel. Joseph may have been a dozen years or more older than she, and perhaps even widowed. He is a builder who probably works more likely with stone or dried brick than with wood. Like his neighbors, he's a faithful Jew, a decent man who doesn't stand out. The circumstances of their betrothal (how they met and how long they "dated") are not recorded. Too bad. The planning of a wedding was just as important back then as it is now.

We first meet Mary when she is minding her own business. An angel appears. It's strange, but that is the very moment when angels generally appear. Not necessarily at a convenient time, rather when they are least expected. For Mary, a better time would have been just before she marries Joseph. Then her virgin conception would not have been publicly exposed. But the angel comes, shall we say, at a very inconvenient time.

Should we be surprised that Mary is greatly troubled? Was there no way for the angel to soften the blow? In his most formal manner, he says: "Greetings, you who are highly favored! The Lord is with you."[2] *Say what?* is her response. Had I been instructing the angel, I would have told him to ease in a little, sending greetings to her family as well. Then he could remind her of Isaiah 7:14: "The virgin will conceive and give birth to a son, and will call him Immanuel." I would tell the angel to get her tracking with him before he dumps the whole message on her.

But if the greeting troubled her, how must she have felt about his next words?

> Do not be afraid, Mary; you have found favor with God. You will conceive and give birth to a son, and you are to call him Jesus. He will be great and will be called the Son of the Most High. The Lord God will give him the throne of his father David, and he will reign over Jacob's descendants forever; his kingdom will never end.[3]

Get outta here! she might have exclaimed. But she doesn't. With all the innocence that this chosen teenage girl is imbued with, she simply asks: *How is this possible? I'm a virgin.* The answer the angel gives is less than comprehensible to her—and to everyone who has pondered it since: "The Holy Spirit will come on you, and the power of the Most High will overshadow you. So the holy one to be born will be called the Son of God."[4] Mary, with no further questions, accepts this as God's truth. She assures him that she is the Lord's servant and desires that his words be fulfilled in her. She accepts what is truly an impossibility, as have Christians down through the ages.

The angel actually has given her a bit of extra information—that Elizabeth, her cousin, is also going to have a child and is already six months pregnant. Whether Mary laughs aloud at this, the text does not say. Elizabeth? It's one thing to be chosen to bear the Messiah. That had been a long time in coming. But Elizabeth with a baby! That's as funny as the story in the Torah about Sarah.

It is no surprise that Mary packs her bags and heads off to spend time with Elizabeth in the hill country of Judea. She longs to pour her heart out to someone who will understand. Not only that, but Elizabeth is also having a baby—a miracle in itself. Even more though, Elizabeth is spiritually mature and is also awaiting the Messiah. She is the one person most likely to comprehend this most incomprehensible angelic encounter.

As far as we know, Mary doesn't tell a soul about the incredible news delivered by the angel. Imagine being the virgin chosen to bear the Messiah and keeping it to yourself. Not a word to her folks or sister or girlfriend, and surely not to Joseph. Instead she stifles herself, almost bursting at the seams. So when she sees Elizabeth and is greeted with great joy, she breaks into song. That could happen only in the Bible. In a twenty-first-century scenario, she would be grabbing the old lady, squealing with delight, and dancing around the house. But Mary is a far more proper Jewish girl than that.

We've come to know her song as the *Magnificat*, beginning with the familiar words: "My soul glorifies the Lord and my spirit rejoices in God my Savior."[5] She goes on to note her own humble status, and then with hardly a pause, makes an astounding claim: "From now on all generations will call me blessed."[6] What has happened to the lowly and innocent Mary in the hours or days since the angel appeared? She has taken on the rank of what we would imagine to be that of a great queen. We would expect someone else, however, not the queen herself, to make such a commendation. This is no less than stunning. Mary, bolstered by Elizabeth, now begins to understand and accept her role.

There are other interesting aspects of these lyrics. She is praising God, who has "brought down rulers," even as he "has lifted up the humble." God "has filled the hungry with good things but has sent the rich away empty."[7] These moral impulses will reverberate years hence in the words of her son. It is a song for the ages.

For three months Mary makes her home with Elizabeth and the mute Zechariah. Two talkative women and a silent man, typical situation some would say. Then she returns home, apparently before Elizabeth gives birth. Now some three months pregnant, she has to face Joseph. This could be a very prickly encounter. As it turns out, however, it is not. Could she have known that an angel has gotten to Joseph first? All we know is that he takes Mary home as his wife. We're curious: Is there no grand wedding feast? We imagine Joseph making no eye contact and shaking his head: *Not in these circumstances.* Which is understandable. No sense publicizing what is potentially a serious scandal.

The text in the Gospel of Matthew then tells us that they do not consummate the marriage until after Jesus is born. And that consummation is apparently the seal of their actual marriage. That would make sense, because in Luke's Gospel, we learn of Mary and Joseph going to Bethlehem to register for the census. At that time, only days before her childbirth, Mary is described as only "pledged to be married to him."[8]

The nativity account is very familiar. They travel the dusty road to Bethlehem, some eighty miles on this rocky, winding, well-traveled course. Had they not been in a caravan, bandits would have quickly spied an easy target. We picture Mary on a donkey, subdued and silent, her robe disguising what everyone else knows. Joseph is leading the donkey, with a watchful eye on her and as mute as old Zechariah had been. The exuberant lyrics she had sung so recently must now seem hollow. They camp a few nights along the way and finally arrive to find the town teeming with people.

We all know about their spending the night in a stable because there was no room in the inn. My nativity scene is a rustic little shed, dried moss on the roof and an open front so that we can easily observe and rearrange the figurines, both people and animals. It is a sentimental image that I refuse to give up just because a cave is more likely to be the place where they stayed. (Indeed, I consider the cave-contenders a serious distraction; they ought to keep quiet, at least in the run-up to Christmas.)

So Mary and Joseph find a space in the stable, with a manger nearby. The baby is born. Shepherds stop by. Can't we just picture Mary absorbed by the pain and the mess and the cries of a newborn who is struggling to suckle, then learning from Joseph that shepherds are outside wanting to see the baby? Shepherds? Dirty, smelly shepherds! Any of us would have said, *What on earth are they doing here?* Not Mary. She somehow manages to get to her feet and walk to the opening of the moss-covered stable and let them peer at her whimpering little boy. In fact, she is glad they have come. Someone around here, she must have thought, cares. And their story of the birth being announced to them by angels must have made her shiver with delight.

How long this shelter for animals serves as their home is not revealed, but on the eighth day after the baby's birth we find Mary and Joseph in Jerusalem, making this most decisive stop as they are heading home. Here they dedicate Jesus in the temple and meet Simeon and Anna. Both offer blessings and prophetic words that cause Mary and Joseph to marvel. But there are also words that surely must have made her shudder. What could this old man mean, she must wonder, when he addresses her with ominous words:

> This child is destined to cause the falling and rising of many in Israel, and to be a sign that will be spoken against, so that the thoughts of many hearts will be revealed. And a sword will pierce your own soul too.[9]

A sword piercing her soul. How incredibly prophetic! It's a good thing that Simeon was not more specific. How could she have endured the next three decades if she had known? But even these words, disturbing as they are, easily blot out that joyous hymn of celebration she had so recently sung.

The little family now makes its way amid the noisy caravan back to Nazareth. Everyone wants a peek at the baby, and Mary must surely be eager to get home and shut the door. Mary is no saint. She is much more like us, as we shall see, than some sort of pious holy woman.

Back home she commemorates every little advance: *he's smiling (or maybe just burping), he's laughing out loud, rolling over, sitting up, creeping, standing, taking first steps. Oh my, she can barely keep up with him. What fun!* And then, Joseph's dream and King Herod's horrifying plot. How could anyone be so cruel as to kill all the boy babies? She clutches Jesus close.

A sword piercing her soul. The words ring in her ears. She has no time, though, to ruminate. She's busy packing, and they're out the door headed for Egypt. Egypt? Wasn't there another Jewish mother—Jochebed—who snatched her little one out of the lethal clutches of a powerful Pharaoh in that very realm?

Exactly how long they remain in Egypt and where they find employment and housing are anyone's guesses. The next we hear of Mary, however, she is back in Israel, specifically Jerusalem. It is several years later. They have made the journey from Nazareth for the annual feast of the Passover. It's a celebratory time—kind of a vacation—except for a mother with kids. Now they're headed home, and she simply asks: *Where's Jesus?* She needs help with the little ones. She begins asking around if anyone has seen him. He's twelve now and tends to go off by himself a lot. She's not panicked, just irritated and needs everyone accounted for. Slowly, however, her concern escalates.

Anyone who has raised a boy has been through this. It starts with a simple question of a neighbor or yelling his name while walking down the block. Where is he? As the minutes pass, irritation begins to compete with fear. We're not yet hyperventilating, but the blood pressure is rising. An hour passes—frustration, then nerves on edge, exasperation, fear, anger, dread, outrage. Our emotional synapses are firing at each other. Is he hurt, is he dead? We don't know what Mary's emotions were at this time, but we assume that she was a normal mother. They had been traveling a full day, most likely preparing to camp for the night. But Jesus is simply not there. No one has seen him. So they go all the way back to Jerusalem. It's a big city. They search everywhere, Mary, we can imagine, in a panic by now. Is this the *sword piercing her soul?* After three long days, they discover him in the temple. If we were to ask where he has been spending his nights, it would be extraneous to the issue.

The elders there are very impressed with the boy. Mary is not. If we read her words as cool and collected, we've missed the point. She isn't screaming but her words, measured for the benefit of the temple-elder audience, burn as hot as the incense: "Son, why have you treated us like this? Your father and I have been anxiously searching for you."[10] If the response were not the very words of Jesus, we'd call it flippant: *Didn't you know I must be about my Father's business?* There is silence. She remembers, but she doesn't understand. They return home, and the text says that he is obedient to them.

The next time we meet Mary, we must call up our imaginations even more than we have thus far. She's attending a wedding, as are Jesus and his disciples. It must have seemed to her so long ago when she was that innocent teenager talking to an angel. She's aged considerably now and is a widow; the kids are all out of the house with children of their own. We spot her across the courtyard bustling around, her hair streaked with gray and some added pounds on her stocky frame. She's no garden statue, for sure. The first thing we might want to say to her is: *Chill out, Mary. Everyone's having a good time. Just relax. Enjoy yourself.* But she would pay no heed. She's a good friend of the hostess, and she can't stop herself. She's simply got to be in charge. If she were in our potluck group today, we might call her a *buttinsky* behind her back, while appreciating her hard work at the same time.

She's on top of things until she realizes with horror that the wine has run out. What does that have to do with her? We don't even ask. That's simply Mary. She moves quickly to where Jesus is chewing the fat with his disciples. She pulls him aside, explaining the problem—a major faux pas. Does she expect him to work a miracle? She gives no hint of that. She might rather expect him to run down to the corner pub and make a purchase. "Woman, why do you involve me?" he says in what appears to be a sharp tone. "My hour has not yet come." We can almost see Mary jerk her head and huff. Then turning to the servants, she says sharply under her breath, "Do whatever he tells you."[11]

This sets the stage for Jesus's first miracle—turning water into wine. Whether Mary or anyone else at the wedding, apart from the disciples and perhaps the servants, realize that he has performed a miracle is not revealed. He simply takes care of the problem. And Mary, we imagine, is off putting out another fire and bustling around until the last guest has departed.

In many respects, Mary (like all of us) is a conflicted individual. Years earlier she had a spectacular encounter with an angel, prompting her to sing lyrics that have inspired listeners through the centuries. But then all too quickly, beginning with a dirty stable, the drudgery had set in. There have been good times and bad. Nothing extraordinary. She is an energetic, small-town, poor Palestinian widow, the very sort of woman who would have been miraculously served by Elijah or Elisha. But for her, there are no miracles—except that crazy situation at the wedding. *Where did he come up with all that wine?*

What a great time at that wedding! But now things have taken a different turn. Jesus is going from place to place with his disciples, including her nephews James and John, and she's glad about that. But she sometimes has doubts. If she were in charge, she'd check out the message and their schedule, but she's out of the loop. Then they all come back to Nazareth. Here everyone knows him: "Isn't this the carpenter? Isn't this Mary's son and the brother of James, Joseph, Judas and Simon? Aren't his sisters here with us?"[12]

He preaches in the synagogue, and the neighbors are impressed. Mary must have looked on with pride. But then everything falls apart. Jesus almost seems to taunt them, saying: "Surely you will quote this proverb to me: 'Physician, heal yourself!' And you will tell me, 'Do here in your hometown what we have heard that you did in Capernaum.'"[13] And he blames them, saying that no true prophet is accepted in his hometown. Then he compares his healing to that of Elijah, who healed a widow not in his homeland but in Zarephath. Elijah? Who does he think he is? The people are furious. *Why does he have to offend them?* Mary wonders. To make matters worse, "they got up, [and] drove him out of the town."[14] These are Mary's own neighbors. She's known them all her life. It hurts so terribly bad. The words haunt her, yes, *a sword piercing her soul.*

Soon Mary is hearing of miracle working and large crowds following Jesus, people hanging on his every word. Others, however, claim that he's demon possessed. In fact, Jewish authorities are becoming very upset. She's a good Jew, and it has never occurred to her to challenge the teachings of the law and everything else that she has learned from childhood. She does remember what the angel had said to her so long ago, but she's certain that the real Messiah will be hailed by all the Jews from the high priests down to the lowliest beggar. But the word around town is that many people actually think Jesus is crazy or worse. She worries.

Mary's other sons are concerned as well. She calls them together, and they decide there's no other alternative. They'll do an intervention. True, he's certainly no alcoholic or drug addict, but something seems to be seriously wrong, and they've got to act now. They arrive hoping to catch him alone, but there's a huge crowd. Someone recognizes them and tells him that they want to see him. He might have sent word back that he will see them as soon as the parable is over. Instead, he says in everyone's hearing what might well be taken as a put-down: "My mother and brothers are those who hear God's word and put it into practice."[15] No, Mary is thinking. *I'm your mother, and I'm with your brothers. Please don't ignore us like that.* But she remains silent.

> As Jesus was saying these things, a woman in the crowd called out, "Blessed is the mother who gave you birth and nursed you." He replied, "Blessed rather are those who hear the word of God and obey it."[16]

We know that Mary will become a true disciple of Jesus herself, and that it is critical that Jesus clearly draw the boundaries so that she will not become some sort of Jewish goddess. For Mary, however, this wall of separation is terribly painful.

The next time we meet her, she is bowed in abject sorrow at the foot of the cross. Will the agony ever end? More than once she has felt a fearful numbness rush through every nerve of her body—as all mothers do—when as a boy he had fallen from the roof or sliced his finger. Now, she is in an entirely different realm. She can't bear to look at his body writhing in stark agony. She would trade places a thousand times over. But she can't. Her mind is screaming. Her chest is heaving. She has no tears left to fall, no voice to cry out. She knows exactly what is happening. *A sword is piercing her soul.*

There is no sleep that night. She's numb. She's relieved that a good man has provided a tomb and that others will care for his body. It's over. It hurts so terribly. He was such a good son, but so different in so many ways. She would swear that she never played favorites with her children, never even imagined the possibility. But Jesus in an odd sort of way was never really a child. *Who was he?* She loved him so desperately. Now he's gone.

The text does not say where Mary is when she hears that Jesus has walked out of his grave. She is surely as shocked as are his disciples. She had been right there when he died, and that death was all too real. Now she's being ripped around by this wild claim. She's thrilled, but she's no doubt wondering if these appearances might be a form of collective hallucination. But then there are more sightings. Does she see him and talk to him? If we know Mary at all by this time, we've got to think that she was hot on his trail. And we do hope she found him.

The last time we see Mary is soon after the disciples have witnessed Jesus ascend into heaven on the Mount of Olives. They all return to Jerusalem and gather in prayer with a group of women including Mary and her surviving sons. She now knows what her role is to be. Discipleship must supersede motherhood.

We recall that the last words Jesus spoke before he ascended to heaven were fulfilled in his followers, including his mother. Like them, did she also received power when the Holy Spirit came upon her and become a witness in Jerusalem and Judea, perhaps in Samaria and beyond?

Concluding Observations

It is perhaps more difficult to understand Mary than any other Bible character. The biblical details are so slight, and the church tradition is so massive and overpowering. How do we separate her, this shadowy Palestinian peasant, from all the theological debates and devotional books and legends and festivals and cathedrals and music and art and statues? It's virtually impossible. We can blame the Roman Catholic Church, but it's more than that. Even I find Mary larger than life, tangled in my psyche and clutching me tight. She's a strong woman and doesn't easily let go especially when I also have felt *a sword piercing my soul*.

I cannot exactly explain why this is, but perhaps it is because I have long resonated with Mary as a mother. In fact, once it went beyond that. My son was in his late teens and spinning out of control. I had been out of town and was driving into Grand Rapids in a blinding snowstorm. Traffic had slowed on I-196, and my exit on Fuller Avenue was less than a mile ahead. In a momentary flash I had a vision of Mary. Well, not exactly. I saw Mary in a grotto up on a hill.

I normally would race right by St. Isidore Catholic Church, but the slowed traffic allowed for a momentary glance. I exited on Fuller, and instead of turning south toward my house, I went north and wound my way around until I found the church. Here I was in the snowstorm climbing the steep embankment to Mary, where I knelt in the snow and prayed before a statue of her holding her young son, Jesus. I'm not saying that she answered my prayer, but today Carlton is a fine young man.

I make no effort to justify what I did that day. I simply confess that it happened.

Questions to Think About

Counterfactual questions can help us in our decision making. What are some *what if* scenarios relating to your own life that make you think more deeply about your choices and God's involvement in your life?

Put yourself in Bethlehem on that most momentous night. You are camping out not so far away from the stable. A stranger comes over, informs you that his wife has begun her labor, and asks if you would be so kind as to come and help. How would you describe the scene the next day when you meet up with an old friend? Would you speak of it nonchalantly, or would you proclaim the good news?

Do you see Mary conflicted in her relationship to her oldest son? Might she have later doubted or unconsciously set aside the prophetic words she had heard as a teenager from the angel as well as from Simeon and Anna? Are you ever conflicted in your relationship with God?

Until her son's death on the cross, what do you suspect was Mary's most difficult issue to deal with as a mother? Have you ever experienced *a sword piercing your soul*?

What do you think Mary meant when she sang *all generations will call me blessed*? How do you feel about Mary's celebration as a saint? Do you think that Jesus would have wanted her perceived that way? Is it wrong to kneel in the snow and pray to her statue?

If you could sit alone in your kitchen sharing a mug of coffee with Mary, what would you ask her and what would you most want her to reveal to you? Do you picture her as someone you would enjoy chatting with? Would you invite her out to lunch with a bunch of friends?

20

A Samaritan, an Adulterer, and a Menopausal Woman

Encountering Jesus

*Y*ou *write just like a woman.* That was a student's analysis of me back
in 1982, on the last day of my History of Missions class. It was my
first term at Trinity Evangelical Divinity School as a visiting professor.
For the following seventeen years, I held that post, flying back and forth
from Grand Rapids to Chicago, two days a week, spring and fall quarters.
I was in the process of completing a missions textbook, and my students
were using the yet-unpublished manuscript, spiral bound.

The comment, though coming from a male student, was actually a
compliment. He went on to say that the history of missions came alive
through the telling of stories, rather than through dry historical facts.
That I write *just like a woman* is not a surprising assessment since I am
a woman. But such a statement is not mere anecdotal evidence. Studies
bear this out. In her book *You Just Don't Understand*, Deborah Tannen
has shown that women typically write differently from men because they

think differently. Men tend to be more analytical and fact oriented, while women are more emotional and story oriented.

It's not that men don't have the ability to invent incredible tales. Go to the lists of best-selling fiction, and their names are right on the top. The great Russian novels were written by men. But men have often ignored the story when writing history, religion, philosophy, or science—topics that they easily assume are based on cold facts or analysis. And women in those fields typically follow suit. And, of course, there's nothing wrong with that. It's simply a difference between fact and fiction or between an analytical-based and a story-based presentation, sometimes seen as a masculine-versus-feminine approach.

Jesus told stories and utilized a wide assortment of literary constructions. In fact, a student might accuse him of writing *just like a woman* (except that he didn't leave any writings behind of which we are aware). That is the beauty of the parables and the Gospels themselves. While they cover the *history* of the infant faith, the format is story based.

What made Jesus different was that his teaching so often took the form of stories rather than doctrinal propositions. Even many of Jesus's encounters with people are metaphorical in tone, among them his interaction with both the Samaritan woman and the adulterous woman. Jesus stood out among ancient teachers in his casual acceptance of women. Unlike Aristotle before him and Augustine after, he never seemed inclined to single them out as inferior or as ones who were restricted by their gender. Indeed, there is no ancient record of a conversation between a man and a woman that ranks so high as the one with the woman at the well in John 4. Even if the skeptic were to remove the divine knowledge demonstrated by Jesus and the recognition of the Messiah by the woman, the encounter is certainly unusual.

Jesus interacted with many women, some of them close followers, others in one-time encounters. In addition to fallen women, such as the one from Sychar and the one taken in adultery, Jesus interacted and told stories about other marginalized women. How can we forget the woman who touched the hem of his garment and the woman worthy only of eating crumbs with the dogs under the table? Whether interacting with or defending or healing or telling stories about them, Jesus was at ease with the feminine side of humanity.

The Samaritan Woman

If we put ourselves in Samaria in the town of Sychar, first-century Palestine, we must use not only our imaginations but also our historical background. Sychar, most scholars believe, is the town of Shechem—the very town where Dinah was seduced (or raped) by a young man whose name is the same as the town. We also remember how Jacob's sons took revenge and went on a murderous rampage there. It is outside this village where Jacob's well was located. It is a favorite stop for Christian pilgrims today.

We can easily imagine that if it weren't for the Samaritan woman, there would have been far less savory gossip in this dinky, little one-horse town of Sychar. She's the main topic of conversation every morning and afternoon when the women congregate at the well. But it's surely not women only who spread rumors about her. The men make snide remarks and guffaw every time she is mentioned. In fact, she's the punch line of half the jokes they tell. And virtually every one of them has at one time or another been accused—in seriousness or jest—of having spent the night with her, though they would deny it to a man.

Simply put, she's not a likely candidate to chair the elementary school PTA or coordinate a neighborhood evangelism team. But that is exactly what happens. Indeed, next to the lightning strike that zaps Paul on the road to Damascus, hers is the most astonishing conversion story in all Scripture. And like Paul she is almost immediately transformed into a missionary.

She comes without a name, which is most unfortunate. Her attitude alone begs for a name. If I were to give her one, it would have some edginess and pride attached—no lackluster handle like *Ruth* that drops off the tongue with a dull thud. She is quick-witted and cheeky, and I would give her a name that fits. Maybe *Charlotte*, calling her *Char* for short. Or, better yet, *Isobel*. She's flirtatious. *Lucille*, a friend suggested. Though hardly first-century names, they might help capture her essence as we bring her into the twenty-first century for a short examination.

She has no friends. No decent lady about town would be caught dead conversing with her. They shun her. She knows well the hardness of that word. She likes women. Maybe not as much as she likes men, but she'd like to be invited to the baby showers and Tupperware parties. She'd like to be called on when someone is sick, but that will never happen. Men shun her too—at least outwardly. She wishes so often that men would be interested in her for reasons other than her body. If only she could just sit down and talk with a man about issues of the day and about the laws of God and other spiritual matters. But that will never happen. Or so she thinks.

Then she meets Jesus. It's high noon. He's alone at the well. Strange. He must be with that bunch of guys she met as she was coming out of town. She might have turned around and gone back to her house and returned an hour or so later. But that's not her style. *Who's he to prevent her from drawing water?* And besides, she's curious. So, without a word, she walks right up to the large, deep well and lets down her bucket. She has no more than pulled it up when the stranger clears his throat and asks: "Will you give me a drink?"[1] She couldn't have hoped for more—a perfect conversation starter.

She tosses her head a bit and says: *I didn't think Jews talked with Samaritans. So how can you be asking me for a drink?* We can just hear the pause. Then the stranger responds with a riddle of sorts: "If you knew the gift of God and who it is that asks you for a drink, you would have asked him and he would have given you living water."[2] She suspects he's speaking on a spiritual level, but she plays along just to keep the conversation going. Addressing him respectfully, she answers, *Sir, you don't even have a bucket. How are you going to get any water?* Then she really gets provocative. "Are you greater than our father Jacob, who gave us the well and drank from it himself, as did also his sons and his livestock?"[3]

Again, Jesus tantalizes her with words, telling her that everyone who drinks the water he has to offer will never again be thirsty. His water is "a spring of water welling up to eternal life."[4] She loves his riddles and this whole interchange. She rises to the occasion. *Okay, if you've got this water, give me some. Then I won't have to keep coming out here to this well.* She knows very well that he's talking about more than simply water. And even if he did have some sort of magic drinking water, she still would have to get water to take baths, wash her clothes, and clean the floors.

The stranger now turns the tables on her: *Why don't you go into town and fetch your husband and come on back?* She hesitates, thinking, *What's going on here?* Shrugging her shoulders, she says: "I have no husband."

Without a second's pause, he says: "You are right when you say you have no husband. The fact is, you have had five husbands, and the man you now have is not your husband. What you have just said is quite true."[5]

She's dumbfounded. He literally has silenced her. No one has ever done that. What does she say next? She blurts out: "I can see that you are a prophet."[6] But she does not want to continue the discussion about husbands. She's quick-witted. She has a diversionary topic on the tip of her tongue. *Okay, well, you know, you Jews worship in Jerusalem; we worship right over there on that mountain like our ancestors did.*

She plays right into Jesus's hands. He tells her the time is coming—and, indeed, has now come—when people will worship God neither on the mountain nor in Jerusalem, even though salvation actually comes from the Jews. "True worshipers will worship the Father in the Spirit and in truth."[7] This is the very kind of conversation she's longed for. Now she's tracking with him. She agrees but insists that such worship can only come through the Messiah, who she hopes will explain everything when he comes.

The stranger's next words are electrifying. He tells her that he is precisely that one. Before she can even say, *Wow! You gotta be kidding!* the same guys she'd passed by on the way to the well are straggling back. They say nothing as they approach, but she sees by their expressions that they are put off by this improper interaction. She hastily takes her leave.

But she can't contain herself. She's just met the Messiah—in person! She tells the first passerby she meets. A crowd gathers around. She stumbles over her words to get out the whole story about how he knew all about her, including the men in her life. Word spreads like lava down a holy mountain. A delegation heads out to the well. They're excited. They beg the stranger to come back to town with them. At their invitation he stays on for two days.

The people are ripe for this good news. They hang on every word. Many of them believe that this stranger named Jesus is the Messiah. They emphasize to the woman that their newfound faith is much more than merely accepting her word about him. "We no longer believe just because of what you said; now we have heard for ourselves, and we know that this man really is the Savior of the world."[8] This nameless woman has become the first *Christian* evangelist.

248

The Adulterous Woman

They are in the back of the shed. No one is around. It just happens. Well, no, it actually isn't the first time; twice before. It all had started when his arm touched hers amid the crowds at Passover. She had thought it was nothing more than the usual pushing and shoving, but when she glanced up, he was looking at her—right through her. They had known each other for years but just in passing. Then after that momentary encounter at Passover, he stops by the house one evening, saying he is looking for her husband. She knows it is an excuse. Everyone knows her husband often travels to Tyre, hoping to make a living as a merchant. Lack of money and loneliness have created tension. When he is home, it seems all they do is fuss and fight.

And then he's at her door pretending to be looking for her husband. He lingers briefly, then leaves before arousing neighborhood suspicion. Yes, she does agree to meet him. It is an old cattle shed belonging to his aged father. Filled with junk, but otherwise a secluded spot. And it is right off the alley near the market. She's taken her basket on that early spring morning, looking as though she were eager to meander through the stalls before the crowds arrive. With no one in sight, she slips in the side door of the shed. He is waiting. Nobody has noticed—or so she has thought.

It would be too embarrassing to share the sordid details, but suddenly the door creaks. They hear voices. He is off her in an instant and scrambling out through an opening in the crumbling wall. There she is lying on a pile of musty hay behind a flimsy partition. Before she can even pull her skirts down, they rush to grab her—two of them, yanking her to her feet, hissing the word *harlot*, like venomous snakes.

Our imaginations soar—or should I say, plummet—when we think of the adulterous woman, spoken of in the Gospel of John. The text is straightforward. Scribes and Pharisees bring a woman taken in adultery to Jesus.

> They say unto him, Master, this woman was . . . in the very act. Now Moses in the law commanded us, that such should be stoned: but what sayest thou? This they said, tempting him, that they might have to accuse him. But Jesus stooped down, and with his finger wrote on the ground, as though he heard them not. So when they continued asking him, he lifted up himself, and said unto them, He that is without sin among you, let him first cast a stone at

her. And again he stooped down, and wrote on the ground. And they which heard it, being convicted by their own conscience, went out one by one, beginning at the eldest, even unto the last: and Jesus was left alone, and the woman standing in the midst.[9]

She's now on her feet only a few yards away from him. He's still kneeling, she knows that, but she cannot raise her eyes. In fact, she has not looked up since the moment she had been caught. She is fully aware, however, exactly who is speaking to her. Everyone around town has been talking about him. Jesus, rabbi and miracle worker. He stands up. She sees that much from peripheral vision. He speaks slowly in a low voice—a kindly voice. *Where are your accusers?* She doesn't answer. *Have any of those men condemned you?* Still not looking up, she barely whispers, *No, Lord, no man has.* There is a pause, less than a minute. Again he speaks. *Neither do I condemn you. Go on your way and don't let this happen again.*

She turns and leaves, still looking down. She can't bear to look into his face. His words have touched her—like no one else had ever touched her before. Not her husband. Not the man in the musty hay.

The Menopausal Woman

Three Gospel writers tell the story of the woman with an *issue of blood*. I commend them. They don't find such a matter too unspeakable to record. In my recent experiences, this is a problem that would not be raised in decent company. I taught for six years at a seminary that had never before in its 125-year history had a full-time woman professor (much less a single mom and divorcée). The other professors were all married and obviously familiar with *female* issues, but such things were not the subject matter of lunch-table discussions. Imagine the reverse. We're all women except for one lone male hired a century and a quarter after the school's founding. We would have talked about *issues of blood* as easily as the Gospel writers did.

In fact, I would have explained to my female colleagues (even if the lone male happened to be close by) that the reason I had been walking the halls like an old lady was because of my *issue of blood*. I was menopausal, a part of life we all would have naturally talked about. After weeks of dragging myself around, I made a doctor's appointment. He was shocked. Ordered me immediately to get to the clinic down the hall and receive a transfusion of two units (pints) of blood. I followed orders, and as soon as they released me less than an hour later, I was back at the seminary, now almost skipping down the hall. What fun it would have been to knock on the doors of my *sister* professors and shout the news that I had been healed. But alas, there was no one to listen.

The blood transfusion did nothing to lessen my grand-mal hot flashes, since I had opted not to take hormone pills. My students were used to my carrying on with lectures and class discussion while I walked to the back of the room and opened a window to get a rush of cold air. They took it in stride. Not my colleagues. On one occasion, I left the table at a faculty meeting and went to the back of the room, opened a window, and stuck my head out. The president asked me if something was wrong. I pulled my head back in and responded: *I'm just having a hot flash.* Except for my closest colleague, who was so tickled he put his head down, my colleagues and the president appeared far less than comfortable with the information. Jesus would have taken it in stride.

Except that Jesus doesn't take it in stride when a woman touches the hem of his garment. All we know about her is what the Bible says best in King James English: she had an "issue of blood twelve years." Jesus is on to her. He stops walking and asks who has touched him. The disciples are bewildered. Dozens of people are pushing and shoving to get up close and personal. He is, after all, a healer. Those with afflictions assume they have to make a specific verbal request before any healing can take place. The woman does not.

She has been to physicians, but her condition has only grown worse. This is her last hope, and she assumes that she can sneak through the crowd of curiosity seekers and simply touch his robe. If he is what people have said he is, this may be her lucky day. Luck? Her initial hope may have been based on superstition alone. She touches and "straight-way the fountain of her blood was dried up."[10]

What happens next is one of the most beautiful passages in the Gospels— and a consolation to menopausal women everywhere:

But the woman fearing and trembling, knowing what was done in her, came and fell down before him, and told him all the truth. And he said unto her, Daughter, thy faith hath made thee whole; go in peace, and be whole of thy plague.[11]

He called it a *plague*, knowing full well what some of us endure. In an effort to personalize her, tradition tells us her name was Veronica, and she hailed from Caesarea Philippi. Nonsense. She would rather remain nameless and without an address. So shall she be.

The Syrophoenician Woman

It is difficult to wrap one's mind around the account of this woman recorded in both the Gospels of Mark and Matthew. On the surface it is straightforward. A Greek woman born in Syrian Phoenicia learns from her underground sources that Jesus happens to be just a few blocks away in her hometown of Tyre. She rushes over to the home where he is staying, barges right in, and pleads with him to cast a demon from her daughter. His response has been characterized as rude by a pastor acquaintance of mine. It certainly sounds rude: "First let the children eat all they want, . . . for it is not right to take the children's bread and toss it to the dogs."[12] Is he associating this woman with a mere dog? We easily cringe.

When I think of this woman, however, I'm reminded of another woman we know from the Phoenician town of Tyre. She was a high-class, haughty princess whom her father arranged to marry Israel's King Ahab. There were a lot of rich, if not royal, people living in this prosperous seaport. Is it entirely possible that this woman barges in with a haughty-princess attitude, thinking she's hot stuff? Sure she falls at his feet, but does Jesus sense that her show of humility is just that—a show? If so, his put-down is appropriate. And her reply demonstrates that she is now bowed down in true humility: "Lord, . . . even the dogs under the table eat the children's crumbs." Jesus recognizes her humble spirit and says: "For such a reply, you may go: the demon has left your daughter."[13]

Women in Parables

When Jesus spoke in parables, were the stories fact or fiction? True or false? True, it is not difficult to imagine that they were both fact and fiction. True, they were stories he spontaneously created. True also, they were drawn from people and events he had known well, perhaps even from memories of his childhood.

Does he recall how a neighbor lost a silver coin? She had it hidden away with nine others and took them out of the pouch to count. One slipped out of her hand and rolled across the floor, and hard as she looked she simply couldn't find it. She never did find it. His mother even went over to her house to help her look, and she promised to throw a celebration when she found it. Never did. Word on the street was that she had miscounted. Never had more than nine to begin with.

But Jesus has never forgotten that incident, how everyone was talking about the neighbor who couldn't find her coin. So he uses the memory to launch a parable. In this case the woman actually finds the coin, lets her friends know, and they all celebrate. "In the same way," Jesus tells his listeners, "there is rejoicing in the presence of the angels of God over one sinner who repents."[14]

He recalls vividly another incident relating to a widow who lived in a neighboring town right next door to his cousins James and John. When her husband died, a creditor threatened to take her house from her and actually did come and carry off her three sheep and two lambs. She had told him that she would pay him regularly, even as her husband had done. With profits from her spinning she would weave and sell fabric and pay him each month. But then he showed up one morning and confiscated all her looms. His aunt and uncle and cousins and all the other neighbors were furious, but what could they do about this haughty loan shark?

Neighbors helped out with meals and guarded her house, but she wanted justice. So she went before the judge. Friends had told her not to even bother. *He'll pay you no mind. Who are you that he will condescend to listen to your case?* They were right. The judge obviously had no regard for the law of Moses. He was dismissive, telling her that his docket was too full; there was major litigation coming up, and he simply didn't have time. But she was persistent. Day after day, she was waiting for him, demanding justice. He was rude. *Oh, it's you again. I told you I don't have time. Just forget about it.*

She refused. Finally, realizing that she was never going to go away, and fearing that she would turn everyone against him with her tenacity, he broke. He heard her case, ordered the loan shark to return her sheep, and gave her full possession of the house. He was just glad to get rid of her. In his parable, Jesus gives only the barest outline of what we imagine he might have recalled. Then comes the punch line: "And will not God bring about justice for his chosen ones, who cry out to him day and night? Will he keep putting them off? I tell you, he will see that they get justice, and quickly."[15]

Sometimes Jesus draws his parables from his mother's meal preparation. He thinks back fondly of her and recalls that time she was preparing for a big family gathering. He and his siblings, in-laws, nieces, and nephews had all come home for the day. He remembers the incredible smell of freshly baked bread. Maybe heaven will be the smell of bread right out of the oven, he muses. Sure, now there's a perfect analogy: bread and the kingdom of God. "What shall I compare the kingdom of God to?" he asks his listeners. "It is like yeast that a woman took and mixed into about sixty pounds of flour until it worked all through the dough."[16]

Another parable Jesus tells is about two women grinding at the mill. That story, we imagine, might have been drawn from an incident that his mother had often referred to. A young woman in Nazareth suddenly went missing. It was the strangest thing. The last anyone had seen of her, she was grinding grain at the mill. She was with another woman, each one pulling the handle halfway before the other took over. One of the women got up and left, saying she'd be right back, but she never returned. Imagine that. She was in a small town. No one saw her go. People asked around, hoping to get some word on her. Nothing.

The day and hour of the coming of the Son of Man is just like that. "Two women will be grinding with a hand mill; one will be taken and the other left."[17]

Everyone knows, though, that trying to explain the kingdom of heaven or anything about the end times, for that matter, is complicated. So Jesus tries to get at the subject from many angles with a variety of parables. One relates to ten virgin bridesmaids. He's always been amused by the stories of lavish weddings, certainly nothing like the simple affairs celebrating the marriages of his brothers and sisters. No matter how much money people have, however, and no matter how prepared they think they are, something always goes wrong.

So, as the story goes, the ten young ladies each take a lamp and walk outside town to greet the bridegroom. They expect him soon after sundown. But he doesn't show. (Who knows? Probably a little tipsy after an all-day bachelor's party.) By 11 p.m., the girls are exhausted, and they lie down in the grass alongside the road to get some shut-eye. Then suddenly at midnight, they hear someone shouting that the bridegroom is on his way. But it turns out that only five of the virgins have enough oil in their lamps to light up the night. The other five ask to borrow some, but the ones with sufficient oil insist they have none to spare. So those who hadn't come prepared race back to town to purchase oil and in the meantime miss the procession.

When they arrive at the banquet hall, the bouncer bars them. *Sorry, ladies. You're too late.* They beg him to let them in. Would you believe it? He claims he doesn't even know them. *Folks, I'm telling you,* Jesus warns, *this is like the kingdom of heaven.* "Therefore keep watch, because you do not know the day or the hour."[18]

Sometimes Jesus draws his message from something he observes along the way. On one occasion he is in the temple courtyard with his disciples. People are passing nearby and dropping coins into the money bucket. He notices certain ones dressed in fine robes throwing in large sums of money—throwing in such a way that everyone in the vicinity notices. But then a poor widow slips by with no one paying any attention. She drops in two small copper pennies—a pittance compared with the offerings of the fat cats.

For Jesus this is a teachable moment. The two pennies given by the poor woman add up to more than that which was given by all those rich guys combined. His disciples, though certainly not rich themselves, need to hear that. "Truly I tell you, this poor widow has put more into the treasury than all the others."[19]

Concluding Observations

If Jesus at times appeared to be short with his mother, it was for a reason. His focus was not primarily on family relationships and kinfolk as had so often been true in his centuries-old Jewish tradition. He single-mindedly set his sights on ministry. That is why he so naturally noticed the widow who dropped her pennies into the treasury. It didn't matter whose mother she was or who her husband might have been. That was entirely beside the point. She was giving all to God, and that was all that mattered.

In his parables that feature stories of women, Jesus was not making an attempt to balance the gender scale by referencing female alongside male. Rather, he was telling stories that drew from everyday life. If a woman stole the plotline, so be it. He simply accepted women (and men) as they were and didn't make a big deal about gender issues.

Jesus was very much at ease with the people. Indeed, that detail is striking. When we contemplate how relaxed he seemed to be with the woman who was having an affair, we are amazed. He had no qualms about conversing with a *fallen* woman. In fact, he spoke with her as though she were his beloved sister—and truly she was. He read her mind, and he surely must have known that on that day she truly believed.

But if he appeared to be at ease with her, he was downright cozy with the Samaritan woman—at least that's exactly how it looked to his disciples. She was a clever woman. She had to be, considering her background and lifestyle. But Jesus was every bit her match. Each time she tried to control the conversation, he bested her. In the end, though, she won the jackpot. She found faith in Jesus and brought a village along with her.

Questions to Think About

"What's in a name?" Shakespeare's Juliet asks. "That which we call a rose by any other name would smell as sweet." Why are so many biblical women nameless? Noah's wife, Lot's wife, Potiphar's wife, and on through the New Testament. We can understand why the adulterous woman and the menopausal woman would rather remain nameless, but why the Samaritan woman? Would a name add to her significance? If it were up to you, what would you name her?

Have you ever known a woman with the personality, background, and chutzpah of the woman at the well? Do you know any women at all with skeletons in their closets and women whose lives are a mess? Are all your friends nice Christian ladies?

If you were to complete the story of the adulterous woman, how would you end it? Would she live happily ever after as an ardent follower of Jesus? Would her reputation in town be destroyed? Would her marriage fall apart? Would she go back to her lover? Do you know people who have found Jesus only to seemingly lose him again?

Can you identify with the menopausal woman? Have you or anyone you've known suffered with an issue of blood?

Do you think it is fair to assume that the Syrophoenician woman may have come to Jesus with a superior attitude? If that were the case, was the dog reference appropriate?

Following in the rich literary tradition of Jesus, how might you construct a spiritually oriented parable of a woman today who had lost a precious item? Of a woman seeking justice, having been scammed by a con artist?

How does the woman who gave her widow's mite speak to us today? Can a few multiplied pennies make a difference in God's service? Or does this parable relate solely to one's motive for giving?

21

Mary Magdalene and Mary and Martha of Bethany

Friends of Jesus

My college roommate and dear friend Ann died five years ago. With her went her fantastic sense of humor. If Jesus had met her in person at the gates of heaven, I imagine him throwing his head back in laughter at one of her embellished stories—who knows, maybe about St. Peter not finding her name on his spreadsheet, and her claim of stolen identity.

Ann was a practical joker and the one whose laughter rang out across a noisy, crowded room. Even strangers gravitated to her. It only took a minute for her to make anyone feel welcome and wanted. She spontaneously gave away gifts—often valuable items—particularly to the needy, and always with laughter and a sparkle in her eyes. No record of in-kind deduction for the IRS, no questions asked. Generosity was second nature to her.

To see her was to laugh, her crooked teeth, often-messy reddish-blonde hair, her XL-size clothing. She possessed a beauty that could not be explained apart from her fun and laughter.

Behind the gaiety and laughter, however, was sadness. Life looked good on the surface, but scratch her and you would find sorrow (and not just after she was diagnosed with the breast cancer that would take her life). Isn't that so often the case with comedians and funny people in general? Indeed, how many comedians do we know who have endured terrible grief and who suffer severe depression? Pain is almost a prerequisite for the profession. And so it was for Ann.

When I envision Mary Magdalene, I picture her like Ann. She's the life of the party. She's the one who, by her very presence, can make Jesus laugh in sheer delight. Sure, she has battled seven demons. How bad is that! Depression, mind-altering hallucinations, body out of control, seven times over. But out of the depths of those nightmares comes a way to cope through humor and good cheer. I can just see Mary as the one who plays the practical jokes and jests with the other disciples about their eccentricities and quirks.

She's the generous one, gives away what she has, always with that toss of the head and her exuberant laughter. She's no beauty queen, she may not even be the sharpest pencil in the drawer, but they all love her and are drawn to the contagious good humor that emanates from her like perfume.

But this profile is pure conjecture, though surely no less so than the oft-repeated myth about Mary: *she was a prostitute.* Pope Gregory the Great in the late sixth century accused her of being a prostitute, a label she has carried down to this day. She was no such thing. What a label to live down! In 1969 Pope Paul VI took it back, but not before the label had stuck. Today Mary lives on in fiction, but she may well have been the most real of any of Jesus's followers.

Mary and Martha, as I envision them, are very different from the Magdalene. Though often presented as polar opposites themselves, I do not necessarily regard them as such. Both are serious and straight-faced. Sure they smile and laugh and have a good time, but they are remembered for their seriousness and inability to get along. I picture both Mary and Martha as women with melancholic personalities, given to solemnity and sometimes anger, more than to easygoing laughter and loud talking. Not everyone can be the life of the party, and sometimes those who are not turn out to be the most faithful and loyal friends.

Mary Magdalene

The most striking aspect of Mary's life that we learn immediately from the Gospel texts is that she has endured an apparently lengthy siege of demon possession. Some readers might roll their eyes and say, *Sure she did. And I suppose pigs fly. What a silly New Testament concept.* Historians of the ancient Near East, however, would not see it that way. Demonic attacks were often reported. There were no known cures apart from exorcism. And not only were there Christian exorcists, but also Jewish and pagan as well. In fact, the Jewish historian Josephus credits King Solomon for being the first to get a handle on demon possession.

The existence of demons was widely accepted. How else might one explain an ordinary individual's sudden descent into utterly uncontrolled fiendish behavior? Her arms were flailing, she was frothing at the mouth, shrieking and hurling foul curses in high-pitched tones. Men, as the Gospels confirm, were apparently as susceptible as women.

So Mary's condition is not some sort of historical aberration. She is suffering terribly from what was as difficult to explain back then as it often is today. In ancient times the condition was considered a sickness, with no apparent shame and typically no potions for a cure. If a demon were present, it was simply cast out by an exorcist, and life would hopefully go back to normal.

We imagine Mary, a happy-go-lucky girl growing up in Magdala, a prosperous fishing village, known today as Migdal, on the northwest side of the Sea of Galilee. She's a tomboy always running off to hang around with the rough fishermen. They tease her as much as they look out for her. Even as she reaches puberty, she runs off as soon as the chores are done. But enough is enough. Her mother insists that it is not proper for a young lady to be interacting with these men. But she wants

---

An Ancient *Cure* for Demons

God granted him [Solomon] knowledge of the art used against demons for the benefit and healing of men. He also composed incantations by which illnesses are relieved, and left behind forms of exorcisms with which those possessed by demons drive them out, never to return. And this kind of cure is of very great power among us to this day.

Josephus, *Jewish Antiquities* 8.44–46, quoted in James H. Charlesworth, ed., *The Old Testament Pseudepigrapha*

---

to be a fisherman herself. She's strong, and she can handle the nets with as much heft as any man. She dreams. If only she had her own boat. She could work it off—an old boat and a discarded net. She'd make the repairs and do the mending herself.

Oh, the dreams of a young girl. But then one night something happens. She had sneaked out after everyone had turned in. She'd done it before. The men laugh when she shows up shivering. It passes the time for them, and they can tease her to their hearts' content. But then something happens. She never says what it is, but she would never again hang around the fishing boats.

It is after that when Mary begins twitching and jerking, especially her arms. She tries to disguise it by wearing a heavy shawl, but then she spills the stew right in the fire. Her mother is furious with her; all she amounts to is trouble. *It's high time, young lady, you get your act together. Do you think money grows on trees? You've wasted our evening meal. How do you expect to make up for that?* Mary can do nothing but weep. She weeps that night and the next day. No sleep. She weeps and twitches and jerks.

Now her family is concerned. And her condition quickly deteriorates. She's rapidly descending into delusions, and sometimes shrieking. First, there are spiders on her arms. Then her arms turn into loathsome vipers biting her neck—and not just two arms but seven arms and seven vipers. How else can she explain amid her sobs and shrieking why her neck is scratched and bleeding? Now her parents are holding her down. She's kicking and peeing in her pants. What can they do to help her?

Sometimes the episodes last for hours. It's such a sad situation—such a promising young woman. Now what will happen? She simply can't go on enduring such profound incidents of terror. They fear for her life. She cannot be left alone, not even for a few minutes.

This is not something that can be hidden from neighbors. Everyone in town knows about this poor, afflicted child. They talk in past tense, almost as though she is already dead. She might as well be. It goes on year after year. No one has a cure. That is, until Jesus comes walking into town one day. Give it a try, neighbors say. It can't hurt. Word is he's healed others. See what he can do. *But she's not flailing around now,* her father insists. He won't see anything wrong with her. *It's a waste of time.* Her mother

261

thinks otherwise. *Don't you want to go, Mary?* she begs. At this point Mary is ready to try anything.

And then it happens. Just like that. Jesus casts out not one or two but seven demons. She will forever be remembered as "Mary Magdalene, out of whom he had driven seven demons."[1] These are uncooperative, combative demons that are not merely *cast* out; they are *driven* out. In an instant, Mary is healed. Is it any wonder that the next time we see her she is one of the most loyal followers Jesus has? She becomes one of his disciples and follows him until his death and resurrection, and beyond.

Mary, in fact, along with Jesus's mother, his aunt Salome, and Mary (wife of Cleopas), is right near the cross where Jesus is being crucified. Then two days later just before dawn on the first day of the week, according to John 20, Mary Magdalene comes to the tomb with spices for Jesus's body. She is bewildered, seeing the boulder moved away from the opening, so she runs to inform the disciples. Peter and John return to check out her story and discover that the body is missing.

They leave, while Mary stays behind. Two dazzling angels suddenly appear and ask why she's crying. Before she hardly has time to respond, Jesus himself appears, though she doesn't recognize him. He, too, asks why she is crying and whom she is looking for. Thinking he's a gardener, she asks if he has removed the body. He responds with one word: *Mary.* She cries out in Aramaic, *Rabboni!* (meaning "Teacher"). She recognizes him in an instant. She would have fallen at his feet and grasped him—or given him a bear hug—but Jesus stops her, saying he has not yet ascended.

Can we even imagine her wild glee when she returns to the disciples? Five words tell it all: *I have seen the Lord!*

Mary and Martha

They never got along, not since they were little. As teenagers they fought like a couple of mad cats in a bag. Unlike the Bible's most famous rival siblings, Jacob and Esau, they didn't fight in the womb. Had they been twins, they no doubt would have. They simply could not get along. Like Jacob and Esau, they should have kept their distance. But they didn't. They remained unmarried, living in their parents' home long after the old ones had died. Getting on in years, they were still at it. Who knows, maybe the premature death of poor brother Lazarus was related to the stress caused by his feuding sisters.

This is how I envision Mary and Martha. Is it too unbelievable to contemplate? Can we even imagine sisters today not getting along—sisters who profess faith in Christ? We can. In fact, it's likely that all of us are aware of sisterly feuds in our own families or among our friends. But most Christians are uncomfortable with the idea of two nice sisters in the Gospels going at it tooth and nail. But think about it. They have different ideas about time management and leisure, different concepts relating to housekeeping and entertaining. Different personalities. Add to that their living situation: one house, always doing everything together, not even separate vacations. Is it any wonder that we see sparks fly?

Still another issue that could have easily grated on their nerves was that of home ownership. From the biblical text, it appears that Martha (likely the older of the two) is the owner. Did Mary thus pay rent? Did she agree to do extra chores instead? Did she resent the fact that the home had fallen into the hands of her older sister? Did Martha think her sister was a spoiled brat and freeloader? Did she wish she'd find a place of her own? When we try to imagine their situation in modern terms, we can hardly be shocked if they had difficulties getting along.

Of course, when their good friend Jesus stops by for a visit, they feign friendship, never supposing he notices their glares and barely audible slights. It is easy enough to pretend—to carry on as though everything between them is hunky-dory. Indeed, they hide their hostility as handily as they serve their food, rarely letting it spill out on their honored guests. Except for once.

Jesus and his disciples are in the area, and they show up at mealtime. That alone would stretch the patience of even the most loving of sisters. Don't these men know that setting a place for thirteen extra people requires a little planning—and shopping? They are thrilled to see Jesus and even perhaps his disciples, but how can they properly entertain on a moment's notice? If Jesus stopped by every day, it would be one thing. But he's been so busy lately that he hardly has time anymore. So, ladies, what are you going to do? Are we surprised their choices clash?

This issue, we imagine, has come up before, in fact, almost every week. There's the Sabbath preparation of cooking and getting the house in order, and what is Mary doing? Her nose in a book (or is it a scroll?). *Just let me finish this chapter. And don't try to order me around all the time just because it's your house.* True, it's Martha's house, and she's the one ultimately responsible.

As the text recounts, Jesus and his disciples are seated and are refreshing themselves, perhaps passing around a jug. Someone raises a question, one of those knotty issues that seems always to elude an answer. But Jesus is on it. Now, others have jumped in with follow-up questions and even challenges. The atmosphere is electric. Martha is running around like a chicken with its head cut off, trying to catch a chicken and cut off its head for a pot of stew. Where's Mary? She's supposed to be pulling carrots out of the garden. Martha looks into the sitting room and seethes: *There she is, that lazy little twit, sitting on a pillow right in front of Jesus, as though she doesn't have a care in the world.*

Martha is livid. She tries to signal Mary, who is either ignoring her or totally absorbed in what's going on. The whole room is full of talking and arguing and laughing—and listening. When Jesus speaks, sometimes it becomes so quiet you can hear a pin drop. Martha clears her throat. No one looks her way. She's upset. She races back to the boiling water, dunks and plucks and cleans the chicken, while more water boils, runs to pull carrots and onions, rushes back to the fire—and fumes.

She's had it up to her ears with Mary. *She's not lifting a finger. She knows very well there's a ton of work to do before anyone can eat. How dare she sit there gazing up at Jesus as though she's the only one in the room? I'll show her who's boss. I'll yank her out of there with my bare hands if I have to. And Jesus will side with me.* How could Martha possibly have such thoughts? We don't know. We're not mind readers.

But she does go into the room and interrupt the teachings and interaction, demanding that Mary come out and help. The text offers a tamer version of what happened:

Martha was distracted by all the preparations that had to be made. She came to him and asked, "Lord, don't you care that my sister has left me to do the work by myself? Tell her to help me!"[2]

It was only fair, and Jesus has never showed any favoritism when it comes to the two of them. She expects that Jesus will simply say to Mary that she had best help out. But she has underestimated Jesus. He isn't your ordinary first-century Jewish man. Could she have been surprised that, as was so typical, he would use her very request as a teachable moment? Can you hear him? *Come on, dear Martha. Please. Just relax.* The text gives us a glimpse of vintage Jesus:

> "Martha, Martha," the Lord answered, "you are worried and upset about many things, but few things are needed—or indeed only one. Mary has chosen what is better, and it will not be taken away from her."[3]

Almost miraculously Martha's tension is gone. We can't explain it, but maybe Jesus has mysteriously touched her.

Far more significant in the lives of Martha and Mary than this clash over meal preparation is their sorrow over their brother's death. Some days prior to his death, they send word to Jesus, by way of social media, that Lazarus is very ill. They expect Jesus to come at once, if not simply because he is a widely recognized healer, but because Lazarus is a good friend. But he doesn't come, and their brother dies.

Friends and neighbors arrive not at a funeral home but at the home where the sisters live in Bethany. We can hope that they are bringing casseroles and desserts, and not expecting Martha to feed them all. The body of Lazarus has already been sealed in a tomb, as was the custom. Then Jesus arrives several days after he had been notified of the illness, appearing to be in no hurry.

Martha goes out to meet him. She's more than a little upset. *Lord*, she cries out, *if you had come earlier he wouldn't have died*. But then she adds a caveat: "But I know that even now God will give you whatever you ask."[4] Really? Jesus comforts her by saying that her brother will rise again. She says she knows that "he will rise again in the resurrection at the last day." But before she can go any further, Jesus tells her he is the "resurrection and the life." And more: whoever believes that about him "will never die." We can imagine her looking at him in disbelief, but she can't avoid what comes next—his stark question: "Do you believe this?"[5]

Here Martha makes a profound profession of faith, not unlike Peter's ("Thou art the Christ, the Son of the living God").[6] She suddenly knows full well exactly who Jesus is: "'Yes, Lord,' she replied, 'I believe that you are the Messiah, the Son of God, who is to come into the world.'"[7]

Martha returns to the house and tells Mary that Jesus has come. Mary races outside and falls at his feet. And just like her sister, she says amid her sobs that if he had been there earlier, Lazarus would not have died. Jesus is deeply moved by her sorrow and, weeping himself, he asks her to show him the tomb. They and many other mourners, including Martha, go with him. When he asks that the boulder be rolled away, Martha protests, insisting that the body by this time is beginning to reek with decay. But Jesus persists. Then, in front of all the onlookers, he raises Lazarus from the dead.

Not long after this, Mary and Martha—and the risen Lazarus—entertain Jesus again. This time Martha serves the dinner. No fussing and fighting. Then Mary does a wild and crazy thing. She goes into her closet, gets a large bottle of expensive perfume that she may have received as a gift, brings it into the crowded sitting room, pours it on Jesus's feet, and then wipes his feet with her hair. We imagine Martha gasping. The only one who speaks up, however, is Judas, who says that she would have done better to sell it and give the money for the poor. Jesus silences Judas and tells him to leave her alone because what she has done is a profound act of adoration—anointing him for his burial. Again, a teachable moment.

No one in that room, including Mary and Martha, could have known how short the time was. It was only six days before Passover, then the crucifixion on Good Friday. Were Mary and Martha there at the cross? All we know for certain is that soon after their time of sorrow over his cruel death, Martha's confession is confirmed: Jesus is the resurrection and the life.

Concluding Observations

Readers may fault me for my less-than-complimentary imaginings about Mary and Martha. Why couldn't I have simply left them as best friends and loving sisters who had one little smackdown in front of Jesus? But can we really suppose this was their only quarrel? That women (or men) in the Bible would be at loggerheads should not surprise us. Sarah mercilessly ripped into Hagar. And Sarah, recall, is the patriarchal queen, none other than the wife of Father Abraham. She's not supposed to behave that way.

Indeed, if that account were not in the Bible, who would dare make it up? Unfortunately for us, Mary and Martha are granted only a few short passages in the biblical text. So we fill out their lives with our imaginations.

Although we should not define the sisters' personalities by the one incident of Martha's grievance against Mary, it is natural to observe their differences. Martha, far more than Mary, is driven—a type-A personality all the way. Can we imagine her pouring a bottle of expensive perfume on Jesus's feet and then kneeling down and wiping his feet with her hair? Would the no-nonsense Martha have done that?

The act of anointing Jesus's feet with perfume happened more than once, the most startling of which occurs when Jesus is at dinner in the home of a Pharisee. There a sinful woman—a prostitute—comes in and weeps before him and begins to "wet his feet with her tears." Shocking. "Then she wiped them with her hair, kissed them and poured perfume on them."[8] Jesus, perceiving the Pharisee's disgust, turns it into one more teachable moment.

It is this incident that is most often incorrectly associated with Mary Magdalene. If she were possessed of demons, some would reason, she must have been a prostitute as well. But it is important to understand that this woman "sinner" who anoints Jesus's feet with her tears as well as the "adulterous" woman are included in the Gospels primarily to show us who Jesus is—the compassionate Messiah who saves sinners. Mary Magdalene also serves that general purpose, showing us the compassionate Messiah who heals the afflicted. But she is far more than a Gospel prop. She is a close disciple of Jesus who stays with him to the end and to whom he first appears on that glorious Easter morning. Her words will live forever: *I have seen the Lord!*

Questions to Think About

As the only demon-possessed individual in the Bible to be healed and follow Jesus in ministry, how does Mary Magdalene speak to us today?

Have you ever known of anyone who was believed to be demon possessed? Have you ever known of an exorcism? Was demon possession in the Bible what we today often think of as schizophrenia or another mental illness?

Does it seem odd that, in an era when a woman's testimony was not considered valid in a court of law, Jesus would first appear to Mary Magdalene? It was her testimony that was first believed. Is there a message here for us today?

Does it seem far-fetched that Martha and Mary might have been at each other's throats since they were young? Do you know of any sisters who can't get along even when living in separate homes—or even when living across the country from each other?

Does it seem that Martha has every right to complain to Jesus about her sister, who is not helping her prepare the big meal? Why do you think Jesus was not more sensitive to her plight?

Besides witnessing up close and personal the resurrection of a loved one, what do the two Marys and Martha have in common? If you were granted an hour to spend with one of them, which one would you choose?

22

Sapphira, Dorcas, and Rhoda

Women Associated with the Apostle Peter

*P*aradise. The word can refer to many places, most notably heaven. Jesus said to the repentant thief on the cross, *Today you will be with me in paradise*.[1] When I am using the term to refer to an earthly place and say to my son, Carlton, *This reminds me of Paradise*, I'm referring to a spot on the escarpment of the Rift Valley near Kijabe, Kenya.

I have had the good fortune of teaching courses during the summers of four different years at Moffat Bible College in Kijabe, Kenya. As a seminary professor, I had assumed I had valuable knowledge I could impart to these African students preparing for ministry. But in the end, I'm certain they taught me far more than I taught them.

Some people visit East Africa to tour the incredible game preserves. I've done some of those touristy things, but I always find the people and their various tribal backgrounds and colorful traditions far more interesting. Virtually everyone I ever met (my students included) spoke English as a second (or third or fourth or fifth) language. How embarrassing it was for me to know only one language.

I also learned a lot from missionary kids who attended the nearby Rift Valley Academy. In fact, they were the ones who led Carlton and me along a winding, rocky trail down to Paradise. We could get there in less than an hour, and it was a place of beauty and isolation that almost took my breath away.

One afternoon after I had dismissed class and was chatting with three of my students, I suggested we continue our discussion as we hiked down to Paradise. They had never heard of the spot, but I convinced them to come along. My teenage son was eager to lead the way. The idea of hiking through the woods on a poorly marked trail did not intrigue the students, but they did seem to enjoy being in our company.

As we arrived, Carlton hurried ahead and enthusiastically welcomed them to this beautiful site, pointing out unusual rock formations and crevices that could easily be missed by a first-time visitor. We were both surprised, however, by the students' discomfort. In fact, one of them said that we ought to be heading back immediately. Getting him aside, I asked what was wrong. He informed me that demons made their abode in such places, and that Africans knew by instinct to stay away. I was shocked. Suddenly I was the *visitor*, and they were the seasoned guides.

They had introduced me not to a geographical location but to an African worldview. Were there demons amid those rock formations? I don't know. What I know for sure is that the distance between my students and me was much greater than merely the number of languages we knew. The cultural gap was very wide.

So it is with Rhoda in the book of Acts. We might still be able to visit what is supposedly the house of Mary, mother of John Mark in Jerusalem. This is where Rhoda worked as a servant. But any such geographical location still leaves us two thousand years apart in terms of worldview—Rhoda's worldview may be much closer to that of Africans than it is to Americans'. When Rhoda reported seeing Peter at the door, the disciples said it couldn't be true. She had seen a ghost of Peter. The actual Peter was in jail.

Such a mind-set is a world away from my perspective on life. I see incredible rock formations, not demon abodes, when I'm hiking. If someone tells me Carlton is at the door even though I know he's at a meeting in Detroit, I immediately question my knowledge of his whereabouts, not whether his appearance might actually be a ghost. Ghosts are the main characters in stories we tell around the campfire. First-century ways of thinking are foreign to most of us today. Rhoda is a reminder.

Sapphira is actually far better known to us than Rhoda. Any reader who comes upon her story for the first time is shocked. How does she merit the death penalty for lying, they would ask. She wasn't even lying under oath. How do others, especially in the Old Testament, get by with lying? Father Abraham, for one. And he goes right on living.

Dorcas is the opposite of any woman we might find in the Old Testament, except perhaps for Hannah or maybe Ruth. Not a negative word is said about her. She and Sapphira play opposite roles in the biblical drama, one known only for good, the other for bad.

Sapphira

Would I ever lie to the Holy Spirit and to a church leader about money that I had promised to give to the Lord's work? Would I lie if it were the entire amount I had received for a land sale and I had no other stocks, bonds, or savings? Not for another pair of shoes, I wouldn't. Not for nicer furniture. Certainly not for a new vehicle. For a February vacation in Florida—to get out of Michigan? I surely hope I wouldn't lie for that. For some funds squirreled away for retirement? Don't push me on it.

I like to think of myself as a straight-up, honest person, but I have on occasion succumbed to temptation. So did Sapphira. That is the single factor that has made her name a byword in Christian circles for two thousand years. She always, however, plays a supporting role to her husband, Ananias. Whether he would have wanted it or not, he gets top billing. And for good reason.

The setting is Jerusalem. Before he ascended into heaven, Jesus had commissioned his followers one last time to take the gospel to Jerusalem, Judea, Samaria, and to the uttermost parts of the world. Next we witness the Holy Spirit coming at Pentecost in tongues of fire. Peter then addresses the teeming crowds with a fiery sermon. Thousands believe and are baptized. *So now what do we do? How do we educate and organize all these people?*

They devoted themselves to the apostles' teaching and to fellowship, to the breaking of bread and to prayer. Everyone was filled with awe at the many wonders and signs performed by the apostles. All the believers were together and had everything in common.[2]

It sounds good, but there are problems from the get-go. Sure, Jesus had said to go out and preach the gospel and heal the sick. But he's no longer with them. What's next for them? Peter and John are locked up in jail and then hauled before the Sanhedrin. Filled with the Holy Spirit, they testify of Christ. The rulers and elders are more than mildly impressed. Of course, their words are nonsense, but they certainly have a lot of courage. So the authorities let them go, with a warning to quit their preaching and healing. But as soon as they're released, they go out into the streets and go right on preaching while the authorities debate what to do. Considering the popularity of this new movement, punishing them could lead to serious unrest.

In the weeks and months that follow, there is an uneasy tension between the leaders of this new faith and the religious authorities. More converts are added daily. It's a movement that simply cannot be stopped. Not by outside forces anyway nor by rigorous demands made on the new believers. Those with money are expected to share. And it works—so well "that there were no needy persons among them." Here we have a form of socialism that works: "For from time to time those who owned land or houses sold them, brought the money from the sales and put it at the apostles' feet, and it was distributed to anyone who had need."[3]

One of those who sells land is Barnabas, and he publicly lays the money down, as the leaders stand by to accept it. So also Ananias. He and his wife are new believers, mentioned only in the book of Acts. He sells a piece of property, perhaps only a few acres. He may have owned land elsewhere as well. Is it jointly owned with Sapphira? Unlikely. Land ownership was solely in a man's name back then. In a typical marriage, he alone would have the authority to buy and sell land and then sock away or give away the proceeds.

The text tells us that with her "full knowledge he kept back part of the money for himself, but brought the rest and put it at the apostles' feet."[4] He does not bring the money while she trails behind him. Indeed, she is nowhere in sight. It is apparent that he alone gives everyone the impression that he is donating the full amount of the sale to the cause. Peter, you would think, would have been pleased to get the money. Whether a thousand dollars or five hundred, it's an impressive contribution. But honestly, not money, is Peter's top priority. He tells Ananias that Satan has filled his heart and prompted him to do a terrible thing—lying to the Holy Spirit. Ananias drops dead. He's carried away and buried.

Some three hours later, Sapphira comes walking by. She doesn't have a clue what has happened. Peter asks her about the land sale and whether they donated the entire amount as Ananias had claimed. *Of course*, she says. Peter asks how she could conspire with her husband to lie to the Holy Spirit. He tells her that her husband is dead and buried, and before she can cry out, she too is dead, soon to be buried alongside her husband.

Was it fair, I once asked in a class, that she was treated as severely as her husband? What rights did she possess in the ancient world where women were generally denied the freedom of land ownership? She had *knowledge* but no *rights*. I make no such attempt to excuse her today. In fact, with my imagination in full throttle, I'm wondering if it very well might have been her idea in the first place to keep back some money.

Indeed, it's entirely possible that he came to faith before she did and was more enthusiastic about this new community of believers. Perhaps she was the skeptic. Maybe she thought Peter was a windbag, or maybe she was scared silly of the authorities and was determined to keep a low profile. Whatever the details about this conspiracy, Peter knows she's got just as much manure on her boots as does her husband. Thus, she drops like a stone even as he did.

What was accomplished? A flippant response would be: *Well, it sure scared the hell out of this budding Christian church.* And that it did. Indeed, we might be surprised by how fearsome, and real, hell is to these early believers—as real as the hope of heaven. The story of Ananias and Sapphira was not soon forgotten: "Great fear seized the whole church and all who heard about these events."[5]

Dorcas

I know Dorcas. She has been part of my life now for several years, and there's no one (at least whom I have known) who approaches her in pure

273

goodness. She's a living saint, though hardly a veiled, praying nun in a cloistered convent. She's an ordinary-looking woman carrying on as though her daily course of kindness were routine behavior for everyone.

Her name is Rose. I'm not lying when I tell you that, like Dorcas, she actually fashions items of clothing, sewing and crocheting little dresses, aprons, purses, baby bibs, quilts, comforters. You name it, she can make it. And she gives them away to needy people. She is truly a modern-day Dorcas. In many ways her personality is the polar opposite of mine. I am argumentative and opinionated and more than once have said things that are a bit shocking in polite company. In fact, I was once accused, in writing no less, of "contrariness" (in the fine tradition, I presume, of *Mary, Mary, quite contrary*).

Not Rose. She is the sweetest person you'd ever meet. Never a bad word about anyone. Sympathetic, understanding, upbeat. Almost unbelievable. I actually find myself mirroring her when she's around. Her presence is good for me, but I can't handle her sweet, soft kindliness for too long. I need to get back to my dear straight-talking, crusty husband John. *Tart* is a better word than *sweet* for him.

We desperately need the Dorcases and Roses in this world, now nearly an extinct species. Indeed, I think that is one reason that God, through Peter, brought Dorcas back to life. Not necessarily for her friends and neighbors, who so appreciated her humble service in that particular place in Palestine of the first century. Rather, I believe she was healed so that she and her life of good deeds could be forever highlighted in Scripture. When we read through the book of Acts, we encounter many very powerful men whose words and writings would last for millennia, Peter and Paul among them. In comparison to her, they wielded authority and influence. Dorcas was essentially a nobody.

She's a disciple living in Joppa who is also called *Tabitha*, her Greek name. "She was always doing good and helping the poor."[6] Everyone knows her, and she's the most beloved person around. Then one day, just like that, she takes sick and dies. It happens today, and it happened back then.

Friends and neighbors grieve. They wash her body and take it to an upstairs room. It's a terribly sad situation. Then they learn that Peter is in a town nearby. They send for him. When he arrives, they lead him upstairs. There he finds a delegation of widows who "stood around him, crying and showing him the robes and other clothing that Dorcas had made while she was still with them."[7]

Peter asks them to leave, gets to his knees, and tells her to get up. She opens her eyes, apparently startled to see Peter in her bedroom. He grabs her hand and helps her up. Then he calls out to everyone, especially the widows, and gives a toast—or at least presents her to the crowd. She becomes a bit of a celebrity in Joppa. Many people believe the gospel message because of this great miracle.

Rhoda

Who has ever heard of Rhoda in the Bible? Her name means *rose*, and she is tucked right in the middle of the book of Acts, allotted only three verses in chapter 12. If we imagine that Dorcas was not an important person in the early church, Rhoda was even less so. She's a mere servant, and her bit part is easily overlooked. But she stands up for what she knows to be true in the face of opposition.

We picture them altogether hunkered down in the house of Mary, mother of John Mark. They're nervous, their minds never far from the crucifixion of Jesus. It could also happen to them. Peter's in jail. What do they do now? He's their leader. Without him no one's in charge. Everyone's talking at once. Of course, they're also praying, but who can concentrate on someone's rambling prayer at a time like this?

Rhoda is praying as well. But for her it's *ora et labora*—pray and work. She's tidying up the kitchen and preparing the next meal. There's a knock on the door. She holds her breath. Should she answer, or should she crawl under the bed? Life is way too scary. She musters the courage. Her heart is pounding. There's no way she can prevent thugs from trying to get by her. She worries for the others. They're sitting ducks—eyes closed in prayer. She goes to the door. Opens it barely a crack.

It's Peter! She recognizes his voice. She spins around and wildly squeals, *Peter's here. It's Peter! He's right at the door!* Now she's panting her exclamations in front of them. They look up startled as though they'd been in a trance (and they were, after all, deep in prayer—praying that Peter would be released).

You're nuts. You're out of your mind! Peter's in jail. Just go back to your sweeping. But she's insistent. *It's Peter. I know it. I'd know his voice anywhere.* They're adamant. *You've seen a ghost, maybe an angel. There's no way Peter's at the door.*

All the while Peter keeps knocking. So someone shoves past Rhoda and opens the door. Would you believe it? It's Peter. And *they're all astonished.* Well, excuse me! That's what she was saying all along. But isn't that the way it often is? Are we surprised that she gets lost in all the commotion of Peter's return? We never hear from her again.

Philip's Daughters

Four sisters. They are daughters of Philip the Evangelist. Were they perhaps half sisters, or did they have the same mother? Was she still alive? Were they Philip's only children, or might they have been teased by a big brother? Or perhaps they toted little brothers in slings on their backs? Did they have other sisters? Were they called by common names of first-century Palestine: Mary, Martha, Anna, Johanna? Probably not Heather, Ashley, Kaylee, or Chrystal. All we know of them besides their paternal parentage (and an interesting detail that they are all virgins—at least at the time of Paul's visit) is that all four of them prophesied. But even this aspect of their lives is without explanation. Did they all prophesy at once? Did they take turns? Were they competitive? Did they each have spheres of expertise? The text does not say. They are mentioned only in passing, barely a footnote in Acts 21. Nevertheless, they have been the subject of controversy over the centuries and particularly in recent years. The issue is the import of their ministry. Do these shadowy virgins who prophesied two thousand years ago open the door for women preachers today? Or did they prophesy in an unusual way, as some have argued, that did not entail *official* prophetic utterings? Or did they simply carry out their spiritual service?

Concluding Observations

Every time I think about Sapphira and her husband, Ananias, I cringe. Would we have any Christians left at all to fill church pews if the same punishment were meted out today? I doubt it. Where would I be? And where would certain Christian leaders be, ones I know personally, who repeatedly lied amid a church-related investigation? The documents proved it. If they were standing before Peter, one, two, three, they'd be dead.

How could I ever explain this passage if someone were talking to me about taking the plunge and becoming a Christian? Let's say this woman I'm talking with has had a tough life and that she's committed far worse crimes—from shoplifting to larceny and a little identity theft for good measure. If she falls back into sin, will she be incinerated on the spot? Times are different, I would say. But why is the passage forever on record in God's Holy Word? she might ask. I can't answer that question, except to say that perhaps it was a loud wake-up call for the infant church—one that should give us considerable pause before we would ever tell a lie.

When it comes to Dorcas (or Tabitha), I'm in awe. If we didn't trust the Bible, we'd say she's too good to be true. What an inspiration, especially to those of us who easily think the life of the mind is about all there is.

The passage in Acts that tells of Dorcas refers to "all the widows" who stood around her body. This, I suspect, is the earliest reference to an actual less-than-well-organized community of widows, perhaps not actually living in community but joining together to do good works.

Rhoda. Don't you just love her? She goes about her work, no complaints. Then, without warning, she's caught up in a wonderful little account that has survived the ages. Who would have imagined that a mere servant girl would challenge the leaders of the prayer band? You can't make this stuff up.

Questions to Think About

Do you expect to see Sapphira (and Ananias) in heaven one day? Is her sin greater than some of yours? Do you expect to be in heaven yourself?

With lying at an all-time high, often taken for granted by those who would call in sick or tell the bartender they're twenty-one, how does the account of Sapphira and Ananias play today? When you look around, do you observe widespread lying "inflation"? Do you ever lie?

Dorcas stands alone. Do you know of any other person in the whole of Scripture who is identified primarily by her good works? Do you know anyone today who would fall under that singular description?

The widows who stood by Dorcas would later join what has become a centuries-long tradition of monasticism, primarily within the Roman Catholic tradition. Have you ever interacted with a nun—a Mother Teresa—whose life is given over solely to service of the poor?

Who is more likely to have visions or hallucinations, men or women? Which gender is more likely to see an angel in the clouds or an image of the Virgin Mary in a tortilla? Do you find it interesting that Rhoda was more grounded in reality than some of the church leaders?

When I contemplate Rhoda, I'm reminded of the Benedictine motto (in Latin) *Ora et Labora*. She worked and prayed. Do you think we sometimes spend too much time on our knees or *prayer-walking* when we might be better off *prayer-working*? How would your church or small group feel about a day set aside for community *prayer-working*—in good Benedictine fashion?

23

Lydia, Euodia, Syntyche, and Junia

Paul's Female Connections

When I speak of people I've known professionally, I'm typically referring to fellow academics—colleagues I would see every day at schools where I have taught over the past decades. But there is another association of people in the business world with whom I have worked now for nearly twenty years. Stepping from the academic world into the business world is to cross a wide chasm, and there is often a feeling of disconnect.

I look back to 1995 and wonder about my decision to establish a retail business. When people ask, my only excuse is to plead insanity. My motivation at the time was fueled by the sort of guilt that often envelops single mothers. My son, three years out of high school, had not yet completed his associate's degree from our local community college. He had purchased a house, rented it to college students, and was eyeing a second one, with the intention of establishing a housing business. If it sounds like he was on the road to great success, such an assumption would be unwarranted.

He'd had some great employment opportunities, only to squander them. I blamed myself. Guilt-ridden, I decided to help out and set up a partnership with him. I convinced myself that if he had been an eager student, I would be helping him out with his college tuition, so why not help him in business? Besides, he was the perfect person to team up with. Hadn't neighbors said they had never known a kid to work so hard for them at various odd jobs? Wouldn't he work just as hard for his mother? The short answer is *no*.

By the fall of 1996, Carlton Gardens had opened as a legitimate retail establishment, though I could write a book on the downside of going into business when a person doesn't have a clue what she's doing. But too proud to simply close down and become one more retail casualty, I plugged along. Carlton has long since gone on to bigger and better ventures, though keeping a close eye on the shop named for him.

For a time the business was all but shut down due to an unexpected opportunity to teach full time at a nearby seminary. Now I run the business and write books. When customers stay away in droves, I make great progress with my writing. When the parking lot is full, my writing suffers. I wonder if that is how it was for Lydia, also involved in business. Did she sometimes wish clients would just go away? Did she ever dream of throwing in the towel?

I often think how interesting it would have been to shoot the breeze with Paul and argue about double predestination and total depravity. But if I had had the chance, I would have wanted to take a break and spend some time with Lydia as well. We'd trade insider stories on the perils of retail during a recession and how irritating it is when someone tries to take advantage of us simply because we're women. I would want to know how she got into business in the first place. Please tell me it was not because she had a son who was screwing up his life. At any rate, I think I would discover that I have a lot in common with this seller of purple.

Like Jesus, Paul served alongside many women. He had no qualms about such associations and never bothered to tell them they couldn't be missionaries like him, traveling the dusty byways preaching the gospel. He was just glad for their help. Paul was driven. He would have had no time for massive megachurch building projects or sitting on a worship committee deciding when the choir should change stoles from purple to green. You mention Lent to him, he doesn't know what you're talking about. A pope? *You gotta be kidding!*

280

Reaching the Mediterranean world with the gospel was his passion. He obviously couldn't do it alone. He eagerly signed up anyone who would serve. "There is neither Jew nor Gentile, neither slave nor free, nor is there male and female," he wrote to the Galatians, "for you are all one in Christ Jesus."[1] So besides Lydia, there were many others, including these little known women: Lois, Eunice, Euodia, Syntyche, and Junia.

Lydia

Today there is an outdoor amphitheater and chapel in the ancient city of Philippi, where it is believed that Paul baptized Lydia. I've never visited the site, but I would like to someday. For now, I live there in my imagination. Actually, I prefer it that way. In my mind's eye, I see the spot where she was leading a prayer group along the riverbank, and I see the overhanging willows and rippling water where she was baptized. I don't need a lovely stone walkway, manicured lawns, and a Greek Orthodox chapel of St. Lydia to bring me back there. I'm virtually certain no one had cut the grass before they sat down to pray and study the Scriptures.

Lydia reminds me in some ways of my part-time business partner. Alex has a larger inventory of high-end textiles than anyone else in western Michigan. She can spot an inferior fabric twenty feet away, and she knows dyes and clothing as well. There's hardly a label that she can't deliver an opinion on. She's an expert who speaks with authority. Yet she's the most down-to-earth person you'll ever meet. Clients love her quirky personality and find her great fun to be around.

That's how I see Lydia, seller of purple. She knows her business like no one else. She has connections and can get her clients whatever they need. She's a professional in the classiest sense of the word, but when she gets started, the conversation could go on for hours. She's the polar opposite of Paul. He's doesn't stretch out conversations, has little time for small talk. But he knows in a heartbeat that she's missionary material.

Lydia meets Paul apparently for the first time at a Sabbath-day prayer meeting. She, along with friends and family, have taken advantage of the nice weather. No pews or pulpits, no stained glass or steeples, just fresh air. Are they expecting company? The text does not say. But no sooner have they begun taking turns in spontaneous prayers than Paul and his entourage show up. She welcomes him, and without wasting a moment he sits down and begins his "power-point"—powered by the Spirit and pointing the way to Jesus.

Lydia is captivated. It's fair to assume that she had known of Jesus, though probably not during his lifetime. But Paul is relatively well known in Philippi, and another name for Paul might well have been the *Jesus-Man*. Everywhere he goes, he speaks of *Christ, and him crucified.* He will later write to the church he had established in Philippi. Here in this letter are some of his most succinct teachings—teachings he may have summarized on that summery day along the river:

If there be therefore any consolation in Christ, if any comfort of love, if any fellowship of the Spirit, if any bowels [of] mercies, fulfill ye my joy, that ye be likeminded, having the same love, being of one accord, of one mind.

Let nothing be done through strife or vainglory; but in lowliness of mind let each esteem other better than themselves. Look not every man on his own things, but every man also on the things of others. Let this mind be in you, which was also in Christ Jesus: Who, being in the form of God, thought it not robbery to be equal with God: But made himself of no reputation, and took upon him the form of a servant, and was made in the likeness of men: And being found in fashion as a man, he humbled himself, and became obedient unto death, even the death of the cross.

Wherefore God also hath highly exalted him, and given him a name which is above every name: That at the name of Jesus every knee should bow, of things in heaven, and things in earth, and things under the earth; And that every tongue should confess that Jesus Christ is Lord, to the glory of God the Father.[2]

Is it any wonder that Paul was the greatest missionary this world has ever known? And is it any wonder that Lydia cannot resist his extraordinary message? There along that riverbank she commits herself to this new faith and is baptized. She had already been a worshiper of God, but she is now a follower of Jesus, the One whom God had highly exalted. There she confesses Jesus Christ as Lord to the glory of God the Father.

As a seller of purple, Lydia encounters wealthy clients, and she herself may very well have been rich. And we have no reason to believe that she abandoned her profession after her baptism. We can, however, imagine Paul encouraging her to do some serious "tent making." She would not actually be making tents with her expensive fabric; rather she would combine her profession with mission outreach as he had done. We picture this rich lady sharing the gospel with rich clients, ones often as needy in spirit as any poor beggar. Her message—as Paul writes in his letter—would offer another form of riches: "But my God shall supply all your need according to his riches in glory by Christ Jesus."[3]

When Paul had initially encountered Lydia and her companions along the riverbank, he was accompanied by a young man, shy but well spoken. His name is Timothy, son of Eunice, grandson of Lois.

Lois and Eunice

The apostle writes a second letter to his dear "son" Timothy. In a previous letter he had told him not to let anyone put him down just because he is young and inexperienced. Rather, he should set an example to the older folks. Timothy, we can imagine, is shy and awkward, no fiery preacher like Paul. In this second letter he remembers fondly Timothy's grandmother and mother:

> Recalling your tears, I long to see you, so that I may be filled with joy. I am reminded of your sincere faith, which first lived in your grandmother Lois and in your mother Eunice and, I am persuaded, now lives in you also.[4]

Lois, Eunice, Timothy. Three generations. Jennie Carlton Stellrecht, Ruth Stellrecht Tucker, Carlton Tucker. Three generations, one set forever immortalized in the Bible, the other firmly established as an essential part of my family tree. Why, I sometimes ask myself, do I continually thrust myself into these biblical accounts? Is it pure self-promotion? I hope not. In fact, it is my wish that all readers enter into these stories. Only then do we begin to fully grasp their significance.

Timothy had the good fortune of growing up with two mothers, albeit one *grand*. Carlton did not. His grandmother, for whom he is named, was killed in an auto accident five years before he was born. But that surely is not the only difference in these two sets. In fact, I would imagine it might be difficult to find two sets of three generations with greater differences. If the three of us were to somehow be reassembled to play the parts of Lois, Eunice, and Timothy, we would no doubt be unrecognizable. But I nevertheless cannot help but find space in their story for my mother and my son as well as myself.

Actually, when he was in middle school, Carlton did receive a coveted Timothy Award in our church Awana ministry for completing a series of workbooks and memorizing hundreds of Bible verses. And he has those verses on the tip of his tongue today. Wouldn't that make Timothy's mother and grandmother proud? I can just imagine the teenager Timothy eagerly going through workbooks and memorizing verses, mother and grandmother encouraging him every step of the way. He's a sensitive boy not afraid to weep, as Paul recalls. In his little family, a boy's tears did not make him a sissy.

The name *Lois*, meaning "desirable" or "agreeable," appears only once in the Bible. More significant is the name *Eunice*. It is a Greek name, perhaps indicating that Lois is (or was) married to a Greek man, and thus their daughter was given a Greek name. Paul's commendation suggests that she was a devout Jew and had raised Eunice in the Jewish faith; both of them, however, had since become believers in Christ. In the book of Acts, Luke offers further information:

> Paul came to Derbe and then to Lystra, where a disciple named Timothy lived, whose mother was Jewish and a believer but whose father was a Greek. The believers at Lystra and Iconium spoke well of him. Paul wanted to take him along on the journey, so he circumcised him because of the Jews who lived in that area, for they all knew that his father was a Greek.[5]

Our primary interest in this short passage is the fact that Eunice seems to have married a man just like Daddy—a gentile or Greek. If only she had left behind a memoir. We might wonder, first of all, why her Jewish mother married a Greek, and then why she followed suit. Had her husband himself been a believer in Christ, we assume both Luke and Paul would have indicated that. Thus, we must assume that they are both "unequally yoked" to husbands who do not follow Christ.

It is clear from this text and in Paul's other writings that people think highly of Timothy, as does he. These women, and particularly Eunice, have done a good job in raising him. Furthermore, we dare not dismiss his father and grandfather. Though unbelievers, they may have also influenced his good reputation.

What most baffles scholars who read this short passage is why Paul, who had strongly insisted that gentiles need not be circumcised, would have circumcised this young man. Was it at the urging of his Jewish mother and grandmother? Paul, remember, testifies to his willingness to make exceptions: "I have become all things to all people so that by all possible means I might save some."[6] We don't easily abandon rituals and beliefs when we convert. Often the new is influenced by the old, and that may very well have been the case with Eunice and her mother, Lois. Had they refused to give their blessing on Paul's conscripting their son unless he were circumcised—a rite disregarded by his Greek father?

Eunice and Lois leave us with so many unanswered questions. Why, we ask, with two of them in the house, couldn't at least one of them have left behind some letters or diaries? Or did they? Were they simply discarded as the scribblings of a woman? Or were both Eunice and Lois unable to write? We'll never know.

Euodia and Syntyche

> I plead with Euodia and I plead with Syntyche to be of the same mind in the Lord. Yes, and I ask you, my true companion, help these women since they have contended at my side in the cause of the gospel, along with Clement and the rest of my co-workers, whose names are in the book of life.[7]

Two women who simply cannot get along: Euodia and Syntyche. It's gotten so bad that Paul asks others to help mediate their dispute. With no further explanation, we are left to our imaginations. The whole mess is complicated. They're neighbors, not related, both very competent and dedicated to ministry. Paul often wishes he had more coworkers like them. But they have come to the faith from very different perspectives. And their different personalities have caused nothing but grief from the beginning.

There had been a need for a house church in their district in Philippi, and it seemed logical that they would be the ones to organize it. They are both competent women who had been eager and attentive students and able church workers. But their inability to cooperate has created tension in the congregation, and the community is no longer growing. In fact, people are leaving in droves.

The issues, however, are larger than either one of them. We imagine that Euodia, a stern no-nonsense woman, has come to faith through the ministry of Paul. She looks up to him as a profound theologian who can condense tough concepts and make them understandable. His passion is mission outreach, and that is exactly what this little house church must be about. Syntyche is also one of Paul's converts. She is concerned about doctrinal issues as well, but she draws deeply from the well of the Spirit. If the Spirit doesn't spontaneously move among the people, how can it be called *true religion*, and that term, she points out, comes straight from Paul.

Besides, we've all heard what happened at Pentecost. The Spirit descended in tongues of fire. They all spoke in tongues. Should we shut out the Spirit in our own little meetings? It would be unconscionable, Syntyche insists.

Sure, there were tongues of fire, Euodia argues. *But that was a singular occasion when the Holy Spirit descended as Jesus had promised. Remember what happened next. Peter stood and preached up a storm. What a sermon it was. Everyone was riveted by his words. Do you think they were interrupting him every two minutes to go off on some sort of prayer language? How are we ever going to teach these people anything if you and your bunch keep interrupting, claiming special words of knowledge?*

Syntyche waves her off. *If you think I'm going to turn into some sort of schoolmarm shutting down the Spirit, you'd better think twice.*

But Paul himself said to do everything decently and in order. No one interrupts Paul when he's preaching.

286

If you could teach like Paul, we wouldn't be having this discussion. Besides, didn't Paul get swept away into a third heaven? Paul has never silenced the Spirit. You need to just quiet yourself and let the Spirit work in your own heart, Euodia. Some of us have been praying for you, that God will truly fill you with the Spirit.

Praying for me? Excuse me! You should be praying for yourselves! With all the navel-gazing you and your bunch are into, nothing's ever going to come of this church! Look at what Hermes and his community are doing. After their meeting they all go out with cakes and rakes and help the needy and bring people back to their homes and teach them from the letters of Paul. They're not into their own individual spirituality. How can anything be accomplished if we don't reach out in community?

Well, look at what's happening with Lucas and Mary and the church meeting in their house. It's bursting at the seams. People come to them because they hear of what the Spirit is doing among them. In fact, they're now meeting every night of the week.

I'd be ashamed to be part of that wild charismatic bunch. They're a disgrace to everything Paul has ever taught. . . .

And so the world turns. Do Euodia and Syntyche realize that both sides of the spiritual equation are needed, and do they work together in their house church? Do they split the church and go their separate ways? Do they come to blows and beat each other bloody, get hauled off to prison, where they form a cell group and lead the jailor and all the prisoners to Christ? Stay tuned.

Junia

Could she ever, in her wildest dreams, have imagined that one day twenty centuries hence, she'd be caught up in a controversy about her gender identity? Sounds way too contemporary for the Bible, but that's exactly what has happened. Is she male or female? The issue relates to her name. Is it Junia or Junias? Most scholars have concluded it is the former. But even with that issue aside, another one emerges. She's numbered among the *apostles*. How could a woman possibly be regarded as an *apostle*? How scandalous is that!

Poor Junia. We imagine how she hated controversy. All she ever wanted was to serve the Lord and be a missionary like her beloved friend, the apostle Paul. He's a fanatic, some would say. He's always ready for a good fight. Not her. She is the least controversial of them all. In fact, we imagine her becoming agitated when she hears that Paul and Barnabas have been arguing. And now they've split up. *Oh, dear Lord*, she prays, *why can't we all just get along?*

To comprehend Junia, who merits only a greeting in Paul's conclusion to his letter to the Romans, we must again fall back on our imagination. Paul is not the only fiery preacher who grabs the attention of passersby and can assemble a flash crowd in a matter of minutes. She and her husband, Andronicus, are also engaging street preachers, she no less effective than he. In fact, she has a way of pulling people in, and not because she is an oddity, some sort of female aberration. Nor is it just because of her forceful vocal inflection. She is a natural on the soapbox, often dropping her voice to a whisper, the next moment thundering warnings to those whose attention is slipping.

She can tell a story like no one else, sometimes drawing from her own experience. She has suffered harassment and imprisonment for her faith in Christ. She is not a criminal; she surely is not conspiring to overthrow the emperor. Her record is spotless. Ask her neighbors and anyone who has ever known her. Her sole *crime* is sharing with others the gospel of Christ. Well, everyone in the crowd knows it is more than just that. Who would arrest and incarcerate someone for simply telling people about Jesus? A woman, no less.

She's dangerous; some would say as dangerous as Paul himself. Look at how she has the people in the palm of her hand. They hang on every word. And when she steps aside for Andronicus to take over, people cluster around her, seeking answers and personal advice. No wonder they arrest this classy Roman woman and lock her in prison. People are flocking to her. At this rate, her ilk could multiply so fast that every street corner would have a preacher just like her. Lock her up. That's the only way to solve the problem.

Paul knows her and her husband, and we can only imagine the affection and admiration he has for these two fellow prisoners. They may have spent many hours together sharing their experiences. And he may have written them personal notes, but in his grand Epistle to the Romans, his commendation is brief:

> Greet Andronicus and Junia, my fellow Jews who have been in prison with me. They are outstanding among the apostles, and they were in Christ before I was.[8]

Concluding Observations

To anyone who would accuse me of going on flights of fancy with these women surrounding Paul, I respond: *Don't blame me; blame him. He could have filled out their stories instead of only mentioning them in passing. Or blame Luke for not including details about them in Acts. It's not my fault.*

That's the way it is with so much of what is written—or not written—in the Bible. Just when a particular individual grabs our attention, the fleeting reference is over. But even when we have many personal details, as in the case of Paul himself, we see him, to quote his own words, "through a glass darkly."[9] But someday, he assures us, we will see the Lord face-to-face—even as we hope we will see him face-to-face and Lydia, along with Lois and Eunice and Euodia and Syntyche and Junia. Only then will they be able to tell us how much we have missed the mark, and, who knows, maybe thank us for our taking the time to be interested in them.

In the meantime, we have options. We can attempt to scrape together some scholarly material that may or may not relate to their lives. Or we can join an archaeological excursion where we may or may not discover the site of the actual house or the riverbank associated with them. Or we can take flights of fancy with our imaginations and make up a story line that fits. It's almost like going back to childhood with our paper dolls that have a new set of clothes and hairdos, as well as a new personal profile every time we play with them.

Questions to Think About

Have you ever toured the Holy Land and its environs? Ever visited the spot where some believe Lydia led a meeting along the riverbank? Do you find such visits meaningful? Do you sometimes find it disappointing to discover a cathedral or amphitheater where a tomb or garden or river walk should be?

Have you ever stepped out in a business venture (or some other venture) that might have been considered atypical for someone of your background or gender? Have you ever owned a retail/wholesale business, as we presume Lydia did? Have you ever encountered what you regarded as gender (or race) discrimination in a job or as a student?

Do you identify with Eunice and Lois, mother and grandmother, as spiritual models for children? Do you have a grandmother who has played a significant role in your life? Do you personally know unbelieving fathers—or mothers—who have served as very positive role models for their children?

The matter that divided Euodia and Syntyche is not revealed, but it may have created as much tension as did other conflicts mentioned in Paul's letters. When a church is divided, is it better to split, with each side going separate ways? Have you ever been in the midst of serious church conflict? One similar to that which might have divided these women?

What do you imagine Junia would think if she could know she is the subject of three recent books: Scot McKnight, *Junia Is Not Alone* (2011), Rena Pederson, *The Lost Apostle: Searching for the Truth about Junia* (2006), and Eldon Jay Epp, *Junia: The First Woman Apostle* (2005)? And that's not counting fiction. Might she say, *Enough already*?

24

Phoebe and Priscilla

Ministry in the Early Church

In high school, hoping to improve my grade in biology, I took up taxidermy and mounted a squirrel. I was a hunter back in the day, though the notches on my gun during several deer seasons added up to zero—never even got off a good shot. The .12-gauge shotgun I used had a powerful kick, but it didn't shoot straight. With my .22, I took aim and hit my target every time—mainly gophers. (I recently put a hole in a beer can with my brother's .22 revolver at a respectable distance, impressing both him and my husband, who doesn't shoot.)

I normally didn't hunt squirrels. Any we shot we were expected to skin and cut up to be cooked for dinner—too much bother for me. But a class project was a different matter. I purchased a taxidermy kit and, with my trusty .22, headed into the woods. With one clean shot, the squirrel dropped from the tree with a gentle thud. It was a plump adult with reddish fur and undetermined gender.

I had more than once helped my father skin and butcher a heifer, so I basically knew what I was doing. Within an hour I had disposed of the meat and innards. (Eating my project just didn't seem appropriate.)

291

I mixed the chemicals and more or less followed the directions, having pulled much of the flesh from the inside of the skull. After applying the solutions, I set the two-dollar set of glass eyes aside and let the skin and skull dry for the night.

In the morning, my squirrel skin was stiffer than a board. Now what? Equally problematic was the elongation of the body, which looked more like a weasel's than a squirrel's. This was an unfortunate turn of events. Had I lost my nine-dollar investment in taxidermy supplies, and what about my grade?

Ingenuity, however, has always been the mother of high grades, so I set to work refashioning my squirrel. I had intended to construct a wooden skeleton on which to form the skin. Now I didn't have to. The skin stood by itself. But twenty-three inches high? That wouldn't do. So I borrowed my father's bailing shears and cut the skin horizontally. Using an awl, I poked holes through both the top and the bottom half of the belly, sewed both halves up, the bottom slightly smaller than the top. Then I fitted the top half over the bottom, smoothed the fur, mounted it on a branch, and took it to school.

My teacher and fellow students were in awe. I got an A, but more than that my squirrel took its place alongside the other mounted specimens in our biology showcase. In fact, many years later when I returned, it was still there. Sadly, the squirrel has since gone missing. The old school has been torn down, and apparently the state-of-the-art lab at the new campus was not considered a proper home for my handiwork.

I would have enjoyed spending time with Priscilla. I can't say that about every woman we've come to know in these twenty-four chapters. But I size her up as a working stiff—my kind of lady. And we can imagine her not being squeamish about getting smelly and blood-spattered while skinning critters and tanning hides. She and her husband were tent-makers, fashioning portable homes from leather.

Phoebe, on the other hand, does not seem to be the kind of woman found in the tent-making business. No animal skins for her and certainly no interest in taxidermy. She may very well have been a high-class lady. In fact, if she were around today we might find her shopping in Saks Fifth Avenue wearing Italian-made stilettos, an Eileen Fisher slinky black dress, and a string of pearls from Tiffany's, maybe even carrying a Gucci leather handbag—that is, until her life is transformed, and she begins funding mission outreach.

These biblical women were as diverse as we are today. They are not the interchangeable flannelgraph figures that I used as a teenager when I was teaching beginner's Sunday school class in a little country church. Back then, Hagar doubled as the woman at the well; Jochebed was a perfect stand-in for Dorcas. I resonate with what Annie Dillard has to say about such Bible characters:

> A blur of romance clings to our notions of "publicans," "sinners," "the poor," "the people in the marketplace," "our neighbors," as though of course God should reveal himself, if at all, to these simple people, these Sunday school watercolor figures, who are so purely themselves in their tattered robes, who are single in themselves, while we now are various, complex, and full at heart. We are busy. So, I see now, were they.[1]

Dillard goes on to challenge us to exercise our imaginations when we contemplate these individuals, as we have already been doing beginning with Eve.

> Yet, some have imagined well, with honesty and art, the detail of such a life, and have described it with such grace, that we mistake vision for history, dream for description, and fancy that life has devolved.[2]

As we dive into the lives of Phoebe and Priscilla, as we have done with other women along the way, we seek to *imagine well with honesty and art*, time-traveling to the first century while bringing these women into our own present-day culture.

Phoebe

If I were going to write a novel about Phoebe, I would introduce her as an organizational genius, someone you would retain to get your business in order. She is a consultant whose administrative skills are much sought after among merchants of the first-century Mediterranean world. But she is shifting gears in a midcareer change. The apostle Paul has captured her attention and convinced her to devote her talent to ministry. She's the most competent individual he has ever encountered and exactly the kind of person he needs to keep an eye on the expanding churches and the demands on his own time.

While he travels, she stays on top of things in his wide network of churches and associates. It doesn't hurt that she has available funds when he or others are in a pinch. How would he carry on without her? She's congenial, quick witted, decisive, and devoted to the cause. With hardly a snap of her fingers, she can straighten out and systematize a mess. She's a troubleshooter and is quick to identify shortcuts in a busy schedule. She's absolutely brilliant. There's simply no one like her.

Actually, were I writing this novel, I'd turn it into a bit of a biblical love story. Paul has romantic feelings for her; or if not that, he longs for a wife with all of Phoebe's stellar qualities. She's not beautiful, but to him she's incredibly appealing: tall, slender, square jawed, with penetrating dark eyes, but that's not what attracts him. He finds her irresistibly efficient. He knows, though, that a marriage to her would never work. They both travel too much, and often in opposite directions. They would never be able to have a real life together. And besides he's determined to remain celibate. But if he were to get married, she would be his first choice. What an incredible wife she would make!

Some nights he thinks about her, wondering if she has feelings for him. She's never once given any such indication. But what if? If they were to be married, how glorious that would be. How absolutely delightful it would be to hold her in his arms when he's shivering on cold nights. What if she were to show any sign of interest? How could he resist? But she'd never do that. She's committed herself wholly to God and is too much of a professional to ever let down her guard. So he dreams.

His words about her are crisp, not a hint of anything but a purely platonic relationship:

> I commend to you our sister Phoebe, a deacon of the church in Cenchreae. I ask you to receive her in the Lord in a way worthy of his people and to give her any help she may need from you, for she has been the benefactor of many people, including me.[3]

> **Phoebe and Bible Translations**
>
> Of all New Testament women, Phoebe might be the most hotly debated in terms of her role in the early church. She is described in Romans 16:1 as a *diakonos*, which is generally masked in English translations as "servant." However, *diakonos* is the same word that Paul uses to describe his own ministry. . . . What is more is that the title of Phoebe as a *diakonos* accounts for the "first recorded 'deacon' in the history of Christianity." . . . In addition to being identified as a *diakonos*, Phoebe is also identified as a *prostatis*. . . . The verb form of *prostatis*, *proistēmi*, occurs eight times in three different contexts in the New Testament. These contexts include church leadership. . . . While English translations definitely have their place, they serve as no substitute for reading the original text. As evident from the above research, the roles of Phoebe as a *diakonos* and a *prostatis* in Romans 16:1–2 have often been slighted in English translations, being rendered as "servant" and "helper" respectively.
>
> Elizabeth A. McCabe, "A Reexamination of Phoebe as a 'Diakonos' and 'Prostatis'"

Paul knew precisely what this commendation meant. However, in the nearly two millennia since he wrote it, scholars have locked horns on the Greek translations of words that are often rendered *deacon* and *benefactor*. And not just in recent years. Origen, a third-century scholar, emphasized how Phoebe ministered to Paul as a *servant*. We imagine her to be far more than that, though Paul often identified himself as a servant, as did Jesus.

That Phoebe was identified with the church of Cenchreae adds a significant clue to the mystery of her job description. Some scholars believe that she may have been the leader of that church; others assume she served as an emissary for Paul and was most likely the individual who carried his most significant epistle to the church at Rome. As is true of other briefly mentioned women in the early church, much of what is written about Phoebe is speculation, if not imagination. Joan Campbell in *Phoebe: Patron and Emissary* summarizes the most common speculation: "It has often been thought that Phoebe was the bearer of Paul's letter to Roman Jesus groups and that it was she who read it to them and responded to their questions. It has even been proposed that she agreed to act as the patron of Paul's . . . mission [to Spain]."[4]

Imagine, then, Phoebe as an organizational genius who doubles as an articulate teacher—a teacher who has absorbed Paul's writings, and especially this grand epistle. She is the *point man* who responds to the tough questions:

Circumcision of the heart? What does he mean by that?

No one who has done good, not even one? What about all our charity programs?

Sin entered the world through one man, Adam? Is he talking about original sin? What about Eve?

He's saying that what he wants to do he doesn't do, and he does what he hates to do? Paul, a slave to sin? How can that be? He's the leader of our congregations.

So is Paul saying here that God chooses and predestines only certain ones to believe? Are you kidding?[5]

Just think of Phoebe fielding all those questions. But if anyone can do it, she can. And she's quick to divert the attention of someone who's more a troublemaker than a true student who is eager to learn. She unrolls the scroll to her favorite passage where Paul, to encourage mission outreach, quotes Isaiah's poetry: "How beautiful are the feet of those who bring good news."[6] She looks down at her calloused, dusty feet in her size 9 leather sandals, and thinks *yes, Paul would call them beautiful.* Her job is as difficult as any Paul has ever assigned to any of his coworkers, but she loves every minute of it.

> **Phoebe: A Far-Flung Traveler**
>
> Like many of the earliest Christians, Phoebe may have been a far-flung traveler and it is likely that she was Paul's chosen courier for his Letter to the Romans; his gratitude expressed for Phoebe's generosity, to himself and many others, rings true in the witness of Scripture. In a patriarchal culture, where it was often assumed that women were properly to be considered an invisible component of society and justifiably under-reported, Paul . . . singles [her] out for praise. Phoebe is remembered by Paul—and in the canon of Scripture—as a sister, as a benefactor, and as a deacon.
>
> V. K. McCarty, "Phoebe as an Example of Female Authority Exercised in the Early Church"

Priscilla

Her formal Roman name is *Prisca*, but she is known to us by her nickname. If Priscilla were living today, she might be a seminary professor, running a business on the side, and maybe even churning out a book now and then. An author? Actually some scholars think that she was indeed. What we know for certain is that she was a teacher who was highly regarded by the apostle Paul.

The women surrounding Paul, unlike those with whom Jesus had close associations, were generally more cosmopolitan. With the exception of Lydia, Priscilla was undoubtedly the most business oriented of all. Unlike Lydia, she was a seasoned Christian. But she may not have possessed the high-class sophistication we easily associate with Lydia. Another factor that sets her apart from many New Testament women involved in ministry is her married status. Indeed, she serves as a model today for women who combine ministry and marriage. Motherhood could happily be added to that combination, but there is no evidence that she ever bore any children.

What might her life have been like before her arrival in Corinth, when we first find her in the scriptural text? We imagine her growing up in Rome, with her Jewish parents. In fact, her Jewish ancestors might have lived in Rome for generations. Both Julius Caesar and Augustus had given legal protection to Jews and their synagogues. But by the time that Priscilla is coming of age, conditions for Jews are perilous. Because of their strict dietary and moral code, they typically live in separate enclaves, but they face opposition, particularly in the decade before she and Aquila are expelled in the year 49. There are clashes between Jews and gentiles, in part because Jews are demanding equal opportunities in education and business and cultural offerings. Anti-Semitism is rife in that most cosmopolitan city.

The persecution, however, is sporadic. During long stretches of time, Jews had enjoyed considerable freedom. In the year 49, however, they have no choice but to relocate. Priscilla and Aquila escape to Corinth, where they do double duty in their tent-making business and in ministry, and then after a time are joined by Paul, himself a tent-maker.

Paul by this time is a seasoned missionary who can uncannily turn failures into successes. He's a master strategist who nevertheless stumbles over his own strokes of genius. He would later write that Priscilla and Aquila risked their necks to save his life. Who knows precisely what that was all about? Why would he have put them at risk?

We can imagine that there's never peace and quiet when he's around. Argumentative and inflexible, he is equally emotional and often overly sensitive. And his tics simply drive her nuts. He calls them his "thorn in the flesh," but now they have become her thorn as well. He's got issues. She knows it, though she would no more inquire about his personal demons than she would confide hers to him.

Yet she and her husband have much in common with Paul besides their tent-making trade. More than anything, the three are united in proclaiming Jesus. He stays with them for eighteen months, and with every month that passes they appreciate him more. When he informs them that he is planning an evangelistic trip to Syria, they decide to pull up stakes and go with him. But then they end up settling in Ephesus, while he continues on his journey. In Ephesus they go to the synagogue on the Sabbath, and here they encounter an evangelist named Apollos, a learned and eloquent preacher who speaks boldly in the synagogue, with one shortcoming: he preaches only the baptism of John.

What do you do in a situation like this? You don't want to hurt his feelings. How do you approach him? Today most people would be offended if someone sought to correct their theology on the spot. Back then, however, things were different. With communication lines poorly developed, learning only half the message was not uncommon. So Priscilla and Aquila take him aside and offer to teach him more accurately the way of Christ. In this context Priscilla's name comes before her husband's, suggesting that, of the two of them, she is the teacher, and Apollos apparently is grateful for her efforts.

Another factor in her taking the lead may have been that she was less threatening than her husband. Perhaps she approached his lack of knowledge with a soft touch, probing his ignorance with questions more than demanding that he adhere to Paul's teaching.

After this, Priscilla and Aquila return to Corinth, bringing Apollos with them. Sometime later, after Emperor Claudius dies, they return to Rome, where they hold church services in their home. When Phoebe arrives with Paul's epistle to the church of Rome, they receive top billing in his greetings.

A Mystery of Authorship

In Apostolic times, a remarkable letter was written to a group of Christians by one of their spiritual leaders. A few years later, copies were circulated to churches in other locations. The first-century church was admonished by its zeal and discernment and uplifted by its stirring prose. This letter eventually found its way into the New Testament canon and is known to us as The *"Epistle to the Hebrews."* In a tangled strand of history, deep mystery surrounds the name of the author. A literary and theological masterpiece, the letter was much too good to be without an author. . . . Weigh the evidence, which is cumulative, and consider the line of reasoning in its entirety. Point by point the scale is tipped; Priscilla outbalancing the other candidates. The scale tells us that the *Epistle to the Hebrews* should be ascribed to Priscilla.

Ruth Hoppin, *Priscilla's Letter*

Greet Priscilla and Aquila, my co-workers in Christ Jesus. They risked their lives for me. Not only I but all the churches of the Gentiles are grateful to them. Greet also the church that meets at their house.[7]

What did she do in her spare time? Some scholars make a good case for Priscilla as the author of the book of Hebrews, and not simply because no other individual is identified as the writer. Nor is the claim made solely on the fact that most writers, including Paul, wished to be identified with their works. The fact of its anonymous authorship has led some to believe it might have been written by a woman. Likewise, the author writes in the first person while referring at times to *us*, perhaps in reference to her husband. And at the conclusion of this long letter, the author speaks of returning again to a community of believers, most likely in Rome. We do not know who wrote the Epistle to the Hebrews, but in many respects, Priscilla fits the bill.

Concluding Observations

While I have not studied all the evidence on either side of the debate, from what I know at this point I would put my money on Priscilla as the writer of the Epistle to the Hebrews. In my mind, she's a more likely candidate than the other most commonly suggested authors, including Paul himself. Other names often suggested are Barnabas, Clement of Rome, Luke, Philip, and Silas. That certainly does not mean I take her to be some sort of modern-day Christian feminist or egalitarian. But if we imagine that she's the author, we commend her for including at least two women in that grand Hall of Faith in Hebrews 11, Sarah and Rahab. But had I been writing that epistle I would have included more women—certainly Deborah among the lesser-known judges who are mentioned.

> And by faith even Sarah, who was past childbearing age, was enabled to bear children because she considered him faithful who had made the promise. . . . By faith the prostitute Rahab, because she welcomed the spies, was not killed with those who were disobedient.[8]

Whether or not she wrote a book of the Bible, Priscilla served faithfully in ministry alongside the apostle Paul, Apollos, and her husband. Perhaps she met Phoebe for the first time when Phoebe arrived with Paul's letter, or had they met and traded stories long before that? Either way, Phoebe must have been excited to see Priscilla on her arrival, and we would like to think that Priscilla invited her home as a guest while Phoebe was in that great cosmopolitan city of Rome.

Imagine being able to sit under the Bible teaching of these women today, each assigned to teach a chapter a week. Phoebe offering a sixteen-week course on Romans, Priscilla offering a thirteen-week course on Hebrews. Either one of them would fill the hall with standing room only.

Questions to Think About

Why are some people troubled by the suggestion that Priscilla wrote the book of Hebrews? How would you feel if proof were unearthed that bore that out?

Can you imagine the great apostle Paul sometimes being an irritant to Priscilla during his year and a half as her houseguest? Can you imagine his having some feelings for Phoebe, especially after having spent time with such an effective husband-wife team as Priscilla and Aquila?

If you could choose only one of these two women to teach your church adult education class, which one would you pick? Which book of the Bible would you rather study, Romans or Hebrews?

How do the women surrounding Jesus in ministry compare with those surrounding Paul? How were Jesus and Paul alike in their associations with women? How did they differ?

Who captures your curiosity more, women from the Old or the New Testament? If you were to pair women off as prayer and hospital visitation partners, which New Testament woman would you partner with Sarah, Rahab, Hannah, Bathsheba, Ruth, Esther, Gomer, and other women of the Hebrew Bible?

Let's say there are workshops in heaven featuring personal testimonials, each one led by a biblical woman (with the exception of Jezebel and a few others). Which workshop would you sign up for as your first and second choices?

If all the women we have met along the way had written memoirs, which memoir would you snatch off the shelf first?

Epilogue

We've come through this study together with considerably more questions than answers. Beginning with Eve, we wondered how much knowledge she might have been created with and how her life progressed outside the Garden. And concluding with Priscilla, we pondered whether she might have penned the Epistle to the Hebrews. We are now at the end and are left wanting. All that is left for us then is to dig deeper into the Holy Scriptures and dedicate ourselves more fully to gospel ministry. May we, to quote the last lines of Hebrews 12, "have grace, whereby we may serve God acceptably with reverence and godly fear."[1]

We salute whoever it was who wrote that marvelous letter, now part of the New Testament canon. Its concluding summary has echoed through the centuries—and through this volume:

> Wherefore seeing we also are compassed about with so great a cloud of witnesses, let us lay aside every weight, and the sin which doth so easily beset us, and let us run with patience the race that is set before us, Looking unto Jesus the author and finisher of our faith who for the joy that was set before him endured the cross, despising the shame, and is set down at the right hand of the throne of God.[2]

Notes

Introduction

1. Blanchard, "Fill My Cup, Lord."
2. *Tractatus Theologico-Politicus*, chap. 6, cited in Durant, *Story of Philosophy*, 209.
3. Gen. 2:18; Prov. 31:25, 31.

Chapter 1 Eve and Noah's Wife

1. Gen. 2:23.
2. Gen. 3:1.
3. Gen. 3:2–3.
4. Gen. 3:4–5.
5. Gen. 3:6.
6. Gen. 3:12.
7. Gen. 3:15.
8. Cited in David Scholer, "God's Word to Women." http://www.god swordtowomen.org/scholer .htm.
9. Ibid.
10. Ibid.
11. Gen. 3:24.
12. Gen. 4:1.
13. Gen. 5:4.

Chapter 2 Sarah and Hagar

1. Gen. 11:30.
2. Gen. 12:7.
3. Gen. 12:11–13.
4. Gen. 12:16.
5. Gen. 12:19.
6. Gen. 15:9.
7. Gen. 16:2.
8. Gen. 16:5.
9. Gen. 18:15.
10. Gen. 20:11–13.
11. Gen. 21:6–7.
12. Gen. 21:10.
13. Gen. 21:12.
14. Gen. 16:2.
15. Gen. 16:8.
16. Gen. 16:10.
17. Gen. 16:12.
18. Gen. 16:13.
19. Gen. 21:10.
20. Gen. 21:20.
21. Gal. 4:24.
22. Gal. 4:28.
23. Gal. 4:30.

Chapter 3 Lot's Wife and Daughters

1. Gen. 19:26.
2. Gen. 13:10–11.
3. Gen. 13:13.

4. Gen. 19:8.
5. Gen. 19:17.
6. Luke 17:27–36.
7. Gen. 19:28.
8. Gen. 19:31.

Chapter 4 Rebekah

1. Tucker, *Multiple Choices*, 125–26.
2. Gen. 24:27.
3. Gen. 24:31.
4. Gen. 24:35.
5. Gen. 24:50–51.
6. Gen. 24:60.
7. Gen. 27:28–29.
8. Gen. 27:13.
9. Gen. 27:40.
10. Gen. 27:13.

Chapter 5 Rachel and Leah

1. Gen. 29:18.
2. Gen. 29:20.
3. Gen. 29:31.
4. Gen. 30:1.
5. Gen. 30:23.
6. Gen. 30:24.
7. Gen. 30:27.
8. Gen. 31:14–16.
9. Gen. 31:35.
10. Gen. 35:4.

Chapter 6 Dinah and Tamar

1. Gen. 34:1.
2. Gen. 34:3.
3. Gen. 34:7.
4. Gen. 34:21.
5. Gen. 34:26.
6. Gen. 34:31.
7. Gen. 38:8.
8. Gen. 38:23.
9. Gen. 38:25.
10. Gen. 38:26.

Chapter 7 Jochebed, Miriam, and Zipporah

1. John 3:14 KJV.
2. Exod. 1:16.
3. Exod. 1:19.
4. Exod. 2:7.
5. Exod. 4:25–26.
6. Exod. 15:1.
7. Exod. 15:18.
8. Mic. 6:4.

Chapter 8 Rahab and the Five Daughters of Zelophehad

1. Gen. 27:9.
2. Num. 27:3.
3. Num. 27:4.
4. Josh. 1:11.
5. Josh. 2:9–13.
6. Josh. 2:16.
7. Josh. 3:16–17.

Chapter 9 Deborah and Jael

1. Judg. 2:16–17.
2. Judg. 4:5.
3. Judg. 1:6–7.
4. Judg. 2:17.
5. Judg. 17:6 ESV.
6. Judg. 4:6–7.
7. Judg. 4:8.
8. Judg. 4:9.
9. Judg. 5:2–3.
10. Judg. 5:7, 11–12.

11. Judg. 5:31.
12. Judg. 5:24.
13. Judg. 4:18.
14. Judg. 4:21.
15. Judg. 5:25–27.
16. Judg. 5:28–30.

Chapter 10 Delilah, Samson's Mother, and Other Nameless Women

1. Judg. 13:11, 13.
2. Judg. 13:22.
3. Judg. 15:4–5.
4. Judg. 16:6.
5. Judg. 16:17.
6. Judg. 16:20.
7. Judg. 11:30–31.
8. Judg. 11:35.
9. Judg. 11:36–37.
10. Judg. 11:38–39.
11. Judg. 11:40.
12. Judg. 21:21.

Chapter 11 Naomi and Ruth

1. Judg. 1:8.
2. Ruth 1:8–9.
3. Ruth 1:11–13.
4. Ruth 4:14–15, 17.
5. 2 Kings 3:25.
6. Ruth 1:16–17.
7. Ruth 2:8–9.
8. Ruth 2:10.
9. Ruth 2:11–12.
10. Ruth 2:13.
11. Ruth 2:14.
12. Ruth 2:15–16.
13. Ruth 3:3–4.
14. Ruth 4:11–12.
15. Ruth 4:15.
16. Ruth 1:13.

Chapter 12 Hannah and Peninnah

1. Van Reken, *Letters Never Sent*, 1–4.
2. Ibid., 13–15.

3. 1 Sam. 1:5
4. 1 Sam. 1:8.
5. 1 Sam. 1:11.
6. 1 Sam. 1:12–13.
7. 1 Sam. 1:14.
8. 1 Sam. 1:15–16.
9. 1 Sam. 1:17.
10. 1 Sam. 1:18.
11. 1 Sam. 1:19.
12. 1 Sam. 1:20.
13. 1 Sam. 2:12.
14. 1 Sam. 1:26–28.
15. 1 Sam. 2:1.
16. 1 Sam. 2:20–21.
17. Schram, *Covenant Foundation*.
18. Schram, "Telling Stories at Rosh Hashana."
19. 1 Sam. 1:6–7.

Chapter 13 Abigail and Michal

1. 2 Sam. 16:21.
2. 2 Sam. 20:3.
3. 1 Sam. 25:1.
4. 1 Sam. 25:3.
5. 1 Sam. 25:15–17.
6. 1 Sam. 25:18.
7. 1 Sam. 25:24–27.
8. 1 Sam. 25:28.
9. 1 Sam. 25:30–31.
10. 1 Sam. 25:32.
11. 1 Sam. 25:35.
12. 1 Sam. 25:36.
13. 1 Sam. 25:37.
14. 1 Sam. 25:40.
15. 1 Sam. 25:41.
16. 1 Sam. 27:9.
17. 1 Sam. 30:16.
18. 2 Sam. 3:1.
19. 2 Sam. 3:2–5.
20. 1 Chron. 3:9.
21. 1 Chron. 3:9.
22. 2 Sam. 13:7.
23. 2 Sam. 13:6.
24. http://www.raw story.com/rs/2012/11/04/ smell-of-freshly-baked

-bread-makes-you-kinder
-study/.

25. 2 Sam. 13:12–13.
26. 2 Sam. 13:17.
27. 1 Sam. 18:20.
28. 1 Sam. 19:11.
29. 1 Sam. 19:13.
30. 1 Sam. 19:17.
31. 2 Sam. 3:13.
32. 2 Sam. 3:15–16.
33. 2 Sam. 6:16.
34. 2 Sam. 6:20.
35. 2 Sam. 6:23.

Chapter 14 Bathsheba

1. 2 Sam. 11:2.
2. http://www.babycen
ter.com/babyNameAllPops
.htm?babyNameId=854775.
3. 2 Sam. 11:1.
4. 2 Sam. 23:24, 34.
5. 2 Sam. 11:4.
6. Lev. 15:19.
7. 2 Sam. 11:5.
8. 2 Sam. 12:24.
9. 2 Sam. 12:5–7, 9.
10. Ps. 51:1–2, 10.
11. 1 Kings 1:1–4.
12. 1 Kings 1:5.
13. 1 Kings 1:17–21.
14. 1 Kings 1:31.
15. Prov. 31:1.
16. Prov. 31:10, 3.
17. Prov. 31:8–9.
18. Matt. 1:6.

Chapter 15 Jezebel, Athaliah, and Huldah

1. 1 Kings 11:31–33.
2. 1 Kings 16:33.
3. 1 Kings 18:19.
4. 1 Kings 19:1–2.
5. 1 Kings 20:42.
6. 1 Kings 21:9–10.
7. 1 Kings 21:19, 23.
8. 2 Kings 9:34–37.
9. 2 Chron. 21:19.
10. 2 Chron. 22:3.

11. 2 Chron. 22:10.
12. "Kings of Israel and
Judah," http://www
.biblestudy.org/prophecy/
israel-kings.html.
13. 2 Kings 22:14.
14. 2 Kings 21:16.
15. 2 Kings 22:16–20.
16. 1 Kings 17:12.
17. 1 Kings 17:18.
18. 1 Kings 17:24.
19. 2 Kings 4:9–10.
20. 2 Kings 4:16.
21. 2 Kings 4:23.
22. 2 Kings 4:24–25.
23. 2 Kings 4:28.
24. 2 Kings 4:30.
25. 2 Kings 4:37.
26. 2 Kings 8:5.

Chapter 16 Vashti and Esther

1. Esther 1:3.
2. Esther 1:6–7.
3. Esther 1:16–20.
4. Esther 1:22.
5. Esther 2:2–4.
6. Esther 2:7.
7. Esther 2:9.
8. Esther 2:12.
9. Esther 2:17.
10. Esther 2:19.
11. Esther 2:20.
12. Esther 4:1.
13. Esther 4:8.
14. Esther 4:11.
15. Esther 4:14.
16. Esther 4:16.
17. Esther 5:3.
18. Esther 3:11.
19. Esther 7:6–8.
20. Esther 9:13.
21. Esther 7:4.
22. Esther 8:15.
23. Esther 10:1–3.

Chapter 17 Job's Wife, Proverbs 31 Woman, Song of Songs Lover, and Gomer

1. Job 1:20–22.
2. Job 2:9.
3. Prov. 31:28.
4. Prov. 31:30.
5. Song 1:2.
6. Song 1:5.
7. Song 1:8.
8. Song 1:13, 16.
9. Song 5:2.
10. Song 4:2–5.
11. Song 7:10–12.
12. Song 8:6–7.
13. Hosea 1:2.
14. Hosea 1:4.
15. Hosea 2:2–3.
16. Hosea 2:5.
17. Hosea 2:13.
18. Hosea 3:3.
19. Hosea 14:4–5.
20. Job 42:12–13.
21. Job 42:15.
22. Matt. 1:20–21.

Chapter 18 Anna and Elizabeth

1. Luke 2:37.
2. Luke 2:30–32.
3. Luke 2:38.
4. Luke 1:5.
5. Luke 1:17.
6. Mal. 4:5.
7. Luke 1:25.
8. Luke 1:41.
9. Luke 1:42–45.

Chapter 19 Mary

1. Adapted from
Tucker, *Multiple Choices*,
30–33.
2. Luke 1:28.
3. Luke 1:30–33.
4. Luke 1:35.
5. Luke 1:46–47.
6. Luke 1:48.

7. Luke 1:52–53.
8. Luke 2:5.
9. Luke 2:34–35.
10. Luke 2:48.
11. John 2:4–5.
12. Mark 6:3.
13. Luke 4:23.
14. Luke 4:29.
15. Luke 8:21.
16. Luke 11:27–28.

Chapter 20 A Samaritan, an Adulterer, and a Menopausal Woman

1. John 4:7.
2. John 4:10.
3. John 4:11.
4. John 4:14.
5. John 4:17–18.
6. John 4:19.
7. John 4:23.
8. John 4:42.
9. John 8:4–9 KJV; italics omitted.
10. Mark 5:29 KJV.
11. Mark 5:33–34 KJV.
12. Mark 7:27.
13. Mark 7:28–29.
14. Luke 15:10.
15. Luke 18:7–8.
16. Luke 13:20–21.

17. Matt. 24:41.
18. Matt. 25:13.
19. Mark 12:43.

Chapter 21 Mary Magdalene and Mary and Martha of Bethany

1. Mark 16:9.
2. Luke 10:40.
3. Luke 10:41–42.
4. John 11:22.
5. John 11:24–26.
6. Matt. 16:16 KJV.
7. John 11:27.
8. Luke 7:38.

Chapter 22 Sapphira, Dorcas, and Rhoda

1. Luke 23:43.
2. Acts 2:42–44.
3. Acts 4:34–35.
4. Acts 5:2.
5. Acts 5:11.
6. Acts 9:36.
7. Acts 9:39.

Chapter 23 Lydia, Euodia, Syntyche, and Junia

1. Gal. 3:28.
2. Phil. 2:1–11 KJV.

3. Phil. 4:19 KJV.
4. 2 Tim. 1:4–5.
5. Acts 16:1–3.
6. 1 Cor. 9:22.
7. Phil. 4:2–3.
8. Rom. 16:7.
9. 1 Cor. 13:12 KJV.

Chapter 24 Phoebe and Priscilla

1. Annie Dillard, *Holy the Firm*, cited in Mandelker and Powers, *Pilgrim Souls*, 365.
2. Ibid.
3. Rom. 16:1–2.
4. Campbell, *Phoebe*, 12.
5. See Rom. 2:29; 3:12; 5:12–14; 7:14–15; 8:29–33.
6. Rom. 10:15.
7. Rom. 16:3–5.
8. Heb. 11:11, 31.

Epilogue

1. Heb. 12:28 KJV.
2. Heb. 12:1–2 KJV.

Reference List

Astle, Cynthia. "Giving Voice to Dinah: Dinah's Story Depicts Male-Dominated Biblical Narrative." http://ancienthistory.about.com/od/ancientwomen/a/013111-CW-Dinah.htm.

"Bathsheba at Her Bath, 1654 by Rembrandt." http://www.erembrandt.org/bathsheba-at-her-bath.jsp.

Blanchard, Richard E. "Fill My Cup, Lord." In *Hymns for Praise and Worship*, #364. Nappanee, IN: Evangel, 1984.

Borgman, Paul. *Genesis: The Story We Haven't Heard*. Downers Grove, IL: InterVarsity, 2001.

Campbell, Joan. *Phoebe: Patron and Emissary*. Collegeville, MN: Liturgical Press, 2009.

Charlesworth, James H., ed. *The Old Testament Pseudepigrapha*. Vol. 1. Cambridge: Cambridge University Press, 1985.

Collingwood, R. G. "The Historical Imagination." In *The Idea of History*, 232–49. Oxford: Oxford University Press, 1946. http://www.brocku.ca/MeadProject/Collingwood/1946_2.html.

Cowan, Connell, and Melvyn Kinder. *Smart Women, Foolish Choices: Finding the Right Men and Avoiding the Wrong Ones*. New York: C. N. Potter, 1985. Distributed by Crown.

Darling, Daniel. "The Most Misunderstood Woman in the Bible." *Today's Christian Woman* (May 2011). http://www.todayschristianwoman.com/articles/2011/may/mostmisunderstood.html.

Deffinbaugh, Bob. "The Skeleton in Judah's Closet." In *Genesis: From Paradise to Patriarchs*. http://bible.org/seriespage/skeleton-judah's-closet-genesis-381-30.

Diamant, Anita. *The Red Tent: A Novel*. New York: St. Martin's Press, 1997.

Durant, Will. *The Story of Philosophy*. New York: Simon and Schuster, 2006.

Elder, Gregory. "Ahab and Jezebel, One of the Bible's Most 'Colorful' Couples." *Redlands Daily Facts*, February 1, 2007. http://www.redlandsdailyfacts.com/opinions/ci_5136057.

Epp, Eldon Jay. *Junia: The First Woman Apostle*. Minneapolis: Fortress, 2005.

Feiler, Bruce. *Abraham: A Journey to the Heart of Three Faiths*. New York: William Morrow, 2002.

Flowers, Karen and Ron. "If the Twins Could Talk to Us." http://family.adventist.org/08%20IF%20THE%20TWINS%20COULD%20TALK%20TO%20US.pdf.

Hazleton, Lesley. *Jezebel: The Untold Story of the Bible's Harlot Queen*. New York: Doubleday, 2007.

Higgs, Liz Curtis. *Slightly Bad Girls of the Bible: Flawed Women Loved by a Flawless God*. Colorado Springs: WaterBrook Press, 2007.

Hoppin, Ruth. *Priscilla's Letter: Finding the Author of the Epistle to the Hebrews*. Fort Bragg, CA: Lost Coast Press, 2009.

Hudson, Mark. "Pablo Picasso's Love Affair with Women." *Telegraph*, February 13, 2009. http://www.telegraph.co.uk/culture/art/4610752/Pablo-Picassos-love-affair-with-women.html.

"Judges 11." In *Adam Clarke's Bible Commentary*. http://www.godrules.net/library/clarke/clarkejud11.htm.

Lockyer, Herbert. *All the Women of the Bible*. Grand Rapids: Zondervan, 1977.

Low, Katherine B. "The Sexual Abuse of Lot's Daughters." *Journal of Feminist Studies in Religion* 26, no. 2 (2010): 37–54. http://www.katherinelow.com/sexual-abuse-lots-daughters.pdf.

Maclaren, Alexander. "Josiah and the Newly Found Law." In *Expositions of Holy Scripture*. http://christianbookshelf.org/maclaren/expositions_of_holy_scripture_g/josiah_and_the_newly_found.htm.

Mandelker, Amy, and Elizabeth Powers. *Pilgrim Souls: An Anthology of Spiritual Autobiographies*. New York: Simon and Schuster, 1999.

McCabe, Elizabeth A. "A Reexamination of Phoebe as a 'Diakonos' and 'Prostatis': Exposing the Inaccuracies of English Translations." *Society of Biblical Literature*. http://www.sbl-site.org/publications/article.aspx?articleId=830.

McCarty, V. K. "Phoebe as an Example of Female Authority Exercised in the Early Church." Paper presented at the third annual conference of the Sophia Institute, Union Theological Seminary, Dec. 3, 2010. http://www.academia.edu/1132713/Phoebe_as_an_Example_of_Female_Authority_Exercised_in_the_Early_Church.

McKnight, Scot. *Junia Is Not Alone*. Englewood, CO: Patheos Press, 2011.

Miller, Maxwell. "Moab and the Moabite Stone." In *Holman Bible Dictionary*. http://www.studylight.org/dic/hbd/view.cgi?number=T4370.

Owens, Virginia Stem. *Daughters of Eve: Seeing Ourselves in Women of the Bible*. Colorado Springs: NavPress, 2007.

Pederson, Rena. *The Lost Apostle: Searching for the Truth about Junia*. San Francisco: Jossey-Bass, 2006.

Pelaia, Ariela. "The Jewish Holiday of Purim." In *Judaism*. http://judaism.about.com/od/holidays/a/Purim.htm.

Rhem, Richard A. "The Continuing Adventure of Faith." *Perspectives* (November 1989): 3.

Rivers, Francine. *Unashamed: Rahab, One of Five Unlikely Women Who Changed Eternity*. Carol Stream, IL: Tyndale, 2000.

Roiphe, Anne. *Water from the Well: Women of the Bible*. New York: HarperCollins, 2007.

Schram, Peninnah. *The Covenant Foundation*. http://www.covenantfn.org/awards/past-recipients/awards-1995/peninnah-schram.

———. "Telling Stories at Rosh Hashana: The Orality of Jewish Tradition." *YUTorah Online*, September 16, 2011, 29–30. http://www.yutorah.org/lectures/lecture.cfm/783369/Professor_Peninnah_Schram/Telling_Stories_at_Rosh_Hashana:_The_Orality_of_Jewish_Tradition.

Shaw, Benjamin. "Was Haman Hanged or Impaled?" (May, 2, 2012). *Ligonier Ministries*. http://www.ligonier.org/blog/was-haman-hanged-or-impaled/.

"Shiloh (biblical city)." http://en.wikipedia.org/wiki/Shiloh_%28biblical_city%29.

Shomaker, Cynthia. *From Moab to Bethlehem: Journey to the King*. xulonpress.com, 2009.

Smith, Zadie. "Some Notes on Attunement: A Voyage around Joni Mitchell." *New Yorker*, December 17, 2012, 30–35.

Stewart, Don. "What Is the History of the Old Testament Apocrypha?" http://www.blueletterbible.org/faq/don_stewart/stewart.cfm?id=393.

Tannen, Deborah. *You Just Don't Understand: Women and Men in Conversation*. New York: Morrow, 1990.

Tucker, Ruth A. *Multiple Choices: A Guide for Women; Making Wise Decisions in a Complicated World*. Grand Rapids: Zondervan, 1992.

Van Reken, Ruth E. *Letters Never Sent*. Elgin, IL: LifeJourney Books, 1988.

Wiersbe, Warren W. *The Wiersbe Bible Commentary on the Old Testament*. Colorado Springs: David C. Cook, 2007.

Williams, J. SerVaas. *Abraham and Sarah: History's Most Fascinating Story of Faith and Love*. CreateSpace Independent Publishing Platform, 2012.

Wodehouse, P. G. *The Code of the Woosters*. 1938, 1966. Reprint, New York: W. W. Norton, 2011.

Wright, Howard E. "What Does the Bible Say About Beauty?" http://ezinearticles.com/?What-Does-the-Bible-Say-About-Beauty?&id=4533069.

Index

Also by
RUTH TUCKER

Becoming a Person of Influence

LEADERSHIP RECONSIDERED

RUTH A. TUCKER

RUTH A. TUCKER

THE BIOGRAPHICAL *Bible*

EXPLORING THE BIBLICAL NARRATIVE
from ADAM AND EVE *to* JOHN OF PATMOS